"One of the things that sets VanderMeer apa[...]
His online presence is considerable and includes a num[...]
ging, a short film adaptation of his novel *Sh[...]
band The Church), his Alien Baby photo [...]
tion via Sony PlayStation." —*Wired.com*

"Jeff VanderMeer has written a fascinating [...]
ing promotion, use of new media, career [...]
and — not incidentally! — balancing all of [...]
anyone who writes, wants to write, or has w[...]
—Nancy Kress, bestselling author of *Write Great Fiction*

"A brilliant writer!" —*New York Times* bestselling author Peter Straub

"Many books tell us how to write, but Jeff VanderMeer's *Booklife* tells us how to be an
author…. VanderMeer made me think, question my own path, and make plans for a
more focused move forward."
—Mur Lafferty, host and creator of the podcasts Geek Fu Action Grip and I Should
Be Writing

"Who better than VanderMeer, master of the blogosphere and online innovator, to
guide us through the burgeoning, oft breathtaking realm of new media…. Jeff helps
you hunt down the vast advantages provided by social networks, blogs, podcasts, and
the like. And the best part is the silly pith helmet is optional. If you're a writer who
knows how to use a computer, then this book is for you."
—Joseph Mallozzi, Executive Producer, *Stargate SG-1*

"Jeff VanderMeer's *Booklife* is a frank, revealing, riveting manual by a writer for writers,
not simply on how to be a better wordsmith, but on how to be a better human being.
I'll be recommending it to all my writing students. I don't know how to praise a book
more sincerely than that." —Minister Faust, the BRO-Log

"VanderMeer has struck a new sort of balance with the Internet: charming his dedicated
fan base on the web, creating multimedia promotional tools for his books, and actively
seeking out new readers like me in the digital crowds. One of my favorite writers."
—*The Publishing Spot*

"VanderMeer may be creating the dominant literature of the 21st century."
—*The Guardian*

"Jeff VanderMeer's book will rock your writer's socks off! I've long marveled at Jeff's mad alchemist-like techniques of creation, promotion, and artistic survival through his artful navigation of brambly networks of writers, artists, musicians, historians, hatmakers, bloggers, booksellers, reviewers, and fans. To steal a line from an Eddie Izzard stand-up act, 'No one can *live* at that speed…' VanderMeer lives at that speed and makes it look effortless — and fun!" —Leslie Ann Henkel, publicist, Abrams Books

"Jeff VanderMeer has written a smart practical jungle-guidebook for the wilds of 21st century publishing — its incredible pressures, joys, poisons, and, most importantly, the dangers of a false sense of control…. Floaty creative types — prepare to be taken to task." —Julianna Baggott, author of *Girl Talk*

"One of the most literary fantasy writers or fantastic literary writers we've got working these days, take your pick." —Ron Hogan, Mediabistro's GalleyCat

Booklife is to authors in today's publishing climate what *Writer's Market* was fifteen years ago: essential. A well-organized, lucid guide to social networking, blogging, and the art of being an author in the age of Twitter. Jeff VanderMeer's advice on maintaining one's focus in an era of unfettered public access to the artist's private life comes from his own hard-won experience; he's been a writer at-home-on-the-web since before most of us had websites. With excellent additions by Matt Staggs and others, *Booklife* is a worthwhile addition to any writer's bookshelf.
—Michelle Richmond, *NYT* Bestselling author of *The Year of Fog*

"Jeff VanderMeer is everywhere. He's in your house, frightening your cat. He's on your lawn, and even John McCain can't get him to leave. He's applying the poisonous glands of his tongue to the paint of your vintage Chevy. He's scaling the side of the New York Times building (they'll arrest them when he comes down, but HE'LL NEVER COME DOWN!). He's engorged in the Grand Canyon, entombed in Grant's Tomb, and impaled on the Space Needle. He's in the middle of the world's largest ball of twine. He's a roving mercenary who kills to earn his living (and to help out the Congolese). He put the bang in Bangkok and the joy in New Joysey. John Waters wanted to make a film about him, but was too disgusted. Harriet Klausner has never had anything good to say about him. Osama bin Laden considered endorsing him, but said even he didn't hate Western culture that much.

And now you're taking him home with you."
—Matthew Cheney, the Mumpsimus

OTHER BOOKS BY JEFF VANDERMEER

Dradin, In Love
The Book of Lost Places
The Exchange
Veniss Underground
City of Saints & Madmen
Secret Life
Why Should I Cut Your Throat?
Shriek: An Afterword
The Situation
Secret Lives
Predator: South China Sea
Finch

ANTHOLOGIES

Leviathan 1 (with Luke O'Grady)
Leviathan 2 (with Rose Secrest)
Leviathan 3 (with Forrest Aguirre)
Album Zutique
The Thackery T. Lambshead Pocket Guide to
    Eccentric & Discredited Diseases (with Mark Roberts)
Best American Fantasy #1 (with Ann VanderMeer and Matthew Cheney)
Best American Fantasy #2 (with Ann VanderMeer and Matthew Cheney)
The New Weird (with Ann VanderMeer)
Steampunk (with Ann VanderMeer)
Fast Ships, Black Sails (with Ann VanderMeer)
The Leonardo Variations (with Ann VanderMeer)
Last Drink Bird Head (with Ann VanderMeer)

BOOKLIFE

STRATEGIES & SURVIVAL TIPS
FOR THE 21ST-CENTURY WRITER

JEFF VANDERMEER

WITH CONTRIBUTIONS FROM MATT STAGGS,
NATHAN BALLINGRUD, MATTHEW CHENEY,
JAMES CROSSLEY, CAITLÍN R. KIERNAN,
TESSA KUM, COLLEEN LINDSAY, CAT RAMBO,
DAN READ, JILL ROBERTS, MARLY YOUMANS,
AND OTHERS

• TACHYON PUBLICATIONS •

BOOKLIFE: STRATEGIES AND SURVIVAL TIPS FOR THE 21ST-CENTURY WRITER
COPYRIGHT © 2009 BY JEFF VANDERMEER

PUBLICATION HISTORY: THE CORE OF SOME SECTIONS INCLUDED IN *Booklife* FIRST APPEARED IN RADICALLY DIFFERENT FORM ON THE AUTHOR'S BLOG, WWW.JEFFVANDERMEER.COM. ALL QUOTES FROM WRITERS NOT OTHERWISE ATTRIBUTED ORIGINATED FROM COMMENTS MADE ON THE AUTHOR'S BLOG AND ARE PUBLISHED HEREIN WITH PERMISSION. QUOTES FROM *Shriek: An Afterword* (2006), COPYRIGHT TOR BOOKS, REPRINTED WITH THEIR KIND PERMISSION. PARAPHRASED TEXT AND STRUCTURE IN THE SECTION ON "SUPPORT FROM YOUR PARTNER" TAKEN WITH PERMISSION FROM BRUCE HOLLAND ROGERS' *Word Work* (INVISIBLE CITIES PRESS, 2002). ALL QUOTES FROM FOREIGN LANGUAGE CLASSICS HAVE BEEN TAKEN FROM PUBLIC DOMAIN TRANSLATIONS. ALL OTHER QUOTES FROM TEXTS CONSTITUTE FAIR USE.

TACHYON PUBLICATIONS
1459 18TH STREET #139
SAN FRANCISCO, CA 94107
(415) 285-5615
WWW.TACHYONPUBLICATIONS.COM
TACHYON@TACHYONPUBLICATIONS.COM

INTERIOR DESIGN & COMPOSITION BY JOHN COULTHART
COVER ART AND DESIGN BY JOHN COULTHART

SERIES EDITOR: JACOB WEISMAN
EDITOR: JILL ROBERTS
DEVELOPMENTAL EDITOR: JULIET ULMAN

ISBN 13: 978-1-892391-90-2
ISBN 10: 1-892391-90-2

PRINTED IN THE UNITED STATES OF AMERICA BY WORZALLA
FIRST EDITION: 2009
9 8 7 6 5 4 3 2 1

For Ann,
who rewrote sections, suggested additions/deletions,
and contributed significantly to the book's final shape and structure

■ INTRODUCTION

Are You Ready to Embrace a Booklife? —————————————— 11
How to Use this Book ————————————————————— 12
- Sampling It ———————————————————————— 12
- Following the Structure ————————————————— 13
- Re-imagining the Book ————————————————— 13
What This Book Is Not ——————————————————— 14
Further Resources: Booklifenow.com and Booklife.com ————— 14

■ I. PUBLIC BOOKLIFE

Chapter 1: Building Your Booklife———————————————— 17
The Pillars of Your Public Booklife ——————————————— 17
Creating and Managing Goals ————————————————— 19
- Mapping Your Future: Think Strategically Not Tactically —— 20
- Approaches to Planning ————————————————— 20
- Change Management ——————————————————— 24
- Mission Statements ——————————————————— 26
- Benefits ————————————————————————— 26
- "How Am I Possibly Going to Keep Up With All of This?!" ——— 27
The Discovery Process ———————————————————— 28
- Being Yourself ————————————————————— 28
- Exploring Your Strengths and Weaknesses ————————— 29
- Improving Your Abilities ———————————————— 31
Choosing Your Platforms ——————————————————— 34
- Facebook ———————————————————————— 35
- MySpace ———————————————————————— 37
- Twitter ————————————————————————— 38
- YouTube ———————————————————————— 40
- Other Platforms ———————————————————— 40
Public Platform Example: The Blog ——————————————— 43
- Creating a Blog ————————————————————— 43
- Temperament: Should You Release Your Inner Evil Monkey? — 44
- The Tension Between Ego and Information ————————— 46
- Modeling and Content Development ——————————— 46
- Effective Approaches—————————————————— 47
- Ineffective Approaches ————————————————— 48
- Enhancements ————————————————————— 50

Managing Your Involvement ——————————— 51
• Levels of Involvement ————————————— 53
• Follow Through = Personal Integrity ————— 55
• A Personal Space the Size of a Postage Stamp? ——— 56

Chapter 2: Communicating Your Booklife ——— 59
Networking ————————————————— 59
• How Do You Network? ——————————— 60
• Rules for Communication ————————— 63
• Overcoming Fear of Contact ———————— 64
• Managing Contacts ———————————— 65
Dealing with Editors and Publicists ————— 68
• A Covenant of Mutual Respect ——————— 68
• When Things Go Wrong —————————— 71
• Making Assumptions, and What You Can Do About it ——— 75
Understanding Creative PR ————————— 79
• Universal Elements ———————————— 79
• The Lifecycle of a Book —————————— 82
• Rules of Engagement ——————————— 84
PR Opportunities ————————————— 91
• Blurbs ——————————————————— 92
• Conferences and Conventions ——————— 93
• Readings ————————————————— 96
• Guest Blogging ————————————— 102
• Interviews ———————————————— 103
• Reviews —————————————————— 105
• Writing Your Backstory —————————— 106
PR Tools ————————————————— 108
• Artifacts ————————————————— 108
• Information Retrieval ——————————— 115
• Objects —————————————————— 115
• Samples —————————————————— 118
Leveraging Your Ideas ——————————— 121
• Lost in the Crowd? ———————————— 121
• Successful Example: "The Situation" ————— 122
Creating a PR Plan ———————————— 124
• Your High-Level Plan ——————————— 125
• Your Detailed Plan ———————————— 126
Five Minimum Elements for Success —————— 129

MORE »

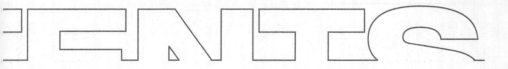

Chapter 3: Maintaining Your Booklife — 131
  Transparency — 131
  Branding — 135
  • Personal — 135
  • Public — 136
  • Managing Perception — 139
  The Importance of Persistence — 140
  Paying it Forward/Community — 143
  Against Trends — 145
  Positive Survival Strategies — 147
  • Multi-purposing the Public for the Private — 147
  • Using Personification — 148

■ BOOKLIFE GUT-CHECK: TOWARD PEACE OF MIND

  The Search for Balance — 153
  Your Health — 155
  • Positive Choices — 155
  • Avoiding the Negative — 156
  Multitasking and Fragmentation — 158
  • White Noise and Dark — 158
  • Managing Open Channels — 158
  • Tolerance for Channels — 161

■ II. PRIVATE BOOKLIFE

Chapter 1: Living Your Booklife — 165
  The Pillars of Your Private Booklife — 165
  Reasons to Write — 168
  Attitude and Creativity — 170
  Finding Inspiration — 172
  • Acknowledging the Passion — 172
  • Strategies — 174
  Being Receptive — 176
  • The Subjectivity of Taste — 176
  • Mastery as Uncertainty — 177
  • The Tactics of Prose — 178
  Room to Think — 182

- Recognizing the Nature of Distraction ———————— 182
- The Other You ———————————————————— 184

Relinquishing All Fetishes ——————————————— 186
Writing and Revision ————————————————— 188
- Testing Your Work ——————————————————— 188
- Poking the Structure with a Stick ———————— 188
- Interrogating Your Characters ————————— 189
- Resources ——————————————————————— 192

Work Schedule ———————————————————— 195
- For Part-Time Writers ———————————————— 195
- For Full-Time Writers (Bowing to Reality) ——— 197

Habit versus Process ————————————————— 200
- Do You Know the Difference? ————————————— 200
- A Novel Example ————————————————————— 201

Permission to Fail ————————————————————— 203

Chapter 2: Protecting Your Booklife ——————— 207
Addiction ————————————————————————— 207
Rejection ————————————————————————— 210
- From Other Writers ———————————————————— 211
- From Editors ————————————————————— 212
- From Reviewers ———————————————————— 213

Envy ————————————————————————————— 215
- The Many Faces of Envy ———————————————— 215
- Difficult Solutions ———————————————————— 217

Despair ————————————————————————————— 218
Revitalizing Creativity ———————————————— 222
Success ————————————————————————————— 224
Support from Your Partner ——————————————— 226
The Long View ———————————————————————— 228

■ APPENDICES

A Note on the Appendices ——————————————— 231
Appendix A: Additional Information on Relevant Roles ——— 233
Agents ————————————————————————————— 233
Booksellers by James Crossley ————————————— 244
Editors by Jill Roberts ———————————————— 246

MORE »

Marketing Versus Publicity by Colleen Lindsay ———————— 249
Publicists by Colleen Lindsay ———————————————— 252

Appendix B: Content-Related ——————————————— 259
Marketing/PR Campaign Summary (Example) ——————— 259
Podcasts ———————————————————————— 266
PR Plan (First Draft Example) ——————————————— 268
Press Releases (Example) —————————————————— 279
Book Reviews ————————————————————— 282

Appendix C: Additional Notes on New Media by Matt Staggs ——— 289
Nodes and Influencers ———————————————————— 289
Reputation Management: Telling Your Story
    Before Someone Else Does ——————————————— 291
Sipping from the Fire Hose: Online Search Tools ——————— 292

Appendix D: Nurturing Creativity ——————————————— 297
Chasing Experience by Nathan Ballingrud ——————————— 297
Luck's Child by Marly Youmans —————————————— 302
Workshops by Cat Rambo ————————————————— 304
Sacrifice: Without Hope, Without Despair by Matthew Cheney —— 306

Appendix E: How to Write a Novel in Two Months ——————— 313
Support ———————————————————————— 314
Writing-Related ————————————————————— 316
Conclusions —————————————————————— 322

Appendix F: Evil Monkey's Guide to Creative Writing —————— 323

Acknowledgments ————————————————————— 327

About the Author ———————————————————— 329

INTRODUCTION

▶▶ Are You Ready to Embrace a Booklife?

THE WORLD HAS CHANGED, and with it the writing life. In addition to the traditional difficulties of putting pen to paper, writers must now consider and internalize a slew of "new media" opportunities — blogs, social networks, mini-feeds, and podcasts, to name just a few. This has forever altered the relationship between writers and their readers, their publishers, and their work.

Booklife will provide you with the strategic and tactical intel to thrive in this new environment. It will help you reach your full potential in both your writing goals and your career goals. Whether you're a beginning, intermediate, or advanced fiction writer, self-published, published in the independent press, or by large New York commercial conglomerates, this book will be of value to you. Nonfiction writers will also find much of use within these pages. All you need to bring to *Booklife* is your own curiosity, openness to new ideas, willingness to work hard, and, of course, a passion for writing.

In addition to helping you become more productive, focused, and savvy, *Booklife* should serve to reduce or remove sources of stress and fragmentation. You *can* balance writing and promotion, interact with the readers using new technologies and keep enough private space to be fulfilled in your creative life. No shortcuts can replace perseverance and hard work, but *Booklife* can significantly reduce your learning curve and give you new, energizing strategies.

I've used the metaphor of a "book life" because I believe in visualization to achieve goals. In addition to the traditional paper-pulp-glue versions, a "book" in the context of *Booklife* can be any creative project that requires text, including podcasts, e-books, and short stories posted online. Anything can contribute to your Booklife in a positive and lasting way, from a series of blog posts to a short YouTube video adapting part of your novel. The term "book" is just the most potent, most concrete anchor a writer can visualize as the end result of his or her labor.

I've tried hard to be honest in writing this book. In support of that goal you won't find slick slogans, seven steps to success, or other facile ways of expressing ideas. For this reason, too, you'll find humor and personal anecdotes where applicable. I've been in this business for over twenty years and I've tried to put that experience to work for you in ways that are helpful rather than insular. *Booklife* is also infused with the spirit of a love for writing and of community. I'm optimistic about the future of the written word, in whatever form it may take, and *Booklife* is a reflection of that optimism.

At this point some writing books would add a rah-rah sentence like "You can change the way you think about your creative life and career, today, this very moment." And you'd either be there with me or you'd be calling bull-pucky. The truth is, you can change your approach and your mindset, but nothing worth doing well is easy. Everything requires work. The good news? By the time you finish implementing the strategies and tactics set out in *Booklife*, you will know you've *earned* your success.

▶▶ How to Use this Book

■ Sampling It

Depending on your interests and level of experience, you can dip into this book at any point. Many of the topics covered are universal — issues that creative people have faced for thousands of years, discussed in the context of our modern era, including new media.

One of the great comforts of encountering discussion of, for example, something like writer envy is remembering that all writers at some point in their careers have gone through similar experiences. Unless otherwise noted, comments from other writers, editors, and readers originated on my blog or in private email conversations. But you'll also find wisdom from the classics, from Sun Tzu to John Ruskin, Seneca to Jonathan Swift. My hope is that you'll enjoy finding so many other voices seeded throughout the text, and that they create an interesting dialog.

None of us are alone in this.

■ Following the Structure

Although you can always dip into this book at any point to address your specific needs, I suggest you consider giving *Booklife* a careful read from beginning to end. I've separated out career-oriented information from creativity by structuring this book around your Public Booklife and your Private Booklife. I've even included a Booklife Gut-Check section between the two because I believe so strongly that you must have a partition between what you do "out in the world" and what you do while you're writing.

This point I cannot emphasize enough: your Public Booklife and your Private Booklife work in tandem — throughout *Booklife* I am careful to provide private context in public sections and vice versa — but you must separate them out for balance and peace of mind. Writers get into trouble otherwise. For example, the minute you start thinking about how to market or leverage something while writing it, you've lost the focus you need to make your work reach its full potential. Many of the ideas in this book are ultimately about strengthening your ability to be two different creatures at very different times. You'll even note that the tone of *Booklife* changes between the Public and Private sections, because the needs of writers, and the approaches, also change radically between the two.

■ Re-imagining the Book

Information and advice has no effect without what the reader brings to the experience. To breathe life and energy into your Booklife, re-imagine *Booklife* and make it your own by customizing it to your own specifications.

How does this work? As a beginning writer I often took a chapter of a favorite novel, photocopied it, set it on the typing stand, and retyped it. By re-typing it, I experienced the text in a different context, and in some ways made it my own. Then I would set aside what I'd typed and re-type the chapter from memory.

You can do much the same thing with this book, as a way of personally visualizing its real-world application to your life and work. Take the sections that you find most useful, make a list of bullet points, and rewrite them from memory, adding in your own personal anecdotes and experiences. Then compare what you've written with the original. In the gap between my text and your reworking of it, you may find much in the way of previously hidden information and understanding.

The idea is not to blindly copy the strategies set out in *Booklife*. My job is just to give you a head start. Question *everything* in this book. Every writer is unique, and every piece of advice has a different meaning to the individual as a result. Part of achieving your unique Booklife will be to reject parts of *Booklife*, too.

Always remember: *Keep one eye on the matter at hand, and the other on the horizon...*

▶▶ What This Book Is Not

Booklife functions as a strategic and tactical guide to being a writer. It is not a technical manual on how to set up a blog, website, MySpace page, or Facebook account. Such information quickly becomes dated due to the way even established web tools change and evolve — within days, weeks and months, not years. *Booklife* is also not a writing instruction book, although the Private Booklife section includes topics like how to recharge your creativity and approaches to revision.

▶▶ Further Resources: Booklifenow.com and *Publishers Weekly*'s Booklife.com

For more information, please visit booklifenow.com. The website not only supports the publication of *Booklife* but continues, in online form, to support the theme of "sustainable creativity, sustainable careers." On the site you will find entries on a variety of related topics, as well as a list of other resources. Given the rapid rate of change in new media, a printed list of other resources in the appendices would quickly become irrelevant. At the website, we can provide a continually updated library of resources to better support you and your developing Booklife. The site will also provide you with information about the workshops run by my wife and I, along with other opportunities to bring *Booklife* to you.

We're also pleased to be affiliated with *Publishers Weekly* and their excellent BOOKLIFE.COM web portal, which provides you with some of the finest literary sites on the Internet. Between the dynamic information on BOOKLIFENOW.COM and the access created by Booklifenow, you should be covered for most of your needs.

You can also check out my personal blog at JEFFVANDERMEER.COM for a running commentary on book culture, writers, and other subjects related to creativity.

I. PUBLIC BOOKLIFE

Chapter 1
Building Your Booklife

▶▶ The Pillars of Your Public Booklife

MORE THAN TWO thousand years ago, the strategist Sun Tzu wrote that the warrior skilled in indirect warfare is as inexhaustible as Heaven and Earth, as unending as rivers and streams, and passes away only to return like the four seasons.

Curiously enough, these classic lines could as easily describe the relationship between you and the Internet, given how quickly a writer must adjust to and take advantage of opportunities. It also reflects the ephemeral quality of the Internet. Because of the vast amount of information and opinion posted every single day, every hour, every minute — supplanting the information posted a minute, an hour, a day before. To exist in this world you need to be fluid and flexible while retaining inner calm and balance.

Traditional strengths like being fleet of foot, working hard, creating something seaworthy and imaginative, and finding interesting opportunities for collaboration still tend to be rewarded in the marketplace. However, the traditional career and promotional models that once helped you to brand and leverage your creativity often don't work today.

The modern context requires from a writer some combination of the following qualities or abilities to achieve lasting, sustainable career success:

- VISION. Look five or six moves ahead, like a chess player, and recognize opportunities to diversify while remaining focused on the main goal.

- CENTEREDNESS. Understand that committing to objectives does not mean giving up balance in one's life.

- **ADAPTABILITY.** Have the flexibility to turn on a dime and reverse course or pursue some new course, depending on new intelligence.

- **RISK-TAKING.** Be able to leap into the unknown, although not without a bungee cord or safety net.

- **HONESTY.** Have the willingness to open yourself up to self-analysis and criticism from others.

Thinking about and nurturing these traits will be invaluable in your journey toward a sustainable Public Booklife.

▶▶ Creating and Managing Goals

The gap between the "professional" and "amateur" writer has been forever muddled by the advent of new media and the ability of individual content providers to find, at the very least, a niche audience. The situation in the writing world now more closely mirrors the way things work in the world of music. Many bands, including several that have hit it big, work from indie labels or create their own labels. A form of "self-publishing" is common and respected — an attitude we're only beginning to see gain traction in a writing culture that largely discourages any do-it-yourself efforts by individual creators.

While I don't believe anyone will ever completely replace gatekeepers in the publishing world, neither is that world the same as it was just ten years ago. Whether you've just self-published your book, or have a contract with an independent or commercial publishing house, you have a greater ability now to control the path of your career and the breadth and depth of your opportunities than ever before in the history of publishing. That amount of freedom can be frightening, and the complexity of possibilities mind-numbing.

That's why establishing goals is one of the most important tasks you can ever undertake for your writing career. Spending a little honest time in this area can sometimes save you years of misguided or misplaced effort.

Creating and managing goals isn't difficult or scary as long as you break it down into its component parts. *A goal must be specific, measurable, and be attached to a timeline.* Each goal should clearly state what you want to accomplish, and by when. Think in terms of declarative sentences like: "I will [achieve something] by [a specific date or time]. For example, "I will sell one novel to a commercial publisher by 2011." Make sure to write your goals down.

In updating my short-term and long-term goals document recently, the simplicity of my bullet point list struck me again — even the details of how I intend to achieve my goals are simple. But when I mention this idea to beginning and even experienced writers many of them look at me as if the problem is actually that I'm *too* organized. Sometimes that look also says, "I'm a starving artist — my genius lies in my disorganized random approach to life, not just my art."

I don't actually buy this argument. Down through the ages, more than one creative juggernaut, including the Renaissance artist Gregorio Comanini, has counseled the equivalent of "Live an ordinary, regular life so you can be irregular and brilliant in your creativity." Deep down, we all know that that focus — knowing where you want to go and how you want to get there — is extremely important to success. Having a document you can refer to that helps focus your efforts, even, perhaps, your behavior, seems ever more vital in this new world we live in — one so wonderful and yet so dangerous due to a combination of limitless possibility and limitless opportunities for distraction.

Providing yourself with positive structure is one way of affirming that you respect your own imagination and creativity enough to set yourself up for success.

■ Mapping Your Future: Think Strategically Not Tactically

Because writers often work organically and hate doing mechanical things like detailed novel outlines, they sometimes also shy away from creating actual lists of long-term and short-term career goals. Instead, many of my colleagues have daily, weekly, or monthly "to do" lists that help keep them focused but also keep them stuck in a tactical mode, which makes it hard to engage in strategic thinking. Yes, you know what you want or need to do for the next thirty days, but what about for the year? What about for the next five years? How do your daily/weekly/monthly tasks feed into short-term goals, and how do your short-term goals feed into your long-term goals?

Many writers never progress in their careers — except in a shambling, two-steps-forward-one-step-back way — because they always focus on the moment, and the moment after that. Their maps lack all kinds of details essential for finding their way toward a destination. Even if you self-define as a "disorganized" writer and believe you could never focus on the "big picture," you can benefit from taking a stab at a loose plan.

■ Approaches to Planning

When I wrote briefly about this topic on my blog, the idea resonated even with those who had been skeptical. Writer Michele Lee, for example, had this to say:

I love making lists and organizing and goal making. But I wasn't sure how much it would help me seeing as I'm only half a step into my career. But it really has helped. I got serious about it at the beginning of last year and wrote up a business plan. While a lot of the goals changed due to outside events and agent/editor feedback it's still helped a lot to have goals. I break mine up into three categories; Private, Public, and Uncontrollable Goals. I highly recommend others sit and work out where they want to be and what they can do to get there. It also helps letting go of the things you can't control.

I like how Michele acknowledges that even if you can position yourself to be successful some things will always be out of your control. Identifying those elements and acknowledging them in your list of goals will alleviate certain types of career frustrations. (See also Marly Youmans' essay on luck and the writer, in the appendices.)

Another way to organize your goals is to create one-year and five-year plans. Your one-year plans should support your five-year plan. Each five-year plan should build on the last, if possible. It also shouldn't result in the equivalent of crop failures or massive purges, like most of the Soviet Union's five-year plans.

Here's a simple strand of a plan, one I created when I was seventeen and beginning to think about my long-term goals. At the time I was going to college and had just transitioned from writing poetry to writing fiction. For me, short stories made sense because I couldn't even comprehend creating something as long as a novel.

- **FIVE-YEAR PLAN:** Publish one book, possibly short stories, from an independent press.

- **ONE-YEAR PLAN:** Publish at least one story in a publication with greater prestige or circulation than any of my previous credits.

- **MONTHLY TASK:** Write at least half a short story per month. Complete one story every two months.

- **WEEKLY TASK:** Keep finished short stories in constant rotation, submitting each to the top markets and working my way down until acceptance.

Usually, barring acts of God and the tender mercies of editors looking for the hot new author, you cannot walk before you crawl. The simple fact is: if you don't write stories, you can't publish stories. If you don't publish stories, you usually can't find a publisher for a collection of short stories — just as you cannot build a wooden house without wood, and you cannot build the ceiling to keep out the rain until you've built the walls. It sounds simple, but many writers neglect this basic element to keeping their careers on track. (The same principles apply to novels, of course.)

Notice, too, that I gave myself more time for the act of creation, but that the pace quickened with regard to the task of getting my stories out there. One task simply requires more mental space than the other. As for meeting my five-year goal, I missed it by one year: it took six years before my first collection came out (although I self-published a chapbook before that).

What do my current goals look like? Here's a peek at just a few, with most of the specific names left out. I wrote these down in early 2008 and each had a deadline of the end of 2009. Two have already been achieved as I write these words, in early February 2009.

- Acquire at least one speaking engagement with higher brand-name recognition (corporate but creative).
- Create a graphic novel with an artist and sell it, to diversify portfolio and form new creative alliances.
- Write one novel in the mystery genre.
- Write reviews for *The New York Times Book Review*.

Each of these goals has a timeline and tasks associated with it, as with the example from when I was seventeen. The only difference is I have many more goals now, some of them long-term and some of them short-term. You'll also notice that my goals, even in this limited sample, are a mixture of career and creative. The goals document isn't the place to map out what you want from your Private Booklife, but it should acknowledge that you want to grow as a writer, and push yourself to do new things. Diversification, if you have the temperament for it, is one of the ways in which you can best take advantage of the opportunities that have opened up in this century. It also limits your susceptibility to those elements outside of your control — like a weak economy, for example.

On a tactical level, you can use a high-level task list to encompass general activities that support your goals. These are things you weave into your month as time and opportunity allow, and which feed into your overall efforts. Here are a few examples of high-level tasks connected to my current goals:

- Consolidate gains in getting better speaking engagements by re-evaluating criteria for acceptance and rejection of opportunities.
- Leverage contacts that occur due to the release of new books and made through writing workshops to acquire information about potential speaking engagements.
- Determine stakeholders, allies, neutrals/potential allies, and detractors/ obstacles to current goals (assess which obstacles to engage and which to ignore).
- Research potential collaborators for a graphic novel.
- Pursue higher-profile book reviewing opportunities by leveraging the *Huffington Post* and *Washington Post* gigs.

Those high-level tasks feed into low-level general tasks like the following:

- Repurpose my own author's note and the combined bio for Ann-Jeff.
- Research new up-and-coming comics artists.
- Update the Services section of my website.
- Get video equipment for webcam.

Low-level general tasks get worked in with daily/weekly project-oriented tasks on a document tracking a month's worth of effort. Remember I said weekly or monthly task lists are no good without additional structure? Within that structure they work marvelously well to focus you on important deadlines while not losing track of the bigger picture. *Keep one eye on the task at hand and one eye on the horizon.*

Here's an example of a typical day's task list for me:

Saturday, January 17, 2009
- FOCUS ON *BOOKLIFE*

- 60 in 60 Amazon entry, plus more Amazon entries, for coming week
- Deadline for getting sample project to Artisan Books
- Get the *Third Bear* story collection contract from Tachyon
- Go through and organize/archive email
- Go through contacts for Matt Staggs and delete those that are out-of-date
- Podcast "The Situation"
- Figure out *Booklife* PR schedule

Notice how the emphasis is on the creative work first and foremost. Also notice how simple this list is — and I make it even simpler by keeping it in a standard Word document rather than in a spreadsheet. You need to be able to easily update the list for it to have value. The danger of using Windows project management software or some other organizational tool is that you'll find yourself spending more time and energy creating your schedule than actually accomplishing the tasks associated with that schedule.

Ironically, many modern inventions designed to streamline our lives, such as time management software, can actually be counterproductive to creativity by being too complicated or automated. Simple actions, however, like using an automated reminder for deadlines or storing documents can be very helpful. You just have to experiment until you find the mix of tools that makes you efficient without distracting you from your goals.

■ Change Management

As my friend *New York Times* best-selling author Tobias Buckell reminded me recently, "No battle plan survives contact with the enemy, but you at least need a battle plan!" To put that comparison in writing terms, strategic goals are almost like a novel outline: the story always changes when you actually write it; or, in this case, live it. One of the trickiest things to determine is when to change your goals. You must continually revisit your progress, your level of happiness, and your interest level. Sometimes you just need to tweak your goals — or the tasks associated with them, if those tasks aren't fully supporting your goals. Other times, you'll need to perform a complete overhaul, especially if the law of diminishing returns has come into play. Here are some scenarios in which you may want to consider a change:

• **You have new priorities or responsibilities.** We all experience life changes, and when we do, we have to modify our goals to reflect those changes. Each change carries with it a range of pitfalls and opportunities. When I quit my day job and began to live off my book and reviewing income I took advantage of that opportunity to make my goals more ambitious, because I had more time to work on them. But one thing I discovered is that without the structure of the day job I also had to be more focused and work harder than I ever had before. Because I was used to the time it took me to do things with the day job, I had no idea how long things took when I could work on them 24–7 — or how important taking breaks would become. As a result, I missed several book deadlines before I adjusted to the new rhythms of my life — and had to go back and adjust my goals yet again.

• **You haven't made progress on the tasks associated with the goals.** While you're busy berating yourself for being lazy, maybe something else is going on. Maybe you really don't like doing the tasks associated with your goals. In fact, you dislike them so much, you can't bring yourself to follow through in any consistent way. At that point, you have to change your goals or you'll continue to be frozen. (If, on the other hand, you haven't even attempted the tasks, maybe you just need a swift kick in the pants. After all, as the Romanians say, "A kick in the pants is just another step forward.")

• **You haven't met any of your goals.** Sometimes elements of what you need to happen to reach your goals will be beyond your control. If you don't meet your goals in a reasonable time try to be patient and give yourself a few more months or even a year. Then consider either re-evaluating your goals entirely or amending them to be more modest. If you take a few steps at a time, you might soon be at the top of the stairs.

• **You aren't happy with your life.** If achieving your goals doesn't make you happy on some level — if you don't feel fulfilled creatively — then you need to do some serious thinking about your life in general, and how your goals either support or do not support your happiness. There can be a huge difference between what others want for you, or what you think you want for yourself, and what the hidden core of you needs for happiness. Sometimes, too, talent is a curse. You may be talented in an area that doesn't actually bring you happiness or balance.

■ Mission Statements

Sometimes when I lead workshops on sustainable writing careers I find it easier to start with goals than with mission statements. A mission statement is a high-level strategic view of your goals. For this reason, many writers feel uncomfortable with mission statements. They'd rather start with something more piecemeal — even if it means changing their goals once they've established a mission statement. This might sound backwards, but sometimes focusing on the details of goals helps you decide what's important to you in a very real way — something grounded in the practical. You can, of course, do what's more traditional and create a mission statement first, but, either way, make sure the mission statement and the goals are mutually supportive. You can have multiple mission statements to support different sets of goals, but I prefer having one mission statement to work with all of my goals:

> I want to improve and challenge myself creatively and career-wise by diversifying my portfolio across genres and types of media — and use that diversification to drive a higher profile in terms of speaking engagements, book reviewing, and other opportunities.

If your mission statement is longer than one paragraph, it's probably too long. Once you've settled on a statement that resonates with you, I strongly recommend printing out a copy and displaying it prominently in your workspace. Having a visual reminder of the "big picture" reminds you of what you've self-identified as important and reinforces the story of your unique Booklife.

■ Benefits

The benefits of such planning extend beyond making progress toward career and life goals. Yes, with a solid mission statement and a focused list of short- and long-term goals, you can achieve amazing things. But more importantly for many creators, this kind of approach also takes away the stress of endless decision-making.

What do I mean? Half of the fatigue you feel in a given day comes from what Jorge Luis Borges called "the garden of the forking paths." *Do I do X or Y? Do I veer off toward Z or stay focused on A?* Irritation and anxiety often originate from our fear that we've chosen the wrong path, even if the decision is minor.

However, if you have a mission statement and goals, you immediately know if you should take advantage of an opportunity. You can easily recognize when an opportunity is not for you. You can even make a list of things you *won't* do. For example, you won't write a short story for a non-paying market. Or, you won't accept a speaking engagement for expenses-only. Soon you'll find that your mission statement and goals will *make decisions for you*, and each time you keep your focus on what you've already outlined as important, you take a big step toward fulfilling those goals. Sometimes an opportunity is an opportunity — and sometimes it's just a distraction or even a trap. One of the hardest things for some writers to do is say no, especially early in a career.

■ "How Am I Possibly Going to Keep Up With All of This?!"

The complexity of an integrated approach to establishing long- and short-term goals isn't about any one part of the process. It's more about what looks overwhelming overall. If you think of a goal's plan in terms of its parts, the idea, it becomes more manageable because you can probably face a daily task list or even a yearly goal without too much stress. Let's review:

- Create a mission statement to keep focused on what's important. (Revise annually.)
- Create long-term and short-term goals documents. (Revise quarterly, but look at daily.)
- Create a general task list associated with these goals. (Revise monthly as necessary.)
- Create a specific tasks list associated with these goals. (Revise quarterly.)
- Work the general and specific tasks into a monthly document broken down by week and day. Include in this monthly document any deadlines and any tasks that you need to perform but that are not connected to your long-term and short-term goals. (Review/revise daily.)

You'll note that after the initial set-up, the only document you need to update on a regular basis is your monthly task list. With this structure in place, you can relax into a productive schedule that supports daily creativity and where you want to be in a year, or five years. (Although you'll need to regularly re-evaluate your progress, make sure you don't re-evaluate so frequently that it becomes an obsessive, self-defeating act.)

In all of this, too, there is still the human element. The simple truth is: no one reaches all of their goals, and no one has the inhuman ability to stay on task all the time. But making the attempt to articulate your dreams in this way means you *will* accomplish more than you would otherwise.

Finally, remember that living a productive Booklife requires a certain amount of introspection. After finishing any project or major task, take the time to reflect on and analyze your efforts. Try to identify factors that helped and hindered those efforts, and apply what you've learned to whatever you tackle next.

▶▶ The Discovery Process

▦ Being Yourself

It's certainly possible that in the distant past you did not need to promote your work. It's possible that in the past all writers needed to do is turn in the manuscript and let the reviews, the interviews, and the incoming royalty checks wash over them. But today, unless you're Salman Rushdie, Stephen King, or Margaret Atwood, you do need to be able to promote your work. Even if you have a contract with a major publishing house, you will need to coordinate some efforts with that publisher's publicity department. You will need to become accustomed to the uncomfortable feeling that you are somehow being less than true to your core creativity while out hawking your wares.

There's definitely a potential disconnect here. As my friend and writer Marly Youmans put it when she saw this section listed in the table of contents: "The more I consider this idea, the less I grasp it, because I start thinking about that weird division between the daily self and what Proust called '*le moi profond*.'" The inner self, Youmans argues, "is subject to all of the disorder and pain of life, and doesn't have to do the dishes or get the kids on the bus, doesn't have any of the clutter that keeps our outer selves busy."

For this reason, you need to find the level and the type of engagement that makes sense for you and your life. You need to be able to reflect your true personality, you need to find strategies that suit what you're "selling," and you need to find ways to separate your writing from your promotional efforts.

If you can do that, you will minimize the frustrations of promoting your work, the most basic of which is that it takes you away from your writing. There's also a certain frustration in the fact that it's often easier to joyfully recommend someone else's book than it is to recommend your own. Still, part of success in this area means finding ways to have fun promoting your project. There's no reason why self-promotion *shouldn't* be enjoyable. You're telling people about something in which you believe deeply. As we'll also discuss, there's no reason why everything you do has to be purely functional. You can use your imagination for PR in ways similar to how you use it for your writing.

Perhaps the most important advice I can give is *just because everyone else does something doesn't mean you should do it too*. Question and research all "opportunities" touted as "bleeding edge" or "innovative" and make sure (1) using them fits your goals and (2) using them makes sense for you as a person. That process includes rigorous testing of the advice set out in *Booklife*.

◼ Exploring Your Strengths and Weaknesses

Not every writer is good at everything. You might be shy. You might be bad over the telephone. You might be unable to type a concise email. However, before you rule out certain approaches to promotion you're going to have to really analyze your core strengths and weaknesses, not just rely on random self-perception. You might be shocked or delighted at what you find out as a result.

For example, I'm assuming you're good at writing—but what kind of writing? Writing nonfiction is different from writing fiction. Writing advertising or PR copy for your own work is different than writing general nonfiction. You might find out that what you think is a strength is actually a weakness. In writing about your own work, you might tend to be more modest or, conversely, too bombastic. You might make assumptions and leave out information because you already know it. In short, it can be as hard to write about yourself as it is to keep putting yourself out there for publicity purposes.

An important component of your analysis will be getting honest feedback from friends and colleagues, as well as giving yourself the distance to make your self-analysis valuable. For example, if you think you're bad over the phone, tape a conversation and play it back to not only make sure you're right but to identify exactly *why* you're bad at phone calls. This process may be challenging or unsettling to you. If so, good! It's supposed to be uncomfortable, but better for you to feel foolish or exposed in your own home than to look foolish or be exposed in public.

After you've completed this analysis you'll still want to concentrate on what feels comfortable to you and doesn't stress you out too much...but you'll also want to confront one or two things that *do* make you uncomfortable so you can grow and change. If you can compartmentalize the unfamiliar in this way, it should also reduce the "sweat factor," as I call it. Simply put, other people will sense when you're uncomfortable, when you're nervous, when you don't really have confidence in what you're doing. If they sense that, then they're going to associate the lack of confidence with your book as well as you.

The good news is that you can find other people to do those things that make you really uncomfortable. If following a traditional publishing route, you have access to a publicist at your publisher, and you probably also have friends with different skill sets willing to help out. And, if you have enough money, you can always hire someone.

Sandra Ruttan, a mystery novelist with savvy in this area, writes:

Not every writer can be a shining web presence. Not all want to be, some don't need to be, and some recognize that they can't be good at it precisely because they can't engage in the social interaction needed to network effectively.

On panels at conventions and on posts online I've said myself that if you can't chat with strangers, if your body language is going to speak of distance and discomfort, you either need to take some public speaking classes and join a few groups where you have to work on interacting with people, or you should seriously consider not attending conventions or doing book signings. There is something worse than not doing an event, and that's being there and doing it terribly. People will notice, and they'll remember, and they'll tell other people.

A few years ago I was at a convention. I was leaving an event with another author when we were intercepted by a blogger. The person automatically engaged in conversation with the author I was with. I hadn't met the blogger, but knew who they were from the Internet, so extended my hand and said, "I'm Sandra Ruttan" and they said, "I know," didn't shake my hand and just carried on with their chat. And, boy, did people talk to me about how I was snubbed later.

On the other hand, I met [mystery author] Lee Child that weekend, [and] he [not only] took the time to talk to me about my web presence, but at a convention this fall, walked down the hall, saw me for the first time in two years and said, "Sandra Ruttan. How are you?"

Lee Child: best-selling author, not a snob, great at remembering people and taking the time to say hi. And on the other hand, blogger with a handful of short stories published...I tell the story for one reason, and that's to illustrate that how you treat people matters. Others notice.

In extreme cases, you may just have to avoid certain situations, the key being to *not feel guilty about it.* Just as Ruttan relates above about her experiences, I have one colleague who used to force herself to go to conventions and meet people because she felt she had to for her career. But, as she herself admits, this did her more harm than good because she gave off an aura not just of shyness but of extreme, intense, debilitating nervousness. She doesn't do many conventions any more. That decision has helped her personally and with her career.

◼ Improving Your Abilities

How can you work on problem areas without being overwhelmed? Make a list of your strengths, your weaknesses, and those gray areas in between — things you're not terrible at but not great at, either. Even though you've presumably had others help you evaluate your strengths and weaknesses to get to this stage, take this list and give it to a couple of friends or colleagues you *didn't* include in your original analysis. Ask them if your list is accurate. After you've included their feedback, and been *totally honest* with yourself, do the following:

- Break the Strengths list down into subcategories, rating yourself in each, so you have a better idea of what those strengths mean. Be aware of your strengths even as you work on your weaknesses and make sure shoring up weaknesses doesn't negatively affect your strengths.

- Select two items from the Gray Areas list that you think you can easily improve and that would help your writing career. Make sure your short-term and long-term goals include ways to better yourself in these areas.
- Select one item from the Weaknesses list, even if it's something that also scares you. Add elements to your short-term and long-term goals that give you opportunities to make this weakness a strength, or at least something you're not bad at anymore.
- Select one item from the Weaknesses list that you don't want to work on improving. This advice especially applies if something on your list scares you too much. Setting it off to the side is about preserving your mental health. You can always revisit it in the context of success with some other weakness.

Live radio interviews (which now include podcasts) fit into the category of a weakness that scared me to death. The first time I was on, I mumbled and I could hardly breathe. Because I was so nervous, I wound up saying something like "You're as stupid as I want to be" to the host, which was meant as a joke but came off as insulting and bizarre. The second time I was on the radio, it went fine. Until the host made a strange comment about whether or not I lived in a cave, which threw me off so much the rest of the interview entered a decaying orbit. The third time, I got the hiccups from drinking too much coffee. I spent the whole hour making sure the cadence of my speech allowed me to turn from the microphone just as I was about to hiccup. This worked better for the interview portion than for the reading I did afterwards.

What was my particular remedy? I relied on repetition and experimentation. I just kept accepting radio and Internet podcast interview requests. I also experimented with different kinds of preparation. Eventually, the combination of finding the best way to prepare and doing more interviews made me more comfortable with the format. I can't tell you I'm the best radio interview ever — I still get nervous — but when you hear me on the radio these days you're unlikely to say to yourself, "Wow! That guy was horrible."

As for a gray area that I've turned into a strength, public readings fit that category. Unlike radio station show appearances, readings never scared me. However, I didn't have a good sense of performance so my readings were serviceable but nothing to excite anyone. Over the past few years, I have worked hard to add an element of performance to my readings, along with humorous anecdotes. Part of that growth process meant watching myself on video giving readings. Another part meant being more careful about my selection of material and how long I read. Now, most people come away from one of my readings entertained, and I generally see comments on blogs afterwards along the lines of "Wow — that guy really put on a good show."

Not only will you remove stress from your life by confronting some of your weaknesses and gray areas head-on, you'll also learn a lot in the process. Like anything else in your Public Booklife, you just have to approach it systemically and incrementally.

▶▶ Choosing Your Platforms

In the past, a writer had limited ways to convey content to a source or sources. Most methods involved dealing with a gatekeeper in the form of an editor or other entity that would accept or reject content, or ask for changes. If someone wanted to bypass these gatekeepers, he or she had to expend a ridiculous amount of time and energy in endeavors such as traditional models of self-publishing.

Today, the situation is much reversed, as the Internet houses dozens of free, unrestricted platforms that act as conduits of information from the creator to an audience and from the audience back to the creator. A platform can manifest as a social network, a variation on a blog, a microblog (for example, Twitter), forums, or even a channel of direct one-on-one communication (like Instant Messenger). Linkage between these platforms means that it's no longer possible to define them as just one thing — no longer possible to set clear boundaries as to whether, for example, Facebook is a social network, a blog, or a form of direct communication. However, all of these platforms give you *access* to a wider world of readers and contacts.

Many of these platforms were intended to be, and remain, *communities,* and were not specifically built to allow writers to disseminate either creative or promotional content. Still, that is one benefit of their existence from a writer's point of view.

At the same time, you cannot be everywhere at once, unless you're able to download your brain into the Internet — something that looked very cheesy in the movie *Tron.* Be aware when considering these platforms that some will fragment you more than others.

What do I mean by that? From using all of these approaches at one time or another, I know that each puts a different strain on your attention span. Some require only a sliver, but that sliver can devour your day. Others require much more than a sliver of your mind but don't give you the feeling of being nibbled to death by tiny sharks. For this reason, where relevant, I've discussed the fragmentation level of a particular approach. You will have your own unique perspective on how to use or not use each, and the interplay between them. Later, too, you'll combine platforms with opportunities and tools to create a larger plan. Please note that (1) although an email could be considered a kind of platform, I haven't included it here because so much of what I discuss elsewhere involves use of email, (2) podcasting is covered in the appendices because I believe for most people podcasting constitutes a form of blogging or providing book samples, and (3) blogs are covered extensively in "Public Platform Example."

Here, then, are a few examples of platforms. I'm fully aware that even this relatively high-level analysis may be dated by the time you read *Booklife*. However, discussing current popular examples still provides you with information on the general value of platforms.

■ Facebook

Facebook allows you to connect with other professional and personal friends and share parts of your life with them. At first, I didn't use Facebook because I already had ways (through my blog, MySpace, and email) to keep in touch with friends. It also seemed like just another thing to keep track of during an already busy day. However, once I had a chance to explore Facebook I began to understand its appeal. In fact, I have now abandoned MySpace entirely — which shares some commonalities with Facebook but is much more cumbersome (see below) — and focused my effort on Facebook.

Why? First, the light, delicate interface in Facebook creates a sense of calm in keeping with the platform's primary purpose. You can easily upload videos, photos, and audio, as you can with most platforms. But more than this, I find that Facebook provides an opportunity that is different than a blog. You can post updates and links that give the people you allow to be your friends an opportunity to check out what you're up to, but those people don't have to make the effort to visit your blog specifically — they have a constantly updated list of all of their friend's efforts, usually with a bite-sized sample, and can pick and choose.

Another great feature of Facebook is that each account comes with an embedded inbox for receiving private messages. You have the anonymity of exchanging messages without divulging your personal email account. This makes superstar creators who might otherwise not interact with the public able to communicate without fear of it turning into a commitment or, even worse, a liability.

For example, a creator responsible for a series of incredibly successful comic books and movies friended me on Facebook recently. This is someone I would have had to go through an agent or manager to contact otherwise. Any email I sent through those gatekeepers might or might not have gotten through. In the context of Facebook, this person and I had a friendly conversation, with the added benefit that they enthusiastically agreed to contribute to a new anthology project being edited by me and my wife.

But even if Facebook didn't include this functionality, it would've proven immensely useful to my career and creativity. Eric Orchard, a Canadian artist who has done amazing work for children's books, made a comment on a link I posted indicating he'd read and enjoyed my work. I checked out his art, fell in love with it, contacted him, and within a few days we were collaborating on a graphic novel version of my novella "The Situation," which we subsequently sold to a major website. Eric read my blog but had never commented there. Facebook, because the format is informal and fluid, encourages people to comment who might not communicate through your personal platform.

You can also schedule Facebook events, create mini-forums around your book, and use a chat function much like Instant Messenger. (Just as with Instant Messenger, this last functionality can be annoying, and I usually turn it off.)

The biggest downside to Facebook right now is that too many writers are being aggressive in using the site for promotion. After a while, an invite to a Facebook party for a book becomes more like spam than anything personal. In fact, any generic invite or promotion across the Facebook email account becomes white noise quickly, and is not effective PR. Some writers set up their account so their name reads "*Novelist* John Doe," annoying at the very least and not recommended unless your first name really is "Novelist." In addition, unless you're a seasoned pro with a couple dozen books out, it might not be the best idea to set your account so your friends have to become your fans. That approach reeks of pomposity, and creates a distance between you and other people on Facebook that can be off-putting.

It's precisely the open, comfortable format that makes aggressive PR seem more obnoxious on Facebook than on other platforms. If you simply express your normal interest in what other people are doing, don't overuse Facebook to promote your work, and let things develop naturally you'll get good value for your time investment. Despite its penchant for providing multiple opportunities to post small amounts of text, I also find visiting Facebook incredibly de-stressing. In fact, during much of the writing of this book, under a strict deadline, I visited Facebook to let off steam. What I found there is a positive and uplifting community made that way in part by the vision of the people who created the platform. Facebook's very look-and-feel discourages flame wars and most other negative behaviors.

Will Facebook prove to be the MySpace of its web generation? As it continues to provide more and more functionality in reaction to developments elsewhere on the Internet, Facebook may become too complex for new users — or it may evolve into a "one-stop shopping" platform that evolves into the dominant life form. Regardless, the potential of Facebook to influence and drive both careers and creativity has not yet been fully explored, and I expect it to be a major force for several years. You'll find endless combinations of ways to make it work for you — limited only by your imagination.

■ MySpace

Although MySpace recently updated its look-and-feel, it still contains the seed of its legacy function as a groundbreaker among Web 2.0 platforms, and one that gained attention mostly because musicians love to use it. Musicians, however, don't have a need to leverage MySpace to post different kinds of text. Therefore, it's still easier to upload a video or audio file to MySpace and create a fan site if you're in a band than it is to post text in a variety of contexts. For me, there's little about MySpace besides its dedicated blog feature (which you can use to mirror your main blog) that can't be done more efficiently, with less of a time drain, on Facebook. This sense of awkward functionality means that MySpace fragments me while multitasking much more than Facebook. The feeling is exacerbated by the fact that MySpace allows more opportunities to receive spam and other empty communiqués.

That said, I do maintain a MySpace page and you may find that you have the exact opposite reaction and like MySpace much more than Facebook. It all depends on what you want out of the platform, and how your brain is wired to appreciate one or the other. I would recommend, however, that you choose one as your primary time commitment and the other as a backup, as maintaining both, especially if you also have a blog, can be a daunting time drain.

Despite the reputation these services have as being the sole domain of teenagers, you'll find that plenty of influential and well-known adults have Facebook and MySpace pages, making them both premium sources for networking and customer outreach.

▪ Twitter

Twitter is a microblogging platform that allows you to update the world on your daily activities via one-hundred-forty character posts sent by cell phone or through an Internet browser or software client. People can choose to "follow" your updates at their option, and you can do the same. It's free to use, and you don't even have to own a cell phone.

You can also synchronize your blog posts to Twitter, so that every time you post an entry it also shares the link on Twitter — you can have your Twitter messages post to Facebook. In a sense, Twitter gains its strength from combining the sense of community associated with a Facebook friend status message with the best elements of the various versions of Instant Messenger.

As of mid-2009, Twitter is the new hot thing online, with people using it as a kind of microblog to write Twitter stories and collaborative novels. Some Twitter accounts serve as communal wisdom about particular topics. Others, like the infamous "Amazonfail" Twitter page, allowed amateur journalists, in real time, to investigate the suspect tagging, and disappearance from search results, of hundreds, perhaps even thousands, of feminist and gay titles.

However, most people use it to tap into a constantly updated news flow, and to communicate with their favorite creators. Ben Templesmith, the graphic novelist and artist responsible for *30 Days of Night*, uses Twitter almost compulsively, and his fans get a level of interaction with him that they wouldn't get otherwise. Pop culture giant Neil Gaiman also has a Twitter account, as do hundreds of others.

The main advantage of Twitter over Facebook is that you don't have to confirm someone as a friend — anyone can follow you if you have a Twitter account. This makes the experience less personal but wider. You can find yourself with immediate access to all sorts of important contacts who might not give you the time of day in any other situation, even Facebook. Just keep in mind that some people use Twitter for creative purposes and others as a microblog for chatting. Chatting into the timeline of someone who sees Twitter as a creative outlet can create conflict.

While I use Twitter by synching it to my blog and Facebook, I rarely update it and rarely check it. For me, making a regular commitment to Twitter fragments my attention too much to allow me to focus on creative projects. It makes it difficult to focus on strategic goals, as it's a very reactive forum. I don't personally get the sense of community from Twitter that I get from Facebook. Facebook also has the advantage of contextualizing the trivial in a larger context. If someone changes their status in Facebook to "Angela just drank a great cup of coffee and went to work," you see that within the continuum of a diverse stream of information about the daily lives, frustrations, and achievements of your different kinds of friends. If someone posts to Twitter "Angela just drank a great cup of coffee and went to work," it's in the context of a dozen other similar Twitter posts, without the benefit of a larger context. Twitter also makes Facebook's anchor — your status message — carry the entire weight of the interaction.

Not everyone shares this view — in fact, by the time you read this book, mine will almost certainly constitute the minority opinion. For example, publicist Matt Staggs finds Twitter much friendlier than I do:

> Depending on your level of commitment, you can indeed build a tight community via Twitter as you interact with your followers. Like Facebook, a certain level of intimacy is engendered by the informal "water cooler" nature of communication in Twitter's social environment; this is compounded by the fact that Twitter users often find themselves talking to the same people every day. Conversations develop at lightning speed as updates prompt real-time responses and reactions throughout the Twitter network. Information spread that way will also often leap from Twitter to all corners of the social web, popping up on blogs around the world.

I understand the value of Twitter, and I expect it to continue to be popular, but some little part of me says it's too early to understand the full effects of Twitter, and whether in four years it will be the Web 3.0 equivalent of Facebook or of MySpace. (Sixty percent of new users don't continue after two months.) Depending on your attention span and your purpose, though, you may find Twitter more useful than I do currently. In theory it's a great networking and promotional tool.

■ YouTube

YouTube is a free video upload service that also includes some social networking options, like comments fields, an inbox for messages, a subscription service, and a few forums. Most writers use YouTube to upload promotional videos or book trailers, which they then leverage across other platforms. Leveraging your video across YouTube itself requires (1) a popular subject and (2) identifying the institutional ways to get the video in front of YouTube administrators. You can also find "communities" through subject matter, but your effort might be better spent on platforms that more naturally lend themselves to communication.

However, you can also use YouTube to supplement your text blogging with video blogging. Web cameras and editing software are cheaper than ever, and with our society becoming increasingly visually oriented it makes good sense to explore that option. You could, conceivably, build a large vidblogging audience through YouTube. As with all such efforts, though, examine whether the time investment is fulfilling or fragmenting, and whether you're getting the desired results.

■ Other Platforms

Other kinds of platforms either have specific targeted audiences or only vestigial social media accoutrements. These include:

• **E-NEWSLETTERS.** An e-newsletter is a self-created platform leveraged through email. These writercentric updates were popular before the rise of new media, and still have their place in a changing virtual landscape. My own VanderWorld Report, set up through Yahoo! Groups, includes more than news about my writing. I add previews of forthcoming books, give behind-the-scenes looks at current projects, and accounts of my travels to conferences and conventions that I might not be comfortable sharing in a more public forum. Follow a few rules and you may find you've created a tool that harnesses the enthusiasm of your core fans. Your e-newsletter should not be interactive — don't make it a discussion group — and it should not be intrusive. Unlike blogs and other new media that require continual updating, an e-newsletter is most effective when delivered only once or twice a month because otherwise it begins to seem like spam. Don't sign up people who haven't expressed interest in your work. Don't make it difficult to unsubscribe, either. The point is, if you keep the list pure, it will become a powerful tool for sales and for dissemination of information. If you dilute it, you will risk irritating people and you'll develop an inflated view of the number of people who really care about your writing.

• FLICKR. Although primarily an image upload service — wonderful if you're going to use photographs on your blog — Flickr does include the ability to share and tag your images, and to comment. Most writers have not explored this functionality, probably because Facebook and MySpace are much more robust.

• NICHE FORUMS AND MESSAGE BOARDS. In addition to communities like Facebook and MySpace, special interest groups and subcultures have set up a vast array of forums and message boards across the Internet. Some are open to the public. Others require you to sign in and meet certain requirements. In many cases you can join a forum and set up your own message board within it. The advantage of going to a niche group is specific to your project. You may be able to find core readers for a particular type of book much more easily in this context. Recently, I participated as a guest in two completely different forums: an Aliens vs. Predators forum to discuss a media tie-in novel and a literary fiction forum to discuss my short fiction. What I found useful about such specific forums is that I exposed myself and my work to people who had never visited my blog or other platforms. These readers otherwise might have remained completely outside the scope of my publicity efforts.

• SECOND LIFE. Some writers have staged readings in Second Life, a virtual reality platform, or even used it for their writing, but its potential for individual creators as opposed to publishers remains largely unexplored due to the huge time commitment. Writer Caitlín R. Kiernan is one of the few authors who maintains an active presence in Second Life, but she has serious doubts about its viability as a tool for writers, despite having been interviewed by the BBC in Second Life:

This is an environment where the lowest common denominator almost always holds sway. Most of SL is a wasteland of virtual strip malls. And even when you get lucky and stumble upon, say, a gorgeously built steampunk city, or a drifting derelict spacecraft, it's likely to be overrun with [characters] dressed incongruously as their favorite manga or video-game characters.

(For more about Second Life, refer to the "Creative Objects" section of "Creative PR.")

• INSTANT MESSAGING. Instant messengers are single-tier pop-up platforms that allow you to communicate with friends and colleagues from a small dialog box you can position anywhere on your screen while performing other tasks. Although many people ignore instant messaging's possibilities as a platform and consider it closer to email, you can have online chats with multiple gatekeepers through an IM and use it to conduct interviews, as I did for a WIRED.COM feature. You can also use an instant messenger's chat room function to have the equivalent of a private conference call via text. Several versions of IM exist, through media giants such as AOL and MSN. Depending on your need to concentrate, you may want to keep Instant Messenger off while working as it can be disruptive. On the other hand, if you have the discipline, it can be a good down-and-dirty way for a gatekeeper to quickly get hold of you.

▶▶ Public Platform Example: The Blog

Multiple platforms or vehicles can carry your persona, your thoughts, and your creative work across the Internet. But the speed of change in new media is fast, and it often adapts to (some say "preys upon") peoples' work habits and their personalities. Today you might be most comfortable with a Twitter account and a Facebook page, or you might want something more substantive. But a year from now your needs or the platforms might have changed again, and you'll be more active somewhere else. Complicating matters, we're overly enamored of blinking lights and bells-and-whistles, like a baby in a crib looking up at a colorful mobile. It can be hard to think strategically in the midst of so much shiny-shiny.

For this reason, try to anchor yourself to shifts in perception rather than trends — and the most potent perception shift right now is the continuing movement toward personal content providers replacing entrenched institutions. As Matt Staggs puts it, "Everyone has become a stakeholder, the monologue a dialogue. Organizations now understand that the power they once held to exclusively disseminate their message via traditional media has come to an end."

Blogs are even now becoming like the castle keeps of yesteryear — a stationary object around which people and armies move — but they're still by far the best way for an individual to leverage content on the Internet.

Because the basic premise of all new media, besides communication, community, and connectivity, is providing some form of content, most of the information I give below about blogs should apply equally well to other platforms. The basics of what people want, what makes them excited, hasn't changed for hundreds of years — just the delivery systems. Although this section deals with text-based blogs, much of the advice also pertains to blogs anchored in videocasts or podcasts. (For more on podcasts, refer to the appendices.)

■ Creating a Blog

How do you create a blog? You can use any number of platforms for blogging, but WordPress is my favorite, as well as Matt's: "I enjoy WordPress for its clean design, integrated stat monitoring and ease of use, but it's really a matter of preference." Blogger provides the same ability to turn your blog into a complete website. You also may prefer a LiveJournal rather than a blog.

Launching a blog or its equivalent is a great opportunity to be creative, interact with your friends and readers, and contribute to the wealth of imaginative, funny, and informative content streams on the Internet. You may even find that your particular niche on the Internet becomes so popular that it not only supports your creative life, it becomes an integral part of that life.

I know that I've gotten so many positive things out of my own blog, Ecstatic Days (JEFFVANDERMEER.COM). Not only have I met many interesting people, but it's fueled my creativity, given me ideas for short stories, and even resulted in the book deal for *Booklife* itself. In addition, it has resulted in collaborations with artists and illustrators, created discussion and discourse in other areas of the Internet, and allowed me to pay it forward by giving me an immediate audience for book recommendations. In one extraordinary case, my blog allowed me to connect a new author, Jesse Bullington, with an agent. Jesse subsequently went on to land a lucrative book deal.

I mention these successes to point out that I've included blogs in *Booklife* as a platform to help your career, but that a blog or other online presence is more than a launch pad for your existing work. For this reason, it's important to think about the kinds of content and behavior you will support through your blog, and what kinds of content and behavior you won't support.

To put it another way, a blog is like a kind of virtual garden. There are an infinite number of ways to make your garden uniquely your own. It's also up to you whether you maintain and add to your garden wisely, in winter as well as in summer — or if you let it become overgrown with weeds and trash. It's also up to you whether your garden fits with the adjacent house that is your Booklife or is radically different from it. In all ways, the choices you make will affect how others perceive you and how you perceive yourself.

▪ Temperament: Should You Release Your Inner Evil Monkey?

In one discussion at Ecstatic Days, my readers talked about the temperament of bloggers. A comment by Graham Storrs struck me as particularly interesting, because I think it does reflect a stereotype about what you need to project as a blogger:

> I find so many blogging writers — the more popular ones anyway — are really upbeat, peppy types. Myself, I'm in a constant struggle against letting out the bitter, cynical old fart within. The peppy ones are obviously more helpful when it comes to community building, encouragement, inclusion, and lots of other good things. Those of us who want to belong but feel that old urge to take our ball and go home have got to be a bit careful when blogging. It is too easy to turn to the dark side. So should I minimize the difference between the real me and what I put out there, or should I try to play nice with the other kiddies?

My answer at the time was:

> Personally, I think you should find a way to balance it. If every time someone comes to your blog it's always to find something negative or dark there, that'll probably turn people off. If they go to your blog and half the time it's sweetness and light — which, c'mon, has to be part of your nature about some things — and the other half it's cynical and whatnot, I think that's just fine.

It's always better to be true to yourself than to contort yourself into some constantly smiling automaton. But that doesn't mean you can't emphasize aspects of yourself that are upbeat and positive — just so long as you don't let a minor part of your personality take over your blog. Otherwise, the disconnect between who you are trying to be and who you are will catch up to you over time.

In trying to find the right balance, I wound up creating an alter ego called Evil Monkey. I use Evil Monkey when my mischievous side comes out and I need to say something that might get me in trouble. Evil Monkey has been instrumental in allowing me to poke fun at bad movies, have complex conversations about politics in fiction, point to hypocrisy in controversial situations, and in general maintain the positive vibe of my blog while still saying many serious things. What's amazing about this kind of displacement is that most readers of the blog *wind up arguing with Evil Monkey* and hold me blameless. This approach also highlights how far humor can take you in the blogosphere. (See also Evil Monkey's Guide to Creative Writing in the appendices.)

Alas, an Evil Monkey doesn't automatically come with your blog when you set one up. You'll have to experiment on your own to find personalized strategies that help turn negatives into positives.

■ The Tension Between Ego and Information

When your ego gets in the way, any writer can turn a blog into a dingy backwater saloon where visitors are wary of getting knifed (or bored out of their skulls) if they linger too long. Especially corrosive over time are blogs that function only as promotional tools for their creators. English writer Chris Billet put it this way:

> I honestly think that Internet/blog interaction is a thing that authors (well, anyone, but authors are in the business of selling to their audience) can really screw up big time. I recently read an author who posted some technical comments regarding spam, and in response to advice on the topic (which I, as a very, very experienced technical analyst can vouch for being good advice) commented something like "do you think the world would be a better place if I wrote less fiction and spent more time mopping up spam?" I rarely let authors' politics or attitudes get in the way of my purchases, but coupled with some other exceedingly arrogant and downright rude comments to well-meaning commenters on the blog, I resolved never to send said author my money by purchasing his books when there are always a thousand others to choose from.

This freedom of choice Chris mentions has been enhanced a millionfold by the Internet. Only a fraction of visitors to your blog will buy your book or other creative project, but that fraction is still significant. Alienate your blog readers with rudeness, haughtiness, or arrogance, and you may well lose readers for your core creative work.

■ Modeling and Content Development

Most blogging platforms like Blogger or WordPress include templates when you're first setting up your blog. You can choose from any of them, or, if you have a budget, ask a web designer to create your own distinctive look. Before you do so, though, you should check out the blogs of creators you admire. Make a list of what you like and don't like, and give the resulting list to the designer. (For more information on this and related topics, I recommend *The Huffington Post Complete Guide to Blogging.*)

Similarly, you should make notes on types of content provided by your favorites. What keeps you coming back to a blog? How could you put your own twist on the same idea? As in writing, the difference between pastiche and a true riff on existing material is how thoroughly you remake something to reflect your point of view. The value of information on the Internet isn't its exclusivity so much as its mutability. However, if you steal something without re-envisioning it, have the decency to note the original source.

At the same time, think about what types of *unique* or fairly unique content you can add to the Internet. I write for Omnivoracious, the Amazon book blog, and one of the best examples of unique content I've seen came from guest-blogger Charles Huston, author of the noir mystery *The Mystic Arts of Erasing All Signs of Death.* His guest-blogging consisted of anecdotes about various crime scenes he'd come across as research for the book, and especially his interactions with crime scene cleanup crews. It made for bracing but entertaining reading. Combining the exotic with concise storytelling is just one of the many ways you can provide enjoyable content.

◼ Effective Approaches

In maintaining an effective blog, it's often less about the information than about how and when you present that information. Being inclusive, being positive, making your enthusiasms other people's enthusiasms, and keeping on topic most of the time are all important. Another key is to post on a regular basis (many successful bloggers suggest at least once a day) without overwhelming your readers.

However, over time, creating a *variety of ways* for your readers to approach your content ensures your blog will garner more comments, more appreciation, and more repeat traffic.

What do I mean by "variety of ways"? If you post a short article about your favorite book, next time you post about a book do so in the context of some larger trend and ask your audience to participate by asking them a related question. If you usually post photographs, mix it up by posting a video. If you have done several serious posts in a row, make sure to mix in some humor. Much as newspaper journalists have to worry about using the same old leads and hooks, you should worry about using the same old visuals and the same templates for your text. Here are a few more ideas that I've found useful:

- Combine image and text as much as possible to break up "gray space."
- Do call-and-response, contests, and posts where maybe you're more serious than usual or give out information where visitors actually learn something.
- Be imaginative and humorous in responding to comments.
- Make sure you usually offer actual content rather than just filler or links.
- When you do link to other blogs, be selective. Make sure it's genuinely good content for your readers.
- Don't be afraid to diversify your content within certain parameters. For example, if I stick mostly to books and things related to books — like movies, comics, etc. — I can post almost anything I want to within that corridor. And I can also venture out from it into politics and other topics every once in awhile.
- Try to make your posts serve multiple purposes. My books-received posts perform the dual service of general entertainment but also making sure almost every book I receive gets some notice/mention, especially now that I've also added a podcast.

Equally as important, *listen to your readers*, whether they make specific suggestions or a telling silence gives you a hint as to direction. Granted, a lack of comments doesn't always indicate a lack of interest, but if you have a sense you're not reaching a wider audience, and you've tried to get media outlets and other bloggers to link to your posts, then you might need to try something else.

◼ Ineffective Approaches

As useful as a blog can be as a platform, certain behaviors tend to make maintaining one a neutral or negative thing for your Public Booklife. Bloggers often get into trouble because of a false sense of entitlement that carries over into how they communicate through their blogs. Avoid the following pitfalls:

- Continually hard-selling your work through your blog. Combine direct and indirect promotion of your work. No one wants to feel like a carnival barker is shouting at them all the time.
- Overreacting to criticism in reader's comments by either suppressing it or responding in anger. Remember that many more people will read your blog than will comment, so do not inflate the positive or negative importance of an individual comment. The majority of people reading your blog may not share the same point of view.
- Being overly aggressive and competitive. As one of millions of voices, you can't really see blogging as a competition. If you do, you'll always lose that contest. Moreover, you'll come across as petty and selfish.

A further note on overreacting to comments, as this is one of the most common ways that flame wars develop on the Internet. Matt Staggs has the best advice on this subject:

> From my experience, fires like these online arguments and spats take fuel to burn, and it's extremely important to weigh what you have to gain versus how much you have to lose before you engage in a conflict. For one thing, criticism is just going to be there. It's the nature of the Internet, an open system through which information flows fairly unimpeded, and efforts on your part to stifle this flow are going to erode your overall appearance of authenticity. No one is going to take good word of mouth about you seriously if it comes out that you actively suppress bad word of mouth. For another, you can't win an argument with a nut. You just can't. It's just best to avoid adding the fuel to the fire which your engagement will ultimately bring. Doing so will just make you look as crazy as the other person in the long run, and you'll erode any sense of authority or respect you have. Just ask yourself before you even type that response: what do I have to gain from this? Chances are, if you're honest with yourself, you'll realize it's not a whole lot.

This advice really applies to any situation, including communication through email or instant messengers. The wise writer remembers to maintain both internal balance and external calm in his or her Booklife.

■ Enhancements

Remember your goals document, and the tasks associated with it? My goals document also includes enhancement goals for my blog, mostly to do with promoting certain types of information and posts, and de-emphasizing others:

Blog Subjects
- Yes
    - Breaking book news first
    - Cultural clearinghouse
    - Fiction
    - Humor
    - Information about my books (reviews, exclusives, contests, etc.)
    - Podcasts
    - Pop culture
    - Progressive politics
    - Reader-immersive posts (contests, etc.)
    - Reviews (movies, books, music, etc.)
    - Strong stances on important issues related to art and creativity
    - Video projects
    - Writing advice
    - Writing process
    - Writing life
- No
    - Prolonged arguments/disputes
    - Links to negative reviews
    - Responses to negative reviews
    - Snark
    - Whining

Depending on how central your blog is to your creative life, you can also create a mission statement specific to your blog. Now, do I always manage to live up to the positive vibe of this list? No, because no one's perfect. However, I try hard, and that's half the battle.

▶▶ Managing Your Involvement

The public presence of a writer today is so different from even a decade ago — the distance between then and now is the distance between receiving a message via the Pony Express in a week and having it emailed to you in a millisecond. You can easily set up a blog, a LiveJournal, or a website in less than 24 hours — and suddenly, *voila!*, you have a public forum. Yes, having a book out is important, but a short story on a prominent website or a clever blog post can be almost as powerful for your career.

This immediacy, this ability to get attention for your work quickly, is wonderful. But it also accelerates the process of *becoming public* before most writers have thought through what kind of longterm commitment they're willing to make to the Internet, and what kind of distance they want between themselves and readers (both readers of your work and of your online manifestations).

Sometimes this idea of distance is critically important, and many bloggers are taken aback once they realize the implications. Silence Without blogger and fiction writer Tessa Kum still struggles with this issue:

> [Readers are] coming to the table under the impression that, because they read my blog, they know me, and thus engage in a level of familiarity that is not at all earned and makes me very uncomfortable. Blogs aren't an even-ended dialog, the information doesn't flow equally both ways. And just because you establish boundaries doesn't mean anyone will recognize them. Although I imagine most people will have less issue with it than I do, there is still an unsettling period where the act of blogging wobbles about, and the purpose is fuzzy. By posting, am I feeding my need to say, or the reader's expectation of something said? One is an act of release, the other is loss.

No matter what you do — no matter how much you think through your approach to the blogosphere — unexpected transmissions of intent and personality will occur, because you cannot control reader perceptions, and *there is no group mind*. Everyone perceives reality in a slightly different register.

Definitions of politeness and intimacy also differ from country to country, complicating the issue further. Still, you can minimize the psychic surprise by periodically measuring the overall effect and reach of your blog through a service like SurveyMonkey or Technorati. Knowing more about who reads your blog may allow you to make a few adjustments along the way.

However, this is not the only potentially serious issue pertaining to your level of involvement. Another concern has to do with the sheer diversity of approaches, in an almost infinite number of combinations. Some people don't even know where to start. Natania Barron, a new writer, wrote:

> It's astonishing [how] the Internet has changed the way writers are connected. I think, at first (speaking as a fledgling) it's a little overwhelming. You move from your own space, your own work, your own thoughts, to a world of such dynamic complexity and variety that it can often cause a bit of paralysis, both creatively and from a networking aspect. You don't know where to go — there are just too many options. And, unfortunately, good advice is just as plentiful as bad advice!

Sometimes this paralysis has less to do about the options and more about personality type. Austin-based writer Jessica Reisman posted this comment after I posted a blog entry about high-level involvement with electronic media:

> My thought is, I agree with you very much, particularly on your things to keep in mind, but I must point out that introverts — who like people and connecting, but like it selective and fairly low-key, and who often do not have the massive output of persona and self that graces and enlivens the pages of some — can end up kind of overlooked and drowned out in this model.

Just about every creative person working today feels some kind of pressure to develop an Internet presence on a platform or platforms — and for good reason. According to Victoria Blake — the founder of Underland Press, the publisher of my latest novel, *Finch* — not being Internet savvy is "practically a deal breaker":

> Publishing is a partnership between publishing house and author. Just as [most authors] can only go so far without the help of a publishing house,

so too a publishing house can only bring the book so far without the help of the author. This has always been true, but it's becoming more true as publishing moves out of the big-house, blockbuster mode and into the small-independent, niche-market mode. Smaller publishing houses need to work with the author more closely to make the most of every marketing dollar and minute.

But what that presence is should and *must* be different for every individual. Not everyone has the ability or desire to engage on the Internet. The critically acclaimed and beloved short story writer Kelly Link, for example, can quite happily have no Internet presence whatsoever beyond a website with a news section. (On the other hand, her husband, Gavin J. Grant, does engage in more aggressive tactics on her behalf.)

Other factors that play a role in your decision include whether you have a book to promote, what kind of book it is, and also the time and effort devoted to unrelated commitments.

■ Levels of Involvement

The majority of people starting blogs or other types of web presence don't think about their long-term commitment to their platforms. They create a blog or LiveJournal because it seems fun, or they think they have to — and because the standards the average blogger sets for him or herself are fairly low, you don't *have* to think about these issues. You can create a useful or popular web presence by experimenting "on the job." However, if you're serious about strategic rather than tactical solutions, you need to think about these issues. Here, for example, are three possible levels of involvement:

• **LEVEL ONE: DISTANT AND STATIC.** At this level, you probably maintain a static website that includes a news update feature or you have a blog or LiveJournal but you only post once a week. Sometimes months go by when you don't post. You'll sometimes comment on someone else's blog, but otherwise you're more or less a ghost on the Internet. You respond to email within a week or two. From a publicist's perspective, this level of involvement isn't recommended. Visitors have no compelling reason to return. Also, most writers provide much more interaction for their readers — to the point that people expect more from everyone. If this is your level of commitment, you'll need to make sure that one visit *does* leave a good impression.

• LEVEL TWO: NEARBY AND AVAILABLE. At this level, you probably use your blog as your website, perhaps through a Blogger or WordPress template. You update your blog at least three times a week and you have either an active Facebook or MySpace page. You might have two of these, but probably not all three. You're likely to use an instant messenger and your blog more than any other platforms. You're likely to have synched up your blog and Facebook to your Twitter account, but you don't post on Twitter very much. You may or may not take advantage of Google searches of your name and related subjects sent to your email account. You may or may not comment regularly on other people's blogs. You tend to answer email within a day or two of receiving it.

• LEVEL THREE: "I ONLY FEEL FULLY ALIVE MANIFESTED ON THE INTERNET". At this level, you update your blog at least once a day and it also functions as a dynamic website — but you also have websites for individual book projects. You may even have multiple blogs to accommodate different kinds of content. You maintain active MySpace and Facebook pages that you visit regularly. You also have a Twitter account that you check twice a day at least, you use an instant messenger for close friends and colleagues, and you receive information directly into your email through Google searches and RSS feeds. You comment regularly in online forums and on other people's blogs. You're online constantly, so you respond to email within minutes or hours.

Every person will create their own unique combination of elements to build an online identity and a corresponding level of involvement. Although consistency is key to building a long-term presence, you can also play with levels. For example, I'm always updating my blog with new entries because that's the bedrock of my online presence, but I'll float in and out of Facebook and MySpace.

The effect of mixing up your level of involvement is to create a new sense of excitement in places long abandoned when you suddenly turn on the lights. Also, given the rate of change and mutation online, visiting a platform you haven't been to in a few months keeps you up to date on any essential changes.

■ Follow Through = Personal Integrity

As you develop your online presence, keep in mind two important rules that will help you in the long-term.

• **AFTER CHOOSING YOUR LEVEL OF INVOLVEMENT WITH THE INTERNET, STICK TO IT.** As discussed, if you want minimal involvement, create a static website about your book or other creative endeavor. If you want medium-level involvement, establish a blog. If you want more, do more — but decide upfront what your approach will be, how much time you can spend, and whether you can actually follow through or not. Any disconnect may determine how much integrity you have in other people's eyes. If, for example, you start a blog and you post a lively selection of entries over the first month, and then… nothing…that makes a statement about you in the public sphere. If you start out making your blog a personal diary and then it becomes basically a place to post information about your book, that disconnect is going to cause you to lose some readers. If you get drunk and post some rambling manifesto, that may also lose you some readers.

Where and how you choose to manifest yourself creates assumptions by the public about you as a writer and as a person, too — just as, in fiction, a wise writer knows that it is what your character *does*, not what s/he *says* that determines whether the reader thinks of that person as good, bad, or indifferent. If you're the crank who always posts negative, cynical comments on writing advice blogs or in online forums, that will affect perceptions. Perceptions become a reality that's hard to shed, and this can hurt the appeal of your work.

• **WHEN YOU CAN, MAKE SURE THAT THE DIFFERENCE BETWEEN WHO YOU ARE ONLINE AND WHO YOU ARE IN REAL LIFE IS MINIMAL.** I used to think that you could control reader perceptions of your online persona if you stayed on message. However, I'm not sure that kind of control is possible. As Tessa points out, some natural dissonance is probably inevitable: "I have come across a noticeable schism in the blogTess readers are expecting and the meTess I've always been. These are people I've met previously, at that. I don't think I can do anything about it, as in both cases I am just being me." The fact remains, she says, that "different forums of communication will always filter a personality in unexpected ways, whether we choose it or not."

Some types of dissonance you may just have to get used to and learn to live with if you want to have a public platform. What I would recommend is that you shouldn't proactively create an online persona for distancing purposes or any other reasons. One danger is that if your platform becomes popular you begin to believe your online persona is your real persona, and usually your online persona is going to be less complex than you as a human being. Another is that the disconnect that occurs when people meet you in the flesh for the first time can be jarring and unpleasant. I remember meeting one blogger who strikes a very aggressive posture online. In person, he looked nothing like his photograph, was meek and mild, and I came away from the experience thinking of the Wizard of Oz for some reason. I never did really regain my respect for that blogger, whether that's fair or unfair.

■ A Personal Space the Size of a Postage Stamp?

Not only is everything you share on the Internet public, but it will reflect on you as a creator. When you create a LiveJournal rather than a blog, it may *feel* more like a diary than a public space, but it isn't — it's still a public space. In addition, many people don't realize how having private information made public invades their personal space.

Always think about what kinds of information you're willing to reveal online, and whether you would be comfortable sharing the same information with a room full of strangers. The Internet can create a premature sense of intimacy. Even if you think that no one at all is reading your blog, a private fact revealed in a careless moment can come back to haunt you years later as readers discover your online presence.

Even if you disable comments, you are still placing yourself in the public sphere. Many people don't understand this, leading to a couple of negative effects. One, they project an unprofessional demeanor without meaning to do so. Two, they put so much personal material on the Internet, and allow themselves to be so available to readers and friends, that they come to feel that their personal space has been reduced to the size of a postage stamp. Not to mention, whether it's fair or not, book reviewers often consider such material fair game in trying to guess a writer's motivations in creating a book. Suddenly that throwaway comment you thought playful and imaginative becomes the horrifying thesis for an excruciatingly incorrect analysis.

Another issue you may need to consider: Will a confessional-style approach to blogging leave enough personal experience in reserve for your actual fiction or other core creative endeavors? The answer will vary for each of you, and may even reflect generational differences.

For example, twentysomething writer Desirina Boskovich, *doesn't* buy into the argument that writing about personal things in a blog format "removes its energy and power and burns up your fuel before you use it."

> For years I kept an online journal that was deeply personal, and I find that the themes I explored and developed there became a major influence on my work. I worked out ideas there in rough form so that I could use them more coherently in fiction. I still look back at it for inspiration because the themes I wrote about — longing, loss, mortality, desire — are still important to me, and I'm still trying to examine the implications.

Still, many creators, without realizing it, may be taking what would be rich mulch for writing stories and novels, and using it instead to fill content gaps. Sometimes, once you've shared a personal experience, you cannot get it back for use in your fiction because, in a sense, you've already told the story. Your subconscious resists going through the process again.

The point is, experiment to find out if your Private Booklife supports sharing personal information as part of your Public Booklife. And, in general, beware of any involvement in new media that takes away any part of your ability to be creative in your core projects. As new writer J. T. Glover wrote, the Internet, for all of its benefits, is also "a demon with anesthetic-laced claws and breath that smells of chloroform." Don't be lulled into thinking that any kind of writing done online is good for you.

Chapter 2
Communicating Your Booklife

▶▶ Networking

HERE'S A PASSAGE from my novel *Shriek: An Afterword* about connectivity. It's from a sister writing to her brother, who she thinks has lost his way:

> Every human being is a puppet on strings, but the strings do not ascend to some anonymous Maker, but are glistening golden strands that connect one puppet to another. Each strand is sensitive to the vibrations of every other strand. Every vibration sings in not only one heart, but in the hearts of many, so that if you listen carefully, you can hear a low hum as of many hearts singing together...When a strand snaps, when it breaks for love, or lack of love, or from hatred, or from pain...every other connected strand feels it, and every other connected heart feels it — and since every strand and every heart are, in theory, connected, even if at their most distant limits, this means the effect is universal. All through the darkness where shining strings are the only light, a woundedness occurs. And this hurt affects each strand and each of us in a different way, because we all hurt and are hurt. And all the strings shimmer on regardless, and all of our actions, no matter how small, have consequences to others...

The word "network" means "a complex, interconnected group or system," but writers often forget the "interconnected" part in their zeal for self-promotion. If you build a "network" that is all about you, that isn't about *people*, then you don't really have a network. Instead, you have a way to send electric telegrams, and you may be perceived over time as white noise or as always carrying a megaphone. That's why you often see writers engage in ineffectual communications — like emailed requests for some sort of action sent indiscriminately to everyone on their contacts list or yet another Facebook request to attend some arbitrary event. In doing so, you ignore the cardinal rule of new media. Every contact is about community, about personal relationships, and the impact of that connection often produces all kinds of unexpected collaboration and creativity.

Here's another way of putting it: If you are on task 24–7 getting your "message" out rather than using your message to meet interesting people, then you've got a backwards idea about "networking." The best networkers, and thus the best promoters of their own work, love people and love to communicate with people — and love to find talent in other people. I cannot tell you the number of times my query to someone to tell them about one of my books resulted in something remarkable unrelated to my original purpose. This process of discovery lies at the core of what makes the Internet so wonderful. Being open to it is paramount.

If writing is a kind of sustained creativity, then inspired networking is as much about sustained creativity in building relationships. It is also, admittedly, as the writer Brendan Connell has called it, "a drop of dew on a blade of grass" compared to the actual task of creating a short story or a novel.

◼ How Do You Network?

Sustainable relationships may sound like a wonderful thing, but how do you go about building them? At its core, networking is about recognizing opportunity and potential — finding sometimes unlikely connections. Yes, you can research contacts for various media outlets on the Internet. Yes, this information can be useful to you, but it's also useful to every other person who can perform an effective search in Google.

If you truly want to form an effective network, if you want "networking" to be personal and your efforts to last, consider this:

• EVERYONE YOU KNOW IS A POTENTIAL CONTACT. This advice applies now more than ever, because everyone is literally connected to other people in a myriad of ways not possible before.

- **Everyone you know is more than one thing.** Always listen to what other people are saying. This advice pertains to networking because you won't understand a contact's potential without some sense of who they are beyond the narrow role you may have assigned them during initial contact.

- **Every book or other project you create is about more than one thing.** Find relevant subcultures. A quick Internet search centered around the genre of your book will reveal a wealth of forums and communities that you can join. Increasingly, too, you can search on topics relevant to your book and find communities with members who don't self-identify as readers but do still read books. They may well be interested in your book because of the subject matter. (For more on this subject, refer to "Nodes and Influencers" in the appendices.)

- **Every person you know knows hundreds more, and they know hundreds more as well.** The cliché "six degrees of separation" is more like "three degrees of separation." Sometimes you'll be approached by a reader who loves your work and they have connections of use to you. Nothing helps more than having an enthusiastic advocate of your work approach a potential contact.

- **Everyone has a different comfort level with types of contact.** I've already mentioned that on Facebook you don't have to give a user your private email address to communicate with them; this makes some people who are otherwise inaccessible more willing to talk to you. However, other people may prefer the telephone or Instant Messenger. Try to approach people in the way that gives them the greatest sense of comfort.

■ ■ ■

Take, for example, Tia Nevitt, who runs a typical mid-tier blog that serves a specific niche audience by only posting information about new fantasy writers. Nevitt's experience with writers is typical of the creative and professional effects of positive networking:

> I run a blog called Fantasy Debut, and in my interactions with authors, it is usually an "all about them" sort of thing. And that's fine; my blog is about debut fantasy authors, not about me. However, every

once in a while, one of those authors will ask me about me. It's always surprising when they do. And it makes the author more memorable to me because they didn't want to make it all about them. Whether they really give a damn or they're just being good communicators — it doesn't matter. They took the time for a personal touch. Such authors will always have a fond place in my memory. And because I remember them, they'll get more coverage on my blog. I understand authors who want to keep a bit of distance. If you have thousands of fans, you can't get close to them all. I respect authorial boundaries. However, in two or three places — perhaps four — true friendships have emerged. I am now even in the position of providing feedback to an author as he writes his book. Which, to me, is very cool.

A contact creates a two-way conduit, not an arrow pointing in one direction. If all of your networking is about the point of that arrow nudging someone else, you're doing it wrong. Or as new writer Natania Barron puts it:

> Consider giving before you get. Has a published writer on Twitter asked for a critique on a new short story? Offer your set of eyes. It's not magic; you have to give to get. Just like any good relationship. Many new writers are looking for handouts and publishing miracles, but aren't willing to do the legwork when it comes to nurturing their network.

At any level, the person you're talking to can usually tell the difference between someone who sincerely wants to communicate and someone who just wants to manipulate a contact. Finding people sympathetic to and interested in what you're doing, who may have something to offer you as well, and communicating with them in the way they're most comfortable with will result in a wider success — and be much more fulfilling than being cynical and just trying to get something from someone. Expectations of reciprocity may result in getting what you want in the short term, but don't build long-term relationships.

Are there dangers to successful networking? Yes. You can become addicted to the thrill of meeting new, dynamic people. Be careful not to develop a network at the expense of your writing. Otherwise, what you have is not a *network* but a social circle. Suddenly, you're spending more time "networking" — translation: "chatting with my friends" — than being creative.

■ Rules for Communication

By engaging with the world on behalf of your book or short story or blog, you will come into contact with a wide variety of people — bookstore owners, reviewers, magazine publishers, website editors, etc. True, your goal is to get these people to review or promote your book in some way. But there has to be an element of honesty to the relationship. Many of these contacts will develop into friendships, possibly even into a romance or two. I met my wife when she came to town to ask my advice about starting a magazine — and that was back in the 1980s, when I still did layouts with an exacto knife, glue, and blue grid paper!

To be a true steward of communication, remember these five rules (which probably apply to life in general, too):

- Be concise and precise with people you don't know, especially if using a method of communication like email that strips out nuance.
- Really *listen* to what the other person is saying and try to understand their perspective. (Visualize their response on a physical level — imagine the context of their job, their surroundings, and in general *empathize* and give the benefit of the doubt.)
- Do not engage in any behavior that would irritate you if you were on the receiving end; politeness and respect are paramount. (If you don't know what this means, buy a book on civility and communication.)
- Try not to deal with people you don't respect just because you need them for something. If you do have to deal with people you don't respect, don't ingratiate yourself with them for PR purposes.
- Respect the privacy of others. Don't give out confidential contact information you've gotten on the side to others unless you get approval to do so from the contact in advance.

An additional tactic that I learned from my publicist, Matt Staggs, is to introduce your contacts to each other. Matt likes to host what he calls "virtual cocktail parties" where he sends an email to two different people and introduces them to each other. Sometimes these introductions go nowhere, but often that initial contact leads to unexpected partnerships and new synergies. This tactic speaks to a larger strategy: Resist the temptation to hoard your contacts. If you connect people, they'll remember you for it.

◼ Overcoming Fear of Contact

Even with clear rules to follow and an idea of the best way to network, you may experience fairly intense anxiety or fear about contacting people. Sometimes this feeling is caused by your assigning an exalted status to the people you're attempting to contact.

When approaching people you believe are unapproachable, try to stop thinking of them as either larger than life or somehow inhumanly devoid of their own insecurities and foibles. Unfortunately, the writer-reader culture, especially in the United States, has a habit of elevating the creator behind beloved works rather than just celebrating the work. As a result, many of us cannot divorce the work from the person. This then manifests in non-concise communication with our heroes — or even just those we see as further up the food chain. In emails, phone calls, Twitter messages, Facebook messages, or face-to-face meetings, we then prevaricate, add disclaimers, and in general undermine the contact's belief in our professionalism. In a sense, we dissolve our true personalities right in front of them as a kind of offering to their reputation.

At one of my first writer conferences, I found out one of my favorite authors was in attendance. I really wanted to meet him, but was too shy. Somehow he found out, and he walked right up to where I was sitting on a hotel lobby couch. He said hello and my first words were "I was expecting someone taller." Now, this writer was very short, and although the intent behind my statement went something like "In my imagination you are ten feet tall, I love your work so much," he did not take it that way. Making matters worse, the next time I talked to him, on the phone, I was so nervous that I laughed maniacally at every little thing he said. After awhile, he paused and said, "Jeff, none of what I'm telling you is funny."

The only antidote for such behavior is finding a way, much as an actor would, to project quiet confidence. Your contacts will respect that approach much more than flattery or any variety of nervous twitches, no matter how endearing when told later in anecdotal form.

How do you project confidence where little exists? I find these three rules work for me:

- Disregard my advice earlier and use only the method of communication with which you feel most comfortable.

- If meeting face-to-face, say less, listen more, and when you do speak start out by asking questions rather than talking about yourself; always remember that you are more likely to look like a fool if you babble.
- Whether meeting in person or through some more remote form of communication, try to have support in the form of a partner, spouse, or friend. Face-to-face, your wingman or woman can take the pressure off of you. In other contexts, your support can actually take the bullet — make the initial phone call or send the initial email.

Always remember, too, that everyone has insecurities, including the person you're contacting, and that most people will be kind enough to try to put you at your ease if you are nervous.

■ Managing Contacts

I've set out the ways in which you can proactively approach networking. Proactive networking best helps you reach your Booklife goals, but the truth is, once you've set up your public self using online platforms, you're going to have trouble *not* making contacts. We make more contacts in the modern age, in a wider variety of ways, than ever before. Every day you potentially make contacts you *didn't even ask for* — through Twitter, Facebook friend requests, emails, or text messages. Information comes roaring at us in a cloud of glittering particles. Which bits are actually valuable, and which are just glitter?

The real problem isn't making contacts — it's identifying and paying attention to the people who really *matter*. That may sound cold or calculating, but it isn't. Preservation of the self is an important part of not becoming too fragmented in our modern world. To better manage your contacts, you should identify the following groups (some people will fit into multiple groups):

- Personal contacts that aren't career/creative contacts (usually certain friends and family members).
- Personal contacts that are also career/creative contacts.
- Direct work-related contacts (the people who give you checks).
- Self-identified fans of your work.
- Professional contacts that constitute "gatekeepers" of some kind (individuals with influence across the Internet or the hardcopy world).

- Professional contacts that constitute entry points to media outlets important to you (reviewers, bloggers, etc.).
- Creative contacts (the people who, although they may also fit into the other categories, represent potential collaboration or some other benefit to your creative life).

These are the people that you should keep in a database of some sort. A simple address book in Microsoft's Outlook or its equivalent might suffice, but for more powerful ways to group, sort, and collect information, consider buying a program like ACT (available from most computer stores); you can also use an online database if you prefer.

For the most effective results, update your contacts list every three or four months, and add new information as you receive it. Our database includes reviewers, bloggers, artists, writers, readers, media outlets, bookstore managers, reviewers, and several other "types," keeping in mind that one person can be tagged as several different types. It's a robust list from which we can call up, for example, "all U.S. reviewers who have previously covered Jeff's books." I even try to keep a log in the notes on reviewers to indicate which books of mine they've enjoyed and, er, which they haven't enjoyed as much. This helps us help our publishers identify who to court and who to ignore for a particular project.

It's worth noting that it took over fifteen years to build this contact list, so be patient. The usefulness and connectivity grows over time. You also need to be willing to devote the effort necessary to keep such a list updated and fresh. In some cases, you might be able to find someone you feed contacts to for their benefit and yours, without the responsibility for maintenance falling to you.

On the negative side, you should also identify and avoid people who have, over time, revealed themselves to be active time-wasters and time-takers. It's never a selfish act to shield yourself from people who waste your time without giving anything back. These types include emotional vampires; sycophants who just want you to validate them; and the guy who every time you get a freelance gig writing for a newspaper, magazine, or online venue emails you to ask if you can get him an "in" too.

There's an uncomfortable truth lurking here. We may think we're truly connecting with other people through the Internet or in the "snail" world, but many of those connections are superficial, and many of them can be seen, from at least one perspective, as moving each of us a step closer to death without any spiritual or creative gain on the individual's part. As Seneca, the Roman Stoic philosopher and statesman (4 B.C. to 65 A.D.), wrote so many centuries ago, some complain that they "have no chance to live. Of course it is impossible! All those who summon you to themselves, turn you away from your own self."

Another way of putting it: whenever possible, only deal with nice, friendly, generous people. Don't sacrifice your well-being or peace of mind for the sake of a "connection." When you can't avoid dealing with a jerk, make sure you're doing it because it's of use to you and not because an email just popped up in your inbox. (See also Matt Staggs' new media essays in the appendices.)

▶▶ Dealing with Editors and Publicists

Although new media has changed the platform-content paradigm forever, relationships with gatekeepers like editors continue to be the most prevalent type of contact for professional writers. In the future, this relationship will remain the same on the creative side, but in terms of the *professional* relationship may morph into something much more like the paradigm in indie or Do It Yourself (DIY) music, where a band hires a producer, creates the CD, and then puts it out on their own label. In a writer context the parallel would be creating the book, hiring an editor, and then releasing the book through his or her various platforms.

Regardless, the general rules of conduct are often the same as for any type of communication covered in the section on Networking. But because the nature of the relationship can take on many permutations, it's important to deal with editor-writer issues separately. Falling into the same category as "editor" for our purposes is "publicist." Your publicist at a publishing house doesn't fit the technical definition of "gatekeeper," but he or she definitely has control over flow of information, and a good relationship with your publicist is in many ways tantamount to having a good relationship with your editor.

■ A Covenant of Mutual Respect

A couple of years ago a writer who used to be a close friend of mine posted a long rant about editors on his blog. In this rant, he tried to justify his inability to find a publisher — and thus explain why he had to post a free PDF of his novel on his blog — by going off on editors and the entire publishing industry.

Now, it is true that publishers can be eccentric, lacking in imagination, and risk-averse. On the other hand, they're absorbing the cost of printing the book, getting it into bookstores, and promoting it. They're also, usually, paying you some sort of advance against royalties.

But the thing about this writer's rant that bothered me the most concerned its assumptions about editors and the creative process. I won't quote it directly, but the gist was: Editors have no role in the process of making a manuscript better — all they do is try to put their frustrated-writer imprint on a book or mess with peripherals like copy edits. Writing is a solitary exercise, and any writer who thinks their editor helped create a better book didn't put in the work on the front end — in fact, bailed on making the tough decisions well before an editor ever saw it.

This rant engendered much debate on my own blog when I linked to it, including this observation from writer Seth Merlo:

> I totally agree with sticking to your creative integrity and vision, [and] I suspect the essence of his argument is that an editor should bring the writer's vision to fruition without interfering with it, but he never actually says as much, and if he does, it gets lost in arguments such as "the writer is always right." It almost comes across as if the writer is/should be his or her own best editor, which would clearly never work.

But the view expressed in the rant isn't as uncommon as one might think, in part because it's one of those received bits of wisdom you hear spouted by people posing as experts at writers conferences. Many times I've heard a so-called expert say something like "Once you get a major publishing deal, you'll need to hire an editor, because no one is actually editing at the publishing houses anymore."

This statement is simply not true. *With few exceptions, every editor I've encountered has made invaluable contributions to my work.* A good editor shares your vision and wants to bring out the best in your work. To accomplish this, they must first understand and empathize with what you are trying to do — and through edits on the developmental and paragraph level make sure that the version in your head actually made it to the page. This process can be time-consuming. It reflects a level of *caring* about your work that you may never get from any other source. In that context, you should at least calmly consider the changes, not reject them outright in the heat of passion.

As new writer Alex Carnegie puts it:

> The ideal of the good editor is the kind of thing I look for in creative writing instructors as well: somebody who can grasp and appreciate what you're trying to do, and yet also look at it with a certain amount

of detachment. They won't pull any punches [and bring new] insights and ideas.

Eventually your text becomes black sticks poking out of a snow storm, no matter what you do. Your gaze cannot get a grip on the page. Sometimes this is true even after you've had time to reflect. A good editor, even just with general questions about the narrative or characters, can allow you to re-imagine and revisit the text in useful ways.

Editors also understand that you may accept a change by finding a third way that neither you originally, or the editor in revision, thought of. Often, this third way creates the bond of collaboration with the editor, because the writer would never have thought of this third way without the editor's prompting. I also can't ever remember getting an editorial suggestion I thought was given in a spirit of making something more commercial. Obviously, there are bad editors and editors who don't really understand the book they've bought, but I've found it's rarely that way.

Besides, ultimately there's going to be a collaborative process going on with your book *anyway*, because *readers* are hopefully going to pick it up. Your personal vision is going to be re-interpreted, changed, and riffed off of as soon as it becomes public. An editor is just there to make sure when that time comes the reader understands completely what you meant to do.

Keep in mind as well that a writer-editor relationship may be long-term, and that person often becomes a good friend. Certainly, in the intense crucible that is a campaign for a book, you come to develop intense respect for these people, who love books as much as you love books, and who must deal with dozens of authors each month. Often, too, they don't get much praise or appreciation for their efforts.

That's why you should always start out from a position of trust and respect that includes an unspoken covenant of communication with your editor — and with your publicist, who will most certainly pop up along the way. The terms of that covenant should read as follows:

I will be courteous, generous, professional, considerate, empathetic, and timely in my communications with my editor and my publicist. I understand that both of them are busy people who may not be able to respond to my email immediately. I acknowledge that they tend to be as passionate about my work as I am, and have my best interests at heart; *at worst, they are not out to get me...*

If you require further clarification of words like "courteous, generous, professional, considerate, empathetic, and timely," you may need another book entirely.

▣ When Things Go Wrong

One useful quality of the Internet is how quickly you can bring people together. When I ran a feature on my blog about "What Editors Hate About Writers" and "What Writers Hate About Editors," everyone got involved, but in a respectful way. It probably helped that I noted in my introductory comments that "The word 'hate' here is not the white-hot hate of a million suns but closer to the disgusted or frustrated 'oh I hate it when that happens' or 'I really hate it when my husband forgets to clean the kitty litter box.'" Besides, there's a certain catharsis in a frank bitch session, or as I put it: "We're a family, and there's a constructive element here in terms of making one family member see another member's point of view. Followed by a group hug."

Time and again, the resulting discussion came back to basic human values, often distorted by impulsiveness, stress, or just being too busy.

• WHAT EDITORS HATE ABOUT WRITERS

An "editor" can be many things, from a gatekeeper at a communal blog to a first reader of nonfiction for an educational website or a professional hired by a New York publisher to acquire books for an imprint.

One type of editor, like my wife Ann, who serves as fiction editor for the magazine *Weird Tales*, may primarily read short stories all week, every week. This job puts her on the front lines with writers every day, and means that many of her reasons for "hating" writers have to do with inappropriate communication. Here are her top five:

- Writers who blast me on their blog for rejecting their story or who send threatening emails because of rejection.
- Writers who query before the published upper limit of my response time.

- Writers who make substantial edits on page proofs after I've told them the time for that kind of editing is over.
- Writers who constantly bug me to tell them *why* I form rejected their story when I have another five hundred submissions staring me in the face.
- Prima donnas, whether unpublished or "famous."

Almost all of these issues reflect a lack of respect on the part of the writer — and emphasize the negative ways in which the Internet has affected communication. It is entirely too easy to fire off an email that a second before was just a burning little thought in your head. By the time you realize what you've done, it's too late. Of course, some people never realize what they've done. Make sure you're not one of them.

On a more general level, having been an editor, here are three things *I* hate about writers:

- Writers who take editors for granted. It's easy enough to show a little love for your overworked editor with a card or small gift, but this doesn't happen often enough. Editors are almost always on the edge of burnout (publicists even more so), and while writers who seem to take and take without ever giving back are the norm, it's a not desirable state of affairs.
- Writers who take advantage of an unequal power structure. Sometimes the worst kind of writer for an editor is an older writer in mid-career, with a wide public following. This means the writer may be more in control than the editor, and may take advantage of this situation to make an editor's life a living hell. Be aware of the power dynamic and behave with restraint as necessary.
- Writers who miss deadlines. Although writing is not an exact science, editors do hate a writer who consistently misses deadlines. Sometimes, editors will, in fact, give such a writer fake deadlines to ensure they get a manuscript by the time they need it…and still not get it.

Victoria Blake, from Underland Press, shared a few more with me for this book:

- Authors should look over every proof the publisher sends them. Publishers send proofs for a reason: we want to get approval for the work. It doesn't do any good to send the proof back with a simple thumbs up. Look through it. Publishers and editors make mistakes. It's your book, and you're responsible for the mistakes, too.

- Though editors often become an author's personal friend, their primary role is to bring the work into being. Don't expect your editor to also be your counselor, and be aware of how personal your emails are, how often you write, and how frequently you expect a long response.
- Make sure you're accessible. After the manuscript is complete, the publisher or editor will be putting the book through its production paces, which includes everything from designing the cover to writing the cover copy to arranging for media interviews. In other words, the work gets more varied and the timeline more complicated. It is important to keep in contact with your editor or publisher. Tell them if you're going out of town, for instance, and give them a way to contact you. Try your best to answer emails within twenty-four hours.

Then, of course, there are the writers who make us all look very, very silly. "I had an author once who wrote his proof marks in red crayon," Victoria writes. "This made every mark exceedingly difficult to read."

• WHAT WRITERS HATE ABOUT EDITORS

On the other side of this issue, writers have their own complaints about editors (and the publishers or other entities they're associated with). It's important that you, as a writer, understand that these are not trivial matters and that you deserve better treatment in such cases. My pet peeves include:

- *Having to ask for payments that are due.* I hate having to ask for what I am owed. There are two components to the high irritation factor: first, it's another thing to keep track of and, second, having to nudge, usually with a "hey, my apologies for asking, but where's the money?" puts you in a position of feeling awkward about asking for what you should've received without asking. It adds stress and becomes just another annoying item on the mental horizon. Any publisher or other entity that regularly pays without a nudge gets extra props, because it's actually not an industry standard.
- *Late payment without communication.* Some people think that if they ignore a problem, it will go away. A freelancer owed money doesn't go away. But

neither do I ever have a problem with an honest conversation about the whens and whys and what-fors and where-fores connected to payment. What I cannot stomach is communication in which the other party tries to will the issue away by just not facing up to their responsibilities.

- *Lack of honesty.* Especially in this era when face-to-face communication is rare, trust can be precarious. Emails strip out a lot of the data by which we decide whether we trust someone or not. All that's really left is saying what you mean and doing what you say you're going to do. As the disconnect between what an editor says and what s/he does grows, so too does my distrust, which ultimately corrupts the connection.

- *Being either too rigid or too fluid.* Having a timeline, a plan, and deadlines are all good things, elements of any successful project. But because writing is a process of discovery, any such structure should allow for variation and exploration along the way (change management, in the business world) — for flexibility. If it doesn't, then creative opportunities that might enhance the quality of your product may be snuffed out before they can be implemented, and the writers involved will probably be unhappy. At the same time, a project management structure that is too hazily defined and defers too much to the creative process risks the diminishment of product quality, or even the lack of a product at all. Finding that balance is key to the sanity of everyone involved, but especially the writer, who flourishes when able to clearly define the objective while also indulging fully his or her sense of play and imagination. (Which, in this context, is not a frivolous thing, but essential to success.)

My readers provided many anecdotes based on similar situations. Kelly Barnhill, one of my favorite short story writers (who also creates instructional books for children), complained about:

Mushy instructions, mushy concepts and mushy feedback. Is clarity too much to ask for these days? Also, when people use jokes in their letters explaining why my check is going to be three months late. Not only jokes, but lame jokes. Honestly. Say what you mean and move on, none of this foot shuffling, cheek reddening, aw-shucks stuff. Besides, some things just aren't all that funny, yanno? Especially when my kid's orthodontics are at stake.

Jess Nevins, author of *The Encyclopedia of Victoriana*, wrote in to say his pet peeve is "Anyone who isn't interested [in your query] who doesn't send a 'No, thank you' e-mail. It takes about five to ten seconds to type and helps the recipient immensely, but far too many people in the industry, from writers to editors, can't be bothered."

And, finally, the ultimate example of lack of communication, ironically from a commenter who only identified "himself" as "Zsetrek":

> Once, a journal published one of my stories without actually telling me as much. I submitted it, a friend on the editorial committee let me know that they loved it, and I didn't hear anything more until the check/complementary copy turned up in the mail. Of course, because they'd never actually gone to the effort of getting into touch with me the whole editing process had been skipped, and the story was a complete mess — up to and including an error in the title that sets my teeth on edge to this day.

Sometimes the writer and editor have an uneven relationship, with the editor having much more power. However, this doesn't mean you should excuse bad behavior on an editor's part. Everyone deserves respect and consideration. If you're not getting it from one editorial source, you'll have to decide if it's worth the stress of continuing to deal with that person and the publisher, entity, or company they represent. As the Internet provides more and more viable ways to bypass gatekeepers (editors among them), you may find alternatives to enduring an unpleasant situation. Remember: if you become so certain that *this* deal or *that* assignment is the be-all and end-all, you have lost the perspective necessary to maintain a healthy Public Booklife.

Hopefully, though, you'll rarely be in one of these situations. The number of positive editor interactions far outnumber the negative.

■ Making Assumptions, and What You Can Do About It

There's a larger issue concerning editor-writer communications that I haven't seen touched on much, and that's the push-me, pull-me aspect of editors not providing writers with enough information about the process of publishing a book — and writers, sometimes as a result, inserting themselves into that process in inappropriate ways.

The truth is, there's very little institutional knowledge in publishing industry. Too many people in the business never realize that the knowledge in their heads, especially information particular to their institution or entity, does not automatically go by way of Vulcan mindmeld into the head of the person they're dealing with. Thus, a lot of time is wasted because of assumptions made to the contrary. Being able to either see things from the other person's point of view or to document your process (and the writer's responsibilities within that process) goes a long way toward preventing communication breakdowns and stress during the lifecycle of a relationship.

Will Hindmarch, an Atlanta-based writer and game developer for White Wolf, shared this alarming story on my blog, one that exemplifies real consequences of the problem:

> A friend of mine...was passed over for a job at a publisher only to learn later that they missed the edits he made on their mock manuscript because they didn't know how to view comments in Word. I suppose that's an example of both parties assuming the other would do things a certain way (e.g. "normally"), but still.

Hindmarch also made the important point that every publishing house has a slightly different process:

> I worked for a publisher whose practices were largely unlike those of every publisher I'd worked with on staff or freelance, but they didn't educate me as to company practices because they figured they just did things the way things were done. Worse, to me, is that these practices were made habit (not chosen) without any intellectual curiosity about how things work in other places. Walking that fine line between appearing informed and doing it right is a curious thing for a freelancer. The fact that asking how a publisher wants something done can ever be seen as a weakness to a publisher boggles me.

Time and again, I've also encountered this attitude. As a freelancer, you can lose a potential job by asking too many questions. Ask too few questions and you may not produce a satisfactory product.

When it comes to book publication, even agents seem to assume a new writer already knows the whole process — including timing issues, like when copy edits or page proofs will arrive, and when to expect a publicist to be in touch. The result? Often, a complaint like Kelly Barnhill's, that "editors fall all over themselves about an unrealistic deadline, and my piece then sits on their desk for four months, and then when they ask for changes, they need a four-day turnaround."

In addition to confusion and stress, not having knowledge of a particular publisher's process means it's more likely that you as the writer will make demands or insert yourself into that process in ways that do not make sense to your editor.

Exacerbating this problem, writers today are taught to be aggressively proactive, which means most editors probably experience more "meddling" now than in the past.

But editors hate it when writers with no idea of what public relations or marketing means make demands that are silly and time consuming. Editors are also frustrated by writers who have no experience with or eye for art or design but still want to have a say in those decisions.

So how can you integrate your efforts and energy into the editor's and publicist's process? Here are some tips that should help during "first contact" with your editor and, later, with your publicist:

- Use the medium of communication with which they're most comfortable, whether that's Instant Messenger, email, the telephone, or something else. If it's a medium you're uncomfortable with, you can always return to your comfort zone later on, when it doesn't matter as much.
- Ask for any documentation on their process, including a timeline for your book, and add on any additional questions you might have in one compact, short email.
- If there is no documentation, query for a short list of specific deadlines. Hold your editor and publicist to those deadlines, and if they slide, make sure that you are also given some wiggle room.
- For those with the time for it, take all the information you have received, assess the strengths and weaknesses of the process, looking for any gaps, and ask additional follow-up questions.

First time novelists or authors especially suffer from not being proactive. Yet the impact of that first book is extremely important to your career. Many authors don't fully understand the process until they've already lived through a book's life-cycle once, or even twice. Although nothing can replace that experience, if you can shorten the learning curve, you'll be better able to take advantage of opportunities. You'll also build a better relationship with your editor and your publicist.

After having gone through this "discovery phase," to get a sense of the publishing company and how it all works, you should then be able to respectfully suggest ways in which you can help the editor and publicist with the book. An editor will appreciate a helpful but not intrusive writer.

Victoria Blake even advises writers to be ambitious in this situation:

> I'm a big fan of free and open idea generation. Practically speaking, that means thinking big and then scaling back for budget and time constraints. If you have a great idea for publicity or for some sort of marketing tie-in, suggest it in a spirit of open idea sharing, and don't be offended if the idea, for some reason or another, doesn't sprout wings. Think about phrasing your emails along the lines of, "Dear X, I was thinking about the publicity for my book and came up with a few ideas that I thought I'd run by you. If these appeal to you, I'd love to talk more about them. If not, no worries." It never hurts to ask.

With the proper knowledge base, you can work alongside the publisher to give your book the best possible shot at success. The keys are the same as they ever were: understanding, respect, and good ideas.

▶▶ Understanding Creative PR

▦ Universal Elements

New media allows for amazing interconnectivity and cross-pollination of ideas. Because the primary purpose isn't for PR, new media has also changed the nature of PR forever. However, some things will always be the same:

• **YOUR SINCERITY AND HONESTY MAKE A HUGE DIFFERENCE.** Try not to act like a telemarketer or a walking infomercial. If you can have fun promoting your book or other creative project, all the better, because that means readers will probably have fun as well.

• **THE QUALITY OF YOUR CREATIVE PROJECT MUST BE HIGH TO GAIN LEVERAGE.** A high-quality creative project could be anything from an esoteric experimental science fiction novel to a heartbreakingly tragic literary novella posted on a website, a book of poems about your neighbor's talking chicken or a techno-thriller about zombies. The genre is irrelevant. All that matters is creating a great book. *If you don't create a good book, most of the advice in* Booklife *won't help you.*

• **THE FORM OF THE CREATIVE PROJECT AFFECTS YOUR ABILITY TO PROMOTE IT.** Currently, it is still easier to get leverage for a "book" that has a physical presence in the world. An electronic version of the book provides opportunities for leverage as well, but despite all of the ways in which the physical book has been put into competition with other forms of itself, it is *still*, as of this writing at least, the anchor and the goal sought by writers and given the most respect by the highest number of gatekeepers. Also remember that although I am defining "book" generally as a creative project, it will always be harder to create ongoing or "permanent" leverage for a short story or an article (and yet simpler because of the limited options) than for the bulwark that is a novel or story collection or nonfiction book.

• **THE INTEGRITY/QUALITY OF YOUR BRAND ACROSS PRODUCTS AFFECTS**

YOUR ABILITY TO GAIN LEVERAGE ACROSS YOUR CAREER. Inconsistency from creative project to creative project breeds indecision among readers. Variety between projects, so long as quality is high, may slow your progress but result in rewards that are just as great. But, again, for the long-term, your work must be high-quality. (Your "brand" across time also refers to your public image and other elements that may not always have much to do with your core creativity. However, these elements have impact because reader perceptions are so often driven not just by their opinion of your writing but of you.)

A writer usually has little effect on marketing or sales, but can have a huge impact on publicity. To be most effective, you must:

• **UNDERSTAND YOUR AUDIENCE AND THE COMMERCIAL OR NONCOMMERCIAL APPEAL OF YOUR CREATIVE PROJECT.** Selling a thousand copies of a nonfiction collection might be an excellent result, while selling a thousand copies of a mystery novel might be seen as a huge failure.

• **UNDERSTAND THE RELATIONSHIP BETWEEN PR EFFORTS AND SALES, PR, AND YOUR REPUTATION.** The simple fact is, your PR efforts can greatly enhance your reputation without having as large an effect on your sales. Good PR is as much about setting you up for future opportunities and making sure you stay in the public eye as it is about readers making purchases. Studies show that readers may need to hear or read about a book as many as seven times before deciding to purchase it. Thus, a strong PR effort will influence sales over time, but the primary impact is to position you in other ways.

• **MAKE SURE TO FIT THE SCALE OF THE PR TO THE SCALE OF THE PROJECT.** You don't send copies of your saddle-stapled 42-page chapbook on armadillo farming to *Publishers Weekly*. Nor do you send a techno-thriller to the book reviewer at *Armadillo Farming Quarterly*. (Except, of course, in the remote eventuality that armadillos play an integral role in the plot.)

• **MAKE SURE TO CREATE QUALITY, PROFESSIONAL-LOOKING MATERIALS FOR YOUR PR EFFORT.** You would be better off not creating that website banner ad if it isn't up to professional standards. Similarly, you will do yourself more damage putting out a boring YouTube book trailer that's four minutes too long than if you did no trailer at all.

• **TEST OUT NEW IDEAS THROUGH RESEARCH AND BY FINDING OTHER EXAMPLES BEFORE IMPLEMENTING THEM.** You can waste a lot of money putting an effort behind "bleeding edge" PR ideas that are in some way faulty in conception or execution. Make sure that someone, somewhere, has been successful with a similar approach. Be very careful to avoid doing anything that makes you look silly or amateurish.

You might be surprised by the kinds of things writers have done to attract attention, only to find that the attention attracted wasn't what they wanted. One writer used to send nude photos to magazine editors along with her stories. Another would review their own work online, using their real name, and describe its brilliance. The worst reading I ever saw — and a reading is a type of PR for your work — included one poor soul who stopped in mid-sentence to reminisce on the glorious day when inspiration came for a particular phrase, making things worse by also stopping to read reviews of the story. One writer's website used to include an image of himself in a stereotypical velvet-Elvis style, with a halo above his half-bald head. Doesn't sound as bad as the other examples? If you'd seen it, you'd put it at the top of the list.

Less heinous crimes include what I call useless PR — like sending readers buttons advertising a book. This is the kind of PR effort that writers often want to focus on — a campaign that actually has little relation to reality. How often have you personally asked someone about a product based on a decorative button they were wearing? And how many times have you been handed a button and thought, "I really don't want to pin something to my clothing."

How did some of these people arrive at such bad places? Horrible advice. Always keep in mind that advice, especially advice on promoting yourself, is often anecdotal or a Received Idea — received from a time machine from the Distant Past. Sincerely-given but idiotic career advice can be a shiv in the side, an icepick through the eye. Worse, it can result in a slow malarial fever from which you never recover, performing actions you later have no good rationale for doing. The worst career advice attempts to separate you from your work, you a shucked oyster wondering what happened, and why.

On the other hand, despite this warning, don't be afraid to test out new things on a limited basis (limited in terms of time and money spent). I've done all kinds of experiments with online media. I've even used talking greeting cards to send out announcements about my books, because nothing gets past a person's defenses like being addressed by an animated squirrel. I've also tried anti-publicity, surprising reviewers and bloggers with an anthology project that was top secret until the day of publication. I'm not saying you should emulate these admittedly risky approaches, but playing around with PR concepts and having some fun isn't always a bad thing.

◼ The Lifecycle of a Book

It's important to understand the elements of a book's "lifecycle" prior to engaging in promotion of your project. Although several graphical depictions of the lifecycle of a book exist in print and online, I recommend the version found in the *Chicago Manual of Style*. A typical textual breakdown of the process — from conception to completion, and based on the traditional model of seeking publication from a New York publisher — might read something like this:

PRE-PRODUCTION DEAL

- Writer finishes manuscript.
- Writer seeks publication by finding an agent or contacting publishers directly.
- An editor accepts the manuscript.
- The writer and publisher sign a contract, usually negotiated by an agent.

BETWEEN EIGHTEEN MONTHS AND NINE MONTHS BEFORE PUBLICATION

- The writer and editor agree on any changes to the manuscript, and the writer implements said changes.
- The manuscript enters into a series of quality control processes, including copyediting, and the writer assists in this process by reviewing the manuscript at various points prior to publication.
- The editor sends the writer a questionnaire that captures all of the writer's thoughts about the public description of the book, unique qualities of the book and author, an author bio and photo, any publicity contacts, etc.

- The publisher begins to work on the book's cover while the marketing department discusses the book in terms of strategies for selling it to booksellers. Other than the questionnaire, the writer may or may not have input with the marketing prior to publication.
- The publisher prepares the book's initial cover and description for its catalog. The catalog is a tool for letting distributors and booksellers know about the book well in advance of publication.

BETWEEN EIGHT AND SIX MONTHS BEFORE PUBLICATION

- Marketing begins to form preliminary advertising plans. The writer provides any ideas now, before the budget and advertising schedules are set.
- Some advance copies, either still in manuscript format or typeset, are sent out to influencers (usually other writers) to collect blurbs that can be used for the cover of the book and for further publicity.
- The editor either puts the writer in touch with the publicist assigned to the book or acts as the contact with publicity. The writer provides input on publicity.

BETWEEN FIVE AND FOUR MONTHS BEFORE PUBLICATION

- The publisher prints Advance Reader Copies and sends them out to early adopters (influencers and gatekeepers) as well as review venues, like the Big Four: library/book buyer publications (*Publishers Weekly, Kirkus Reviews, Library Journal, Booklist*) that require a copy of the book anywhere from four to five months prior to publication.
- The editor and publicist, along with marketing, implement any strategies or advertising to make sure it coincides with (or occurs after) the date the book will actually reach bookstores.

ONE MONTH BEFORE PUBLICATION TO A YEAR AFTER

- The book is published and finished copies are sent by the publicist to relevant review venues and gatekeepers. The writer also receives copies.
- The book is published, reaches brick-and-mortar bookstores and the warehouses of virtual booksellers through the publisher's distributors, and

the writer enters into the public publicity-cycle for the book, which can last for three months (more, if the book has legs). The writer and publicist pursue further opportunities as they arise, although on the publicist's part this will mostly consist of passing on communications from gatekeepers about interview opportunities, etc.

- After the review phase, there will be a period during which the book is considered for awards, and another phase if the book is released in another form. (For example, first publication in hardcover, with a trade paperback published a year later.)
- The writer continues to follow up on opportunities, but most energies will be turned toward the next creative project.

This breakdown provides you with useful information, especially in the context of a prior section of *Booklife* (Dealing with Editors and Publicists). However, it doesn't approach the "book" as a mutable object that can take many different forms in the modern era. If you boil the process down, stripping off the detail and making a "book" a more fluid creature, the lifecycle roughly becomes:

- Creation and perfection of content.
- Acquisition of a platform (or format) for the content.
- Creation and perfection of the "skin" (aesthetic) and context for the content.
- Accessibility to the content.
- Visibility for the content.

In creating your plans for your book, always keep this simplified version of the lifecycle in mind. It helps focus your efforts by reminding you of what's important. For more information on "marketing" versus "publicity" and a writer's duties in the context of publicity, please refer to Colleen Lindsay's excellent essays in the appendices.

■ Rules of Engagement

Without sound rules of engagement — literally the context within which you approach your PR campaign — nothing you do in support of your book will be graceful, artful, or that effective. Many writers live in a world of tactics, in which their PR efforts represent a kind of thrashing, spiking push-and-pull that may seem like progress but is actually disorganized, foundering, and doesn't support strategic goals. Here are some things to remember when putting together your PR campaign.

• ALWAYS COORDINATE YOUR EFFORTS WITH YOUR PUBLISHER'S PUBLICIST

Hopefully, you begin to create your plan after you've had at least some initial conversations with your publicist (if you are working within the traditional model rather than some form of self-publishing). Making a list of the things the publicist plans to do for your book will allow you to fill in the gaps.

If your publicist's entire plan consists of sending out review copies, you have a lazy or overworked publicist — or your book isn't considered a priority. Regardless, though, you'll want to take their plan and, consulting with your editor, develop your own plans of action to present to publicity. (In the appendices, you'll find an example of an effective presentation.)

Because many publishers, especially independent publishers, have limited resources for publicity, this book includes discussion of several elements that traditionally would *not* be handled by the author, just so you have the information if you need it.

• FIND WAYS TO ALLOW PUBLICISTS AND OTHER THIRD PARTIES TO COMMUNICATE FOR YOU

Even though we live in the age of the individual content provider, many media outlets frown on a writer contacting them directly. In addition, some gatekeepers will think this personal contact confirms your low status; if you had "people," you wouldn't need direct contact with the gatekeeper.

Keeping in mind the rules set out in Colleen Lindsay's article on dealing with publicists (see appendices), provide contact information to the best person to make the initial contact, whether your publicist, editor, or someone else assisting in your efforts. If you don't have a publicist or this kind of access to your editor, you may want to make sure none of your friends or colleagues have a connection with the gatekeeper or gatekeepers before you contact the outlet directly. If you ask a friend or colleague to contact a gatekeeper, provide them with a script of what to say and how to say it, to avoid any miscommunication of your message.

As the Internet continues to erode certain kinds of hierarchies, more and more writers will be in direct contact with more and more gatekeepers. However, this will probably increase not decrease the need for third party liaisons, since gatekeepers will need some way to prioritize the flow of incoming information.

• Acknowledge the limits of your skill set

The skills that led you to write a book or story or article are *not* the same skills required to leverage it in the public world. That is a *separate* skill. Not everyone has it, and only some people have it in genius-level quantities. This can work for you in areas where an element of inspired amateurism — the Do-It-Yourself impulse — is appreciated, even expected. However, even in areas previously the domain of amateurs, like YouTube book trailers or podcasts, more and more sophisticated, professional efforts have started to become the standard.

Therefore, to avoid stress and be more successful: *Recognize your own limitations and find others with the required skills and experience.*

You may need a budget to hire someone, but you may also be able to barter for services. The barter system has become more and more common as creative individuals collaborate across the Internet. The best way to find the right people to work for you is to find existing examples of what you want to do, and approach whoever created them — whether it's a banner ad or a website or a short film. In all things remember that a combination of mimicry and your unique vision provides the best chance for success.

Luckily, too, online platforms like blogs come with ready-made templates, and a blog platform like WordPress allows you to turn a blog into something very much like a website. Make sure to let standardization and templates do the work for you where appropriate.

If you cannot find someone to do something you know is not your strength, you may need to decide whether it's worth the effort. An ugly or clunky website or book trailer can be worse support for your efforts at leverage than no website or book trailer at all.

• Define the limits of your effort

There are only so many hours in a day, and you have only so much stamina across a day, a week, or a longer period. Before entering into a campaign for your creative project, decide how much time and energy you can afford to spend on it. Ask yourself these questions:

- How much time will I be spending on this effort and over how many days, weeks, or months? For example, are you going to devote forty hours over three weeks, or sixty hours over three months?
- Will I be traveling as part of this effort, or staying at home? Time spent traveling may not be time spent promoting your work, but it's still time lost.
- Will I be spending money or only using opportunities provided by the publisher as well as free tools and platforms? If you're spending money, what's your budget, and are you buying services, access, or hardware?
- What form of follow-up is required for this project? Whether it's nudging gatekeepers, conducting interviews, or finding ways for people to view your book trailer, every creative project requires some type of follow-up. Follow-up, even if it's just emailing people, takes time and must be accounted for in your efforts. Sometimes this is the most important part of what you will do for your project.
- How much additional follow-up am I willing to do? The "X" factor in all PR campaigns is the exponential way success feeds on itself. If you're successful in your initial efforts, there will almost certainly be additional investments of effort to leverage that success.

These questions and their answers exist in the context of a wider space: your creative life. Some writers can easily promote their work and continue to create by separating "creative" and "career" efforts into separate daily blocks of time. Others require the immersion of total concentration on the act of creation and must acknowledge (without guilt) that focusing on their careers will require not working on creative projects during that time. My own level is that I can't work on a major creative project while also doing PR for one of my books, although I can still focus on blogging and writing nonfiction. Therefore, I adjust accordingly.

Whatever your personality and approach, make sure you know the personal consequences of your decisions in this area. Be prepared to go weeks without working on your fiction, and, if possible, try to make sure those weeks coincide with a time period you planned on recharging your imagination anyway. Given the introvert/extrovert difference between creativity and PR, you may find that the time spent on promoting your book actually helps you get back into your writing afterwards.

• Develop a message and stick to it

Every creative project has two stories to tell. One of them is about the project itself and the other is about you. When you're lucky, both stories are compelling, and both allow you to get leverage with media outlets. When you're extraordinarily lucky, both messages are, in a sense, the same message.

For example, when I used to run a publishing company, we released *The Fourth Circle*, a surreal novel by a Serbian writer named Zoran Živković. Živković lives in Belgrade and had survived the NATO bombardment. His house wasn't far from the Chinese Embassy, which took a direct hit. *The Fourth Circle* was written as a way of distracting himself from a horrible situation. We had a compelling story about the author, and a compelling story behind the book. That *The Fourth Circle* only indirectly dealt with the war actually enhanced the meta-story by demonstrating how the author used writing the book as a coping mechanism, and as a partial escape from his situation.

Make sure you know what your message is, and stick to that message throughout the PR campaign for your book. (A good press release written by your publicist or by you can help in getting your message across. Press releases are dealt with in the appendices.)

• Understand the indirect benefit of your actions as well as the direct benefit

A single PR action may only sell a few books, but if there is a peripheral, or secondary, benefit that either supports your strategic goals or results in some tactical advantage, then that one action may be more worthwhile than another action that "only" sells more books. Most writers, except for those who are bestsellers, need to explore and exploit all indirect benefits of an action, because your best chance of success lies in diversification and reputation as much as in sales. When creating a plan, try to think of all of the indirect advantages of a particular task or action. An advantage might be as small as the opportunity to meet a gatekeeper who can be useful to you.

• DO NOT OVERESTIMATE THE VALUE OF LOCAL COVERAGE

New writers tend to value local coverage because it provides a nice ego boost with their friends and relatives. However, such coverage tends to be of limited value unless you live in a major media market like Boston, New York, Seattle, or San Francisco — or a slightly smaller city that's a hotbed of the arts, like Austin. With falling circulations for newspapers and local magazines, the amount of effort you expend on local coverage should not exceed the expected return.

Also keep in mind that unless you have achieved a huge success — the kind that cannot be ignored — your book or other creative project tends to be invisible to gatekeepers. There's a certain truth to the idea that people respond to the exotic and ignore or take for granted what's right in front of them. For years, I found it much harder to get coverage by the local *Tallahassee Democrat* than from all manner of international media. For a time, I was better known in Helsinki, Finland, than in Florida. A good way to drive your publicist crazy is to insist they spend time trying to talk some overworked, underpaid features editor at a newspaper with a circulation under twenty thousand to run a feature on you or your book.

Leverage always creates exceptions, though. If you've achieved huge success — like winning a major prize — your efforts will be rewarded. Similarly, if you are doing a reading or signing at a legitimate brick-and-mortar location, you may be able to get some limited coverage. It doesn't hurt if a mention or article is also posted online, as this allows you to reap additional benefits from that initial effort throughout the blogosphere.

• RECOGNIZE THAT THE TERM "BOOK TOUR" HAS A NEW MEANING

Due to the influence of electronic media, the idea of a book tour has changed radically. Just doing readings and signings at a brick-and-mortar location is a small part of the total tour. In fact, the online media coverage, fan comments, and your own blogging about readings may be of more value than the actual readings. In addition, your "book tour" might include a series of guest blogging stops, an interview session in Second Life, stopping by the message board devoted to a particular topic or type of writing, and any number of other constantly evolving "events" that have nothing to do with our physical world. Thinking about the book tour in this way may help you to organize your thoughts on the form and timeline of your own unique promotional efforts. (For more thoughts on this subject, refer to the examples in the introduction to "Creating a PR Plan.")

▶▶ PR Opportunities

In this section, you'll find a list of effective PR opportunities to help your cause. Your task will be to combine the ones that work best for you, creating an effective, unified plan that integrates opportunities with the tools discussed in the next section, and that includes leverage across your platforms.

I generally define "opportunities" as publicity on platforms to which someone else controls access, which you can then leverage across your own platforms. Along with the creative project you're promoting, many of the tools associated with your publicity efforts help you to convince gatekeepers to offer you opportunities.

That's a rather clinical definition for a category that includes conventions and readings, but for strategic and tactical purposes it's a clarifying way of looking at the battlefield. In the real, flesh-and-blood world, of course, there are many different perspectives at work here. For example, a reviewer doesn't think of him or herself as a "platform" for publicity. Nor should you, as a writer, think of reviews as just a way to get information about your work to the public. But for now, put on your PR hat.

An opportunity tends to accrete a certain amount of leverage to itself; this is an intrinsic quality of an opportunity. For example, an interview on a website has a built-in audience. The primary value comes from exposing readers who have never heard of you to your work — and reminding others who do know you but may not read your blog or Facebook status that you have a new project out.

You can get additional benefit out of any opportunity, large or small, by sharing the link or information with other gatekeepers (bloggers for media outlets, etc.) and thus magnifying the effect. Writers who, for example, complain that their interviews are always ignored by Internet gatekeepers while interviews with "X" always get additional coverage don't understand that in all likelihood "X" or "X's" publicist proactively sent out the link or information. You'd be surprised at how effective this simple effort can be at generating coverage. Content providers for news feeds in particular are always hungry for links — not because they're lazy but because they're overworked.

That's a tactical example of an advantage you can gain. On a strategic level, remember to integrate new media efforts with more traditional approaches. Why?

If you maintain a foothold through several of the platforms we've discussed (blogs, Facebook, etc.), you already have ready-made conduits through which you can send information related to your books and other creative products.

On the one hand this means you don't have to do as much work to reach some form of an audience from project to project. On the other, it means you run the risk of running a "perpetual campaign," in which you are sending out the equivalent of "PR bursts" across the Internet through multiple platforms on a regular basis. Without finding creative or selective ways to manage, disguise, or "mix up" these bursts, you'll soon find that new media becomes much less effective for you.

This is one reason to mix traditional approaches to PR with new media solutions. Another reason is that not all potential readers of your work like or use new media. If you want to diversify your audience and widen your efforts, explore effective use of traditional approaches, most of which have more to do with the physical world. (An email is not a handshake, and a conversation in a bar is not a chat on an instant messenger.)

Your challenge in promoting any book or other creative project will be to find your comfort level, mixing and matching new and traditional approaches so that you create a plan that fits your personality and doesn't fragment you so much that you cannot get creative work done.

■ Blurbs

In the old days, soliciting blurbs praising your book was almost exclusively the domain of your editor or possibly your publicist. Now, though, blurbs serve a wider function than simply decorating the front or back of a book. Editors and publicists still make the majority of these contacts for you, but asking for a blurb can also be seen as a kind of opportunity, especially since social media has made the "cold call" less of an intrusion. Anyone who has a high enough profile for you to receive a blurb from them probably has an online presence, and may be willing to help you promote your book online.

How do you go about soliciting a blurb?

- Identify those authors you admire and are relevant to your book.
- Check the Internet for contact information, or have a librarian help you look their contact information up in reference books.
- Send a short email, letter, or other message with your contact information indicating your admiration for their work, the fact your book is coming out from such-and-such press, and that you would be honored if they could find the time to blurb it. Include just a couple of sentences about the book itself.
- If you receive no response or a dismissive response, do not press the issue.
- If you receive a friendly reply, strike up a conversation and also contact your editor or publicist about making sure that person receives a copy of your book.

A good author blurb helps sales of the book by functioning as a "word of mouth" that targets the blurber's core audience, as opposed to the broader definition of "word of mouth" that refers to all potential readers. However, it also helps you with reviewers who like the author, and it will help you get more blurbs from authors who are friends of the author who blurbed your book. You can also use it as leverage with bookstores for readings, etc. In short, the right blurb can make people sit up and take notice. If you can't get one blurb from a well-known author, aim for several endorsements from lesser known writers and let the quantity of quotes help you. Sometimes, too, you may be entering a new market in which you are unknown. In that case, seeking out a hot new writer from that genre who may be more approachable can be a stepping stone to acceptance from the giants in that market.

■ Conferences and Conventions

Never underestimate the value of face-to-face time with readers and influencers who have gathered in one place for the purpose of celebrating a particular type of writing. Whether you write fantasy or realism, science fiction or mystery, poetry or manga, you can find a conference or convention worth attending. As you become more established, you will also begin to receive invites to such events, perhaps even offers to be a guest speaker, making it easier to promote your creative projects at them.

Selecting an Event

Here are a few pointers for selecting a conference or convention.

- When researching the best possibilities for you and your project, check with past attendees to get their impressions. (This also gives you an opportunity to network.) Some opportunities actually turn in to literal traps, as when my wife and I attended one supposedly prestigious convention only to find parts of it were held in an old racquetball court and the location was sixty miles from the nearest hotel. If we'd known about the commute we probably wouldn't have accepted the invitation, but by the time we mentioned the gig to prior guests, it was too late to back out.
- Don't rule out events that seem peripheral to your book if you can find the right slant. For example, if there is any pop culture or otherwise "hip" aspect to your creative project, you would probably benefit from attending Comic-Con in San Diego even though it is primarily aimed at celebrating the comics industry.
- Remember that librarians and booksellers have state-based, regional, and national events, and that meeting concentrations of either group can be extremely important to your career. (Even independent publishers are more likely to help send you to one of these events, because of the super saturation of gatekeepers.)
- Be aware that events like BookExpo America are huge, and unless you have publisher support they can be overwhelming to individual writers.
- If you're a new writer, don't waste too much time trying to get on panels. Being too forceful in trying to get on the program will tax the patience of already overworked convention volunteers, and you can gain almost as much by attending panels. Besides, many of the best conversations and networking at these events will occur outside of (or in spite of) the formal programming.
- If you do decide being on a panel is important, try pitching a panel topic to the organizers and volunteer to moderate it if they accept your idea. This allows you to network with the other attendees who happen to also be on your panel.

When you're just starting out, all events look like opportunities. However, you will need to make sure as you progress that you begin to turn down requests to attend events. If you're a freelance writer, you may decide you only attend events where you are receiving a speaking fee or at least reimbursement for all expenses. Or, you may decide that you will only attend a certain type of event. For two years, to get out of my comfort zone of attending fantasy conventions or conferences, my wife and I instead accepted invites from literary festivals and organizations wanting us to deliver a keynote speech or workshop. This allowed us to make contacts with many new and interesting people outside of our main circle of acquaintances. This also led to additional opportunities that would not have materialized otherwise. Always keep in mind your long-term goals when deciding on public appearances, and understand that sometimes saying "no" is a way of saying "yes" to something more important.

ATTENDING AN EVENT

Whether you've attended one event or ten, I may be able to save you from making a few basic mistakes, while also priming you to take advantage of opportunities.

First, if you are new and don't know many people attending the event, try to find a more experienced writer who will go with you. Otherwise, you may wind up wandering lonely as a cloud — especially if you aren't good at meeting people on your own. A convention attended in this context may be a waste of time and money. Similarly, if there are people you would like to meet at the convention, email them ahead of time to let them know you enjoy their work and hope they might have time for a drink. While most will not respond, some will, especially the ones who hold court in the convention bar.

If you aren't on a panel and don't know anyone at the convention, attend as many panels as possible and turn the event into a purely educational experience that aids your Private Booklife.

For most writers conventions may be most valuable for networking, but don't forget that such events also offer unique promotional opportunities. Take PR materials for your project, along with copies of your book. You can usually find a freebies table for the promotional materials. The copies of your book should be given out to attending reviewers, bloggers, and other influencers. Small postcards with your contact information on them are as effective as business cards. Push against the trend toward tiny "strip" business cards, however, as they're easily lost by the recipient.

While conventions and conferences provide wonderful opportunities for making the personal acquaintance of other professionals in your field, don't insert yourself into the ongoing conversations of other attendees. Observe proper etiquette even when itching to do otherwise. Proper etiquette doesn't mean you have to remain at a distance, however. As a new writer with a book out, I did sometimes walk up to my hero — if they weren't otherwise occupied — and say something along the lines of "I know you're busy and I don't want to hold you up, but I love your work and here's a copy of my new book as a thank you for so many hours of great reading." The truth is, the recipient can always toss your book later.

A book is one thing. A manuscript is another. Under no circumstances should you ever try to give a professional attending one of these events your unpublished project. If you have a conversation where you make a personal connection, you can always send an email follow-up after the event with a polite P.S. mentioning your manuscript and asking if the person is willing to take a look at it.

Finally, if the event has a dealer's room with publisher and bookseller tables, be sure to strike up conversations with anyone whose table interests you. Feel free to mention your book. Anyone sitting behind a table is there to sell books and make contacts. I'd advise against buying a table and sitting there with your books, as for an individual writer this is usually a lonely chore self-assigned to the self-published. It can be useful to you, but it also ties you down.

Readings

The creation of the LongPen™ famously championed by Margaret Atwood allows a writer to stay at home and still do bookstore events. According to the website, the LongPen "has an interactive image and voice, as well as the ability to sign. The author will be there, in real time. So the exchange is with the author, not the signing device…In fact, it's quite possible that the screen exchange will be more personal than what exists now."

Despite this cheery sales pitch, I'd argue that you can't really have a meaningful exchange with a robot that creates signatures, even if the robot has an interactive image and voice. Sometimes there's no substitute for getting out there and meeting people. Most of our existence, thankfully, still occurs in the physical world. And, although many brick-and-mortar bookstores are in financial trouble at the moment, readings don't seem to be going out of fashion.

There are several factors you'll need to consider before you decide to commit to using readings as part of your PR plan. Please note that a "reading" might consist of just a signing with a question-and-answer session, or it might be as complex as a presentation of some kind. A "reading" might also be part of a larger book tour that includes both physical and virtual events. A reading might also have a virtual component, such as a nearly simultaneous podcast. At the very least, you can leverage any event by asking your audience to blog about it.

SETTING UP AN EVENT

The mechanics of getting a reading and signing in a bookstore can be murky. First of all, many publishers no longer send any but their best-selling authors on book tours. Secondly, there is a kind of "which came first, the chicken or the egg" aspect to getting a reading or signing. This issue concerns leverage. If you have a substantial body of work behind you, you may not have any problem setting up events, especially with independent bookstores. However, if you are new, bookstores may only greenlight a reading/signing if you can guarantee coverage in local media (a feature or book review). At the same time, local media outlets may only cover your book if you're doing a reading.

This timing issue requires nudging both parties along the path if there's resistance. When just starting, I often went to the bookstore manager and told them that I thought I could get local coverage, only for them to express skepticism. Then I would contact the features editor at the local newspaper, tell that person a little about my book, and indicate the local bookstore was interested in holding an event. If the features editor expressed interest in covering the book in the context of a local event, I would then go back to the bookstore with that shaky reassurance. Several times I got a reading as a result. From that point forward, it's just a lurching dance of shoring up the details on both sides and hoping the covenant holds…

There are easier ways, if you have luck and publisher support. On some projects, my publicist has set up events using time-honored contacts. On one project, I dealt directly with the events organizers for the entire Borders chain and they arranged for a dozen individual stores across the United States to host events. Still, with exceptions pertaining to your outrageously high sales across many projects or the fluke of a high-flying individual book, you will probably wind up doing most of the heavy lifting yourself.

Brickbats and Benefits

It's important to note that most people in the book business are deeply divided over the value of in-store events, and many writers find them time-intensive for little gain. Colleen Lindsay, a publicist-turned-agent who runs a blog called The Swivet, even crunched the numbers and declared that it's impossible for bookstores or writers (other than the Stephen Kings of this world) to make a profit from an in-store event.

It's hard to argue with Lindsay's numbers (and you may not want to), but other factors *do* come into play, even if we put aside the idea of promoting the arts as irrelevant to a discussion of book promotion (but especially because the aim of book promotion is not always direct sales).

From a new media perspective of interconnectivity, in-store events have the following potential benefits:

- Face-to-face meetings with bookstore managers and buyers can lead to long-term relationships. The people on the front lines deserve your support and respect. They're also, along with librarians, the most effective word-of-mouth advocates for your book. A single bookseller can, through his recommendations, hand-sell hundreds of books. While you can meet booksellers at conventions, nothing beats leisurely time one-on-one, especially if your reading was professional and your interaction with customers friendly and upbeat. More importantly, each bookseller is connected to many other booksellers, and they do talk. Booksellers also know librarians and people in every aspect of the book trade.
- Meeting your hardcore fans always helps reinforce that bond (and your brand). Especially as you have more and more books out, you will find that certain readers become bona fide fans. Although there's a lot you can do for your fans through the Internet, getting a chance to meet them face-to-face is invaluable to reinforce their loyalty. People still want to see the writer in the flesh. As your career progresses and you hit the inevitable rough patches, these are the people who will buoy you up and give you the strength to keep going. Also, they're often your fans because they share similar interests and concerns. Like the booksellers, they too belong to related networks of creativity. More than once I have collaborated on interesting projects after talking to someone who came to a reading of mine.

- The bookstore has to not just stock but properly display your title for at least two weeks prior to the event. Even writers with books published by large commercial publishers have difficulty getting prominent placement in most bookstores. Doing a reading or signing usually means the bookstore places additional emphasis on your titles. Most bookstores will also have you sign stock after an event. Readers are more likely to buy a signed copy. On some titles, there's no appreciable up-tick in sales after an event, but on others the bookstore may well sell out.
- The appearance of success promotes and reinforces the potential for actual success. Bookstore events still have a mystique with most readers. Inasmuch as you successfully use your platforms to publicize your in-store events, you're adding to the prestige of your overall brand. As with every opportunity, you should be looking for the indirect benefit as much as the direct benefit. If you have a decent-sized audience through your platforms, you can also provide much-needed general publicity for the bookstores. Blogging about your event, podcasting it, or getting others to do the same increases its value to you.
- Every reader counts. I've done bookstore readings for 150 people and readings for five people, two of whom just wanted to get in from the cold. But picking up even two or three new readers per event can lead to multiple sales. Some will become hardcore fans who buy everything you write. Some will tell everyone they know about your books (and some of those people will tell people they know). Some will turn out to be a gatekeeper you never knew was a fan. A motto I'm fond of is "one reader at a time," because it forces you to focus on the individual.

You may decide that focusing on readings doesn't make sense for you, and in this increasingly electronic world you may have a point. But if you do decide to set up a series of in-store events, here are a few tips to maximize your efforts.

- Focus on major metropolitan areas or places with high concentrations of fans, friends, or family. Bookstore managers don't care who comes to your event, so long as it seems well-attended and they sell some books. Keeping your database of contacts current helps you to identify the best options and allows you to "turn out the vote." You can accomplish this best by sticking to areas with high density populations or by stacking the deck.

- Team up with writers local to the area for your event. In addition to helping you with promotion, local writers bring their own built-in audience. Especially if you've got a tight schedule, moving from city to city, they also protect you against unforeseen flight or traffic delays making you late to an event — whether or not you're there, *they* will be. Finally, they're usually hooked into the local arts scene, so you'll meet other creative people from the area.
- Make sure your event doesn't conflict with another event. You'd be surprised how many times writers forget to check for conflicting events, only to show up at theirs and find out that the, er, Super Bowl is being played right down the street, in an hour.

In addition to bookstore venues, there are many local, regional, and national reading series across the country, receptive to both new and established writers, that you should investigate.

ELEMENTS OF A SUCCESSFUL EVENT

Beginning writers, so often starved for attention, often view readings as an opportunity to cram in as much material as possible. However, out of hundreds of readings, I have only ever encountered two people who could hold my attention for more than twenty minutes: Seamus Heaney and Stephen King.

A reading of no more than fifteen minutes allows you to give your audience an effective sample of your work, without overstaying your welcome. This brevity also allows more time for questions, which is important since many people come to a reading as much out of curiosity about writers and their world as they do to hear you read. While a reading provides you with your identity as a writer, most readers will respond even more emphatically to the wider context of you as a person.

Humor is important in a reading because it engages the audience and allows them to connect with you. If you can read a humorous passage, you should do so ninety percent of the time. But remember that what's humorous in New York City may not be humorous in Huntsville, Alabama, and that what's humorous to an audience of budding writers may not be humorous to the general reading public.

That said, sometimes you must, as they say, stand and deliver. In important venues, or in situations in which you need to assert your authority as a writer, always select something serious that will blow your audience away.

Being aware of your context extends beyond noting the locale and taste of your intended audience. If you are reading with other writers, make sure to research their work and try to create a contrast from that work with the material you decide to read. Understand that a reading is a performance, and attempt to animate your words in that context — just don't overdo it. For example, creating additional voices for different characters, unless you have acting experience, usually backfires on the reader because it distracts from rather than enhances the experience.

Some members of the audience for a reading won't be there to see you specifically — they just want to see a writer because they're curious. A writer in this context is like a five-legged calf or a frog with three eyes. This is one good reason to bookend a reading with anecdotes about the writing of your book or any other interesting or amusing story connected to the book. In doing so, try to emphasize your central message.

Also, as I've emphasized before, take honest stock of your strengths and weaknesses. If your friends and colleagues agree that you aren't a good reader, stick to signings, anecdotes, and answering questions. Answer any and all questions with honesty and without snark, unless you know every member of the audience personally and can guarantee that your sarcasm will be interpreted as benign.

I used to be uptight about readings, because I always read serious material and you cannot predict an audience's reaction to such material. I also chose long segments to read, giving readers no relief from my seriousness. Since I began reading shorter excerpts, weaving in anecdotes, and found humorous passages to present, my readings have become an asset rather than a liability, and I have a lot more fun, too.

Then, too, maybe you might want to be more extravagant. If so, you could do worse than follow writer Catherynne M. Valente's example:

Our most recent tour has incorporated a phenomenal amount of perfor- mance art including belly dancing (with and without live python), aerial rope suspension, fire-spinning, and burlesque. We take a small circus with us, all over the country. I have heard it said that book tours don't make money, in terms of net copies of books sold. And that's true. But you can't put a price on a lifelong fan, and that's what we're creating as we travel — readers and listeners who will stick with us through thick and thin.

For more on these topics please refer to James Crossley's "Booksellers" in the appendices.

■ Guest Blogging

Many of the most visible blogs (or LiveJournals) in your area of emphasis entertain guest bloggers from time to time. In my experience, if approached courteously, most bloggers are open to being contacted about such opportunities. A blog's readers tend to like being exposed to different voices and points of view — as long as they know the blog's creator will be back soon. You can even make several "stops" as part of a so-called "blog tour," during which you post entries on consecutive days on a series of blogs. (Another approach is to have other bloggers all talk about your book on the same day.)

Having your own established blog provides a huge advantage when you approach other bloggers with promotional ideas. As Matt Staggs notes, "At best, they'll see you as one of them — someone with a genuine interest in the online community — and at worst you'll at least be able to better understand the time and effort they take in their own blogs." If relevant, having guests on your own blog post about subjects related to your book may also be beneficial.

If you're interested in pursuing guest-blogging spots on popular and relevant blogs, following a few simple guidelines will make the experience run more smoothly, and minimize any possible friction with the blog's owner.

- Send a cordial query to your favorites with information about your book, along with some thoughts on subjects or themes you might explore as a guest blogger. Don't blast multiple bloggers with a generic email; personalize each contact and stay focused on a reasonable number of blogs.
- If your own blog has some notoriety, make sure that you don't guest blog on a platform that shares much of the same audience.
- Research the blog's archives to find out what kinds of posts have seemed most popular, and plan accordingly, factoring in how most readers who comment engage existing posts.

- Don't violate any rules set down by the blog's owner in advance.
- Don't post questionable content of any kind. In your role as a guest, just do not take the risk, even if meant in a humorous way.
- If you do guest blog, make sure you provide proper context about your work and yourself in your first post.

After you guest blog, find some way to pay back or pay forward the opportunity. This isn't *quid pro quo*, but simply being considerate. Even if you're a small fish and the platform you guest blogged on is run by a big fish, that person will appreciate the gesture.

Perhaps the best way to pay back the favor is to garner so much attention due to the quality and relevance of your guest blogging that you actually enhance the status of the big fish's blog.

▦ Interviews

The release or impending release of most creative projects usually sparks *some* kind of response, whether across the blogosphere or in mainstream media. Thus, you may not have to do much work to get interviewed — a few journalists and bloggers may come to you. If not, however, apply the same standards of research that you would to conferences and guest blogging. Also familiarize yourself with your targeted market, be courteous, and remember that the onus is on you to prove that your story or project has value to them.

FORMAT

An interview can be conducted in many different ways: via email, telephone, Skype, Instant Messenger, webcam, video, etc. It can be live or taped. You should try to become comfortable with all of these methods. However, there are compelling reasons to use email when you have the choice:

- You can schedule when you decide to answer the questions. I've often regretted agreeing to a telephone interview because invariably, when the day comes, I'm so busy that a conversation at a set time is an irritation.
- Email requires less time than audio or video, which often requires additional set-up or equipment.

- Most people take only so-so notes and a feature or article relying on a transcript will likely contain errors.
- You can avoid being "ambushed" by an interviewer.

CONTENT

Although the content of an interview is largely determined by the questions asked, you can also help shape that content through careful preparation. This isn't a problem with interviews through email, Instant Messenger, etc., where you have a chance to gather your thoughts while answering the questions. But for video or audio captures, here are a few pointers:

- Request a list of topics and questions from the interviewer ahead of time.
- Tell the interviewer what topics you are unwilling to cover and which questions you won't answer. (Typically, you should be open to any question or topic, but sometimes your creative project contains personal elements; talking about some of those elements might violate someone else's privacy.)
- Write out a list of talking points ahead of time. Do not include too much information, and do not try to memorize anything.
- Use your talking points not only to stay on message, but to redirect the conversation if you don't like a particular question. Politicians are adept at answering the question they wanted to answer, rather than the question put to them by the interviewer. In your case, the reason is more benign than spin control. Some interviewers will misinterpret your work or ask questions that indicate they haven't done their research. By using your answer to redirect, your main purpose is simply to gently guide the interviewer toward the truth. Always remember not to serve evil gods by using these powers for anything other than to correct an interviewer's sloppiness.

However, regardless of the method of interview, you should go into an interview with a clear plan of what you want to say and how you want to say it. The simpler your message, the more effective, given short attention spans and the vagaries of how your interview may be edited by the interviewer. Judicious use of humor also goes a long way toward making the end reader, viewer, or listener want to pick up your book.

The Right Way to Be Selective

Satellite radio, webcams, and podcasts have all created new venues for interviews. When you're first starting out, you may want to take advantage of every request. However, over time, as you become better known, you will want to be selective with regard to interviews. If you've just been interviewed by the *Los Angeles Times* book blog, do you also want to do an interview for a personal blog that averages one hundred visitors a day?

It's not just a rhetorical question, because the answer might be "yes." Those hundred visitors might all be bookstore managers or professional journalists, for example. I recently answered reader questions for Joseph Mallozzi's blog. When I agreed to the opportunity, it was an off-the-cuff decision. I wasn't busy and readers of his blog had bought one of my books. After I answered the questions, I discovered Mallozzi is an executive producer of several TV shows and that his blog gets heavy traffic for this reason. I'd inadvertently exposed a large, fresh group of readers to my work. It could as easily have gone the other way: I could have discovered I'd spent a lot of effort for little gain.

To echo the discussion of fragmentation and networking, while you can say yes to every interview opportunity if you want to, make sure that's your *decision* and not just a response to stimuli.

Reviews

Most publicists advise writers not to contact reviewers or send books to them directly. There are at least two reasons for this advice: first, writer interference may clash with the publicist's efforts and, second, many reviewers don't take seriously direct contact or a book sent from the writer because they're used to an established hierarchy in which a third party does the contacting. Direct writer contact implies self-publishing, among other negatives.

While generally good advice, the no-contact rule has some exceptions. First, the publishing world is changing and more writers are taking promotion into their own hands, especially writers with independent and boutique presses. This means more reviewers have become used to at least some writer contact.

Second, the definition of "reviewer" has changed over the past few years. It used to mean a writer for a local, regional, or national newspaper, magazine, radio program, or TV program. Now that term might include a Twitter baron with a following of five thousand or a guy named Zanzibar76 who podcasts out of his basement and has an audience of fifty thousand listening in every week. The Twitter baron doesn't care where his information comes from. And Zanzibar76 doesn't know the protocols of contact — he's much more like the guy in the indie rock scene who came out of writing for fanzines to do reviews for *Rolling Stone*.

Third, experience and the length of a writing career eventually come into play. Over time, you *will* meet reviewers in your virtual and physical travels. Some of them will have already read and enjoyed your work. At the point where you have forged a cordial personal relationship that stops short of being a clear ethical conflict of interest, it's your call as to whether you contact that person about your book.

In general, I tend to avoid emails on such subjects because it feels intrusive, but have no qualms about dropping signed books in the mail to reviewers I know are sympathetic to my work and haven't minded the practice in the past. They are then free to open a line of communication with me or not, whereas a direct email to a reviewer seems to require a response.

As for the established hierarchy and protocol at those citadels of established traditional media, a good rule of thumb is that if a media outlet has a books or reviews editor and doesn't divulge contact information for its reviewers, you should assume you need a third party to contact the editor for you.

■ Writing Your Backstory

If your creative project has a unique story behind it, don't just put that information in a press release. Use that angle to pitch an article, essay, or opinion piece to the appropriate newspaper, magazine, or website. A piece that allows you to mention your project, even just in a short author's note accompanying the text, can be a powerful advocate for your work with readers who might otherwise never be interested. You can also release your article for free online and encourage everyone to reproduce it on their own platforms. (The Creative Commons website provides many different ways to release text for reproduction elsewhere, with varying levels of protection for the author of the material.)

If you decide to research possible venues for a pitch, remember that magazines tend to have much longer lead times than most online outlets.

Schedule your pitches accordingly, and weigh the relative value of online versus hardcopy possibilities along with other variables like payment, audience, and relevance to your book.

Also consider having someone else write the story. Pitch the idea to a free-lancer that you know writes for certain publications or websites. You'll give up the possibility of getting paid, but you may also be able to bypass the relevant gatekeepers. (For additional advice, read the applicable information in Matt Staggs' "Nodes and Influencers" in the appendices.)

▶▶ PR Tools

In this section, you'll find a list of effective tools to help your cause. Your task will be to select the ones that work best for you and integrate them into an effective, unified plan that *links use of tools with the opportunities discussed in the last section, and that includes leverage across your platforms*. Every tool has some application not yet thought of or rarely used for book promotion purposes.

I have divided PR tools into the following categories: Artifacts, Information Retrieval, Objects, and Samples. It's impossible to list every permutation of, for example, "artifact" related to promoting your creative project, especially since the possibilities change every year due to the creativity of new media entrepreneurs. But I can make you aware of some of the tools and briefly discuss how they enhance and feed into your overall effort. I've largely avoided discussing tools like magazine, radio, or TV advertising because (1) it's expensive, (2) it's superfluous if you can get free coverage through a review or feature, and (3) you can find information on these traditional approaches in many other books.

■ Artifacts

In the context of your PR campaign, "artifacts" are tangible physical or virtual creations that can be leveraged through a platform or an opportunity. An artifact often enhances your ability to acquire leverage by providing added value to readers or to the gatekeepers who decide whether or not to grant you an opportunity. They also, either directly or indirectly, support your message about your book or other creative project.

Artifacts possess their own aesthetic integrity and can be powerful expressions of the imagination in their own right. Sometimes, they transcend from adjuncts to your main purpose into their own creative projects, and thus support your Private Booklife as well.

Let's explore some examples of artifacts.

Book Trailers

An effective book trailer is short and to the point. A trailer longer than a minute or two must do more than present the book — it must tell a story. Good book trailers also make some attempt to be cinematic rather than static, include music, and mix in humor when possible. Because the classic leverage model is to upload your trailer to YouTube, viewers will tolerate a certain level of amateurism. YouTube is still the home of DIY video.

As both my publicist Matt Staggs and I have discovered, some book concepts better lend themselves to video than others, especially because you have to be realistic about your resources. For example, books with a strong visual component make it easier to create a simple video even if you have little video experience because you can build your narrative around one or two images.

One easy way to start building a video is to make a list of those images, as well as any other elements you think are important. Then search the Internet for public domain still pictures, video, and audio. You should also check with the cover artist for the book, who might well be willing to share more images to help construct the video.

Once you have as much material as you can find, separate it all into high-quality and low-quality buckets, keeping the low-quality images, video, and sound just as back-up. Review the high-quality material and begin looking for the elements you need to put together a coherent video that also matches the story you want to tell about the book. Try to create at least a rough sequence before you begin to put together the trailer.

Even if you only have Windows Movie Maker or some other rudimentary software, you can then begin importing the elements you want to use and arranging them according to your rough order. Depending on how organized you've been this part of the process might take a few hours or a couple of days, especially since you'll need to add additional effects and title cards.

Depending on the book, you can either downplay the amateur aspect or play it up. Both approaches have hidden dangers. On the one hand, people may find your trailer boring. On the other hand, they may find it laughably bad. For example, Matt took a big chance with James Morrow's *Shambling Towards Hiroshima*, a book that mixes satire with spoofs of Japanese monster movies. He found public domain Godzilla footage, interspliced it with passages from the book and images of the book's cover art. He didn't have to deliberately aim for camp in the final product because his core elements already achieved that effect. These very elements might've seemed like weaknesses in a video for a more serious book — in fact, he might not have been *able* to take a DIY approach for a more serious book.

But the *personal* aspects of certain types of DIY can also work to your benefit. One way to get around this is to deliberately embrace and emphasize the amateurism. For an anthology my wife and I edited called *Fast Ships, Black Sails*, Ann had contributors dress up as pirates and send in video clips of them reading from their stories. The personal connection with the viewer created by these very short readings, combined with the charm of seeing the writers with eye patches and, in one case, a parrot on the shoulder, led to the video being picked up by the official *Pirates of the Caribbean* fan website. Did the video fall into the pitfalls of an amateur approach? It's open to debate. We were able to leverage the video to a wider audience, but at the same time some viewers found the approach too uneven.

The fact is, even inspired amateurism can only take you so far. Leveraging a video requires gatekeepers to link to it or embed it. As homemade online video grows more and more sophisticated, you may have trouble getting attention for an amateurish book trailer, even with the anecdotal evidence I provided above. The question you'll then have to ask yourself is: Am I willing to pay to have a professional create a trailer for me? If you are willing, then you need to make sure you have a good plan for how to use the video.

What's an appropriate context in which to leverage a book trailer? One possibility is to create a trailer for a second release of your book. If your book comes out in hardcover and then trade paperback, consider delaying a book trailer for the trade paperback edition. The trade paperback edition of a hardcover has more limited potential for reviews and other types of PR, so generating attention through this option can help with leverage. A good example is Toby Barlowe's recent book trailer for his novel *Sharp Teeth*. It supported the release of his book in trade paperback, it reminded everyone who didn't pick up the book the first time about what created such buzz around its initial release, and it's a beautiful little artistic statement in its own right. The trailer hit the Internet about a week before the trade paperback's publication. Barlowe not only leveraged it across his own platforms, he found ways to get gatekeepers who had loved the hardcover to feature the video.

FILMS AND SOUNDTRACKS

Sometimes, a book trailer turns into something more, although admittedly, the demarcation between "trailer" and "film" is getting blurrier and blurrier.

For example, the three-minute trailer for my novel *Shriek: An Afterword* grew into a fourteen-minute independent short film with a soundtrack by the rock band The Church (a good example of creative networking, as I'd used the opportunity of a visit to Australia to meet with them, and we'd hit it off).

Although created for the Internet, the film was shown at various independent theaters and other venues around the country and the world, at events promoting the novel. One of my favorite photographs of all time shows a double-billing of the *Rocky Horror Picture Show* and *Shriek* at the Clinton Street Theater in Portland. The film was also used by Borders to promote the novel to their subscribers and received Internet exposure far beyond the dedicated website I'd created for the title. The trailer for the movie also wound up being featured on news sites such as Mediabistro's GalleyCat.

But after book promotion was over, the film — experimental and definitely its own entity by that point — engendered a soundtrack for the novel. The Church decided to take the instrumental music they'd created and flesh it out into a full CD with lyrics. I had written the novel while listening to The Church, which only deepened the synergistic relationship. In late 2008, The Church released the CD simultaneously with a deluxe edition of the novel. At this point, it was no longer clear which creative object was subservient to the other. This example also demonstrates the powerful effect of the Internet, as members of The Church lived, at various times, on three different continents during the making of the CD, and the project would not have been economical without access to the Internet.

Sometimes, too, this process can be even more immersive. Remember Catherynne M. Valente from the section on readings? She has a close working relationship with the musician S. J. Tucker. Together, they've collaborated on three full-length CDs intended as soundtracks for Valente's books.

> They stemmed from our friendship and mutual love of each other's work, and have taken on lives of their own. S. J. suggested an Orphan's Tales album in my Ohio living room in 2006 and wrote the first song while I made breakfast — and thus everything began, because if there is music, there is obviously a tour, and we began to figure out how to perform as a reading-concert, alternating readings from the novels and songs from the albums into a single experience. We have traveled all over the country doing this, and have pushed each other as artists in new directions.

How does the process work? Valente delivers the manuscript to Tucker when completed "and I give her complete freedom to write the songs that she wants to write, whatever inspires her within the book. By her music, I often learn a great deal about the book I wrote — each of her songs is a crystallization of part of the novel, and I see it from other perspectives."

From a PR standpoint, Tucker and Valente have, as Valente puts it, "cross-pollinated our fandoms — those who read my books discover her music and those who are avid fans of hers find my books through her songs." They've also built a dedicated audience for their performances, as well as for limited-edition perfumes and jewelry tied to the books. The collaboration even led to a journey of several weeks, across several states, culminating in a special event for "superfans": an intimate multi-day train trip down to New Orleans with both performers, readings, and songs planned the entire way, ending in a sumptuous group dinner at their destination.

ALTERNATE REALITY GAMES

The idea of using the Internet as a kind of meta-notebook across which you scrawl your own choose-your-own-adventure or other kind of alternate reality game, and in so doing engage new readers, still hasn't reached its full potential. Writers keep trying, though, and some day soon the very nature of social media may change to the extent that it makes such efforts easier. Until that time, or unless you perfect some method yourself, you have a couple of possibilities: to work within an existing online reality or to create your own via various platforms.

As mentioned earlier, Second Life — a kind of virtual reality you access through the Internet after subscribing — hasn't been used much as a platform. It also remains underdeveloped as a way to create a PR artifact. For this reason, it may be fertile new territory to explore in the future. Writer Caitlín R. Kiernan has had a presence in Second Life for almost two years and hasn't yet found a way to tap into the potential for creating potent artifacts:

> I've been a "resident" now since May 2007, and I've tried, mainly, to use it for the purposes of roleplay as a writing exercise. Upon discovering Second Life, my first reaction was that it is perfectly suited to this end. And that I could use various roleplay scenarios to work out bits

of story for print, or, better yet, to create stories in an entirely new medium...So, at the start, my hopes were very, very high. After all, this is the closest thing we've seen yet to a "holodeck." Within SL, I can be anyone, any species, any gender, exist in any time, in realistic and in fantastical worlds that, with a little work, time, and money, I can customize to my specific needs. Almost any imaginable interaction can be acted out in SL. Its potential for simulation, full-immersion improvisational theater, and interactive storytelling is enormous. Sadly, it's also mostly untapped. Because, in truth, most users approach SL as nothing more than a chat room/social networking site that just *happens* to offer very fancy avatars that you can move about within very fancy virtual environments. Even those few corners of SL set aside specifically *for* roleplaying and storytelling are usually overwhelmed by users who are actively hostile to roleplaying, who purposefully disrupt it, or who simply cannot grasp what it means to be *in* character.

The hindrance to use of Second Life for Booklife purposes appears to be that success hinges on your audience not only being receptive to the message but also not actively disrupting your attempt to deliver it!

Juliet Ulman, a consultant and editor who used to work for Bantam Books (and the developmental editor for *Booklife*), provides a view of Second Life from a publisher's perspective. She notes that Bantam even established its own cafe and connected virtual bookstore "where they hold virtual readings and Q&A sessions with such established authors as Dean Koontz and George R. R. Martin — after which those who've chosen to attend virtually can purchase the author's works in the attached bookstore."

However, Ulman believes that Kiernan's experience is "not unusual" and that "the direct effect of these virtual events on actual sales is difficult to assess and almost certainly less than one might hope." She also points out that unless you are a "brand-name" author like Koontz or Martin, it's difficult to entice users away from the many distractions of Second Life to engage with what is essentially an old model of author interaction simply transported to a shiny, pixelated stage."

Even Kiernan admits, however, that "Second Life does have a lot to offer writers, in theory, but only if they are willing to invest a tremendous amount of time and energy, endure an unspeakable amount of stupidity, and possess great patience." Potentially, then, a writer could use this advanced form of roleplaying to create interesting PR artifacts while also stimulating creativity in his or her Private Booklife.

On the other hand, you might be better off trying to "go viral" by being a mammal rather than a dinosaur, being small rather than large. To promote her novel *Palimpsest*, Valente built an alternate reality game out of the equivalent of a piece of string, two trashcan lids, and a plastic bag:

> This was [a kind of virtual] "novella" in the world of the novel, accessible by readers through blogs, Twitter feeds, forums, and Facebook profiles. Hidden in the text were links to puzzles, digital art, audio files, video, and music. I created a video trailer for the novel which also served as a gateway to the game. We funneled several thousand readers through the linked sites in the six weeks before the novel came out, and it ramped up the excitement for the book considerably. It was a huge undertaking that involved many writers and artists working in tandem and anonymously, but its success in terms of [establishing an] online presence [for] the book before the book ever existed in the world cannot be overstated.

I find the implications of this experiment exciting because Valente provides a great example of how to create something that enriches both your Public and Private Booklife. From a PR point of view, however, success depends on more than just reader participation.

For example, what kind of press coverage did the ARG experiment get? In other words, the PR value of an artifact lies not just in its connection to a core creative project, but in its uniqueness. The added dimension to an effort of this kind is how you leverage that uniqueness to get the word out to people who never even access the game. Theoretically, three people could "play" the game and if you received coverage from, for example, one major media outlet like WIRED.COM, the benefit to your book would be greater than if three thousand people had played the game and no one had written about it.

■ ■ ■

Artifacts are alluring because they promise to scratch your creative itch even as they help your Public Booklife. However, always remember that creating an artifact can divert time and money away from other, more direct efforts on behalf of your book. It can also skew your efforts toward promotion of the artifact rather than your book if you let it. Make careful assessments of the career and creative value weighed against the depth of the required effort. Also make sure before creating an artifact that you have an effective way to leverage the results.

In my case, creating a short film for *Shriek: An Afterword* raised my profile and led to many other opportunities. In Valente's case, the game she created also raised her profile and reaffirmed her willingness to take risks. However, in both situations the direct impact on the profile and sales of the *novel* the artifacts were built to promote is hard to determine. Perhaps the most valuable benefit associated with a daring artifact is to establish a brand for the author, and that brand may come to be more valuable over the long-term than the impact on the sales of any individual book.

Information Retrieval

Your own database of contacts, as discussed in the Networking section of *Booklife*, provides a valuable source of intel during a PR campaign. You can use your contacts database to target various types of gatekeepers and reviewers, or target various parts of the country. Over time, you can use it to identify key concentrations of your fans, which can help you plan book tours. Always supplement your existing contacts database with information from Google searches and RSS Feeds. (Rather than providing a full exposition of a very technical subject here, please refer to "Sipping from the Fire Hose" in the appendices.)

Objects

Unlike artifacts, objects have no real intrinsic value as creative projects. Imagination is required to envision and create them, but they more directly serve the purpose of promoting your book. Moreover, there is less differentiation between objects than between artifacts. All banner ads look more or less the same. All postcards must follow the same rules about where to put address information. Here are a few examples of objects that can help support your PR campaign.

Dedicated Websites

With the right leverage, a good website can direct hundreds or thousands of readers a month to your work. Find a way to make it different in content or look by researching other author sites. Mimic what you like functionality-wise and then do your own take on it. Use someone with Web design experience, not just someone who knows a little HTML coding. Even if you write the content, use third person for static author biographical notes and other incidental/informational text. Reserve first person for your blog entries and other updates in which you directly address your audience. Make sure the design and functionality is clear, clean, direct, and modern. A website dedicated to your book should include the following basic information:

- A main page with a short description of the book, along with a couple of blurbs or review quotes, a link to preferred sellers, and an image of the cover. If you plan to post news, embed the news section in the main page.
- An "about the author" page with a photograph and short bio note.
- A press kit page that includes downloadable print-quality images of you and your book's cover, along with the official press release, all of the technical information about the book (release date, ISBN number, etc.), and direct contact information for you and your publicist.
- A "contact" page that repeats your contact information and includes a feedback form that sends a message to your email account.
- A "samples" page that includes various excerpts from the book, possibly with audio versions.

I also recommend investing in a book specifically devoted to the mechanics and methodology of website creation, like the excellent *Web Design in a Nutshell* by Jennifer Niederst Robbins. It's worth noting, too, that more and more writers are creating a page for their latest book that resides on their blog. This has the benefit of being easier to maintain and having a more concentrated effect, at the expense of diversity and complexity.

Postcards

There are several advantages to postcards. They're inexpensive, seem less tacky than bookmarks, can be mailed, or can be used as an oversized business card. Unlike a business card, they provide the recipient with concise information about your book. Unlike the abomination that is the button, they serve a practical purpose. You can use them at conferences, but you can also send them to readers willing to pass some on to friends and family. Simple and straightforward, postcards make excellent emissaries for your book in the physical world. I don't even bother leaving space for mailing information, as I leverage postcards as part of a press kit or during public appearances. Several companies have an online presence, the best of which is MODERNPOSTCARD. COM. (One example of a riff on the postcard is to put the same information on a beer coaster or a pack of playing cards.)

WEBSITE BANNER ADS

Of all types of paid advertising, website banner ads strike me as being the most valuable. You can pay to leverage a single advertisement across many sites, but you can send the same ad to friends and supporters who will post it on their sites for free.

One decision you'll have to make is whether viewers click through to your site or to the sales page for your book on Amazon, IndieBound, or other online retailers. That decision should be based on whether your effort is primarily to support the current book or to support your overall brand. As for what makes someone click-through from the ad to information about your book, PUBLISHINGTRENDS.COM notes that one of the most effective approaches is to create an ad that leaves you wanting more at the end. Therefore, an effective technique is to entice the viewer to click at the end to answer a question or "learn more."

Keep your banner ad simple but intriguing. Make sure it is designed by a Web design professional. Avoid complicated animations that may not run on all computers or all sites.

■ ■ ■

Not only are objects usually simpler to create than artifacts, they also tend to have a one or two targeted purposes. For this reason, they're like the foot-soldiers in your campaign. They perform a necessary function, but they're not particularly maneuverable. There's a kind of static quality to them. For this reason, don't try to make objects perform complex tasks. An anvil is not an apple, just as a banner ad is not a book trailer and a website is not an ARG.

■ Samples

One of your most effective tools will always be a sample of your creative project. These samples can take many forms, from the entire text to a selection created in another medium. Presentation and ease of use determine how useful sampling will be to your efforts. However, as Juliet Ulman points out, always check with your publisher first: "Unless you've specifically negotiated it in your contract, you will not have the right to provide a full free download of your book. And, if you haven't retained First Serial Rights, you cannot provide an excerpt without your publisher's approval." Also, if you don't have a publisher and haven't built up at least a modest reputation for your writing, be careful that your offer of a sample doesn't come across with a whiff of desperation, even though the traditional idea of a hierarchy for writers is crumbling.

Free downloads

A download of your book should be in an easy-to-read format that approximates the published iteration. While a simple, easy PDF format works fine for most laptop or desktop computers, it won't translate well to most e-readers. The ability of e-readers and other portable devices is always changing, however, so you'll need to research the current standards before deciding how to release your book.

You can use the information at the Creative Commons site to decide on the level of reader access to the text. Creative Commons just provides a pre-built, universally agreed upon structure to communicate your wishes about access to readers. You can release it for download and printing only, or allow much more interplay with the text.

Cory Doctorow championed the free book download through the culture website Boing Boing a few years ago, and he's had great success. However, a word of caution: his success doesn't mean you too will be as successful unless you have access to many readers. One theory of book downloads is that those who champion them as effective tools already have hugely successful platforms through which to leverage them. It's also still unclear whether most readers who download a novel actually read the entire novel. Presumably, though, most people who download a book at least sample it.

The link between increased sales and book downloads that some writers claim also isn't clear, but even if you assume the worst — that there is little or no link for most writers — leveraging a book download "event" creates all kinds of useful peripheral publicity. Nor is there any evidence that free downloads negatively affect book sales. As Doctorow has rightly pointed out, too, timing is extremely important: you won't generate as many book sales if you release the free online version prior to publication. (Although peripheral to this discussion, pick up Doctorow's excellent *Content*, a collection of essays about copyright and other subjects relevant to the new digital age.)

You can also, of course, offer a download of part of a book if the idea of a full download makes you nervous — or even podcast all or part of your book, if you own the rights (see the appendices for more on podcasting). Free samples can be offered on several sites. Amazon, for example, allows anyone to sell ebooks for their Kindle store. You can offer a free sample there as well as at Scribd and Issuu. Both Scribd and Issuu offer an online interface so readers don't have to actually download the book or sample.

As I discuss in the Leverage section below, book downloads are no longer new and haven't been for a couple of years, but that doesn't mean you shouldn't find effective methods of using this approach.

Published Excerpts

If part of your book is self-contained, consider sending it around to applicable magazines, websites, or blogs for publication or posting. Depending on the circumstances of physical publication, a serialization may even be possible. If you want to get creative, you could even do a fictional blog tour, in which different blogs post interlocking excerpts. (Refer to the section above on Writing Your Backstory, as the advice there also applies to fiction excerpts.)

Print-on-Demand "Catalog."

Most writers think of print-on-demand (POD) technologies as a good way to cheaply self-publish a book, especially since celebrity authors like Wil Wheaton have been so successful using online services like Lulu. However, you can also use POD for PR if you have multiple projects coming out and want a kind of catalog that includes information and samples from all of them. In the past, I have created little ninety-six-page books when I had four or five projects either in print or soon to be in print.

The best use I've found for them is when you're introducing yourself to a new type of audience. When I attended my first Associated Writers Program conference in Vancouver, Canada, a few years ago, I had few contacts in the academic world and knew only a couple of people. I used my panel appearance to hand out about two hundred copies of my little sampler as a way of introducing the audience to my work. That "supplement" resulted in a number of new contacts, two invitations to submit material to literary journals, and at least one speaking engagement. The per-unit cost of the book was about three dollars, so I spent a total of six hundred dollars, but in terms of the long-term value that was incredibly cheap. This is just one example, of course, and you might find some other viable use for the idea — like sending signed, numbered copies to select booksellers.

(Extra) Review Copies

Remember to get a list from your publisher of everyone who received review copies of your book and find any gaps in coverage. Library journals, newspapers, major online review sites, and major traditional magazines that publish book reviews should be covered by your publisher's efforts. The average publisher will send out anywhere from fifty to four hundred advance copies. The contact and the types of venues vary depending on the nature of your book.

Acquire additional review copies to cover any places your publisher deemed too small or not influential enough but that you still want to see covered for your own strategic or tactical reasons. Even with my books from major publishers, I always make sure to have extra copies (at the author discount) so I can personalize them and send them to places not covered by my publicist: mid-level bloggers, smaller media markets, and those peculiar drifters, unassociated with any particular organization or publication, whose opinion tends to influence the opinion of others behind the scenes.

It may seem obvious, but you'll also need extra copies of your book to give to people who helped you on the particular project or during your career to that point. This easy way to say thank you may result in additional coverage if recipients just happen to include people who blog or write for media outlets.

▶▶ Leveraging Your Ideas

■ Lost in the Crowd?

Tools help you get opportunities and can be leveraged across your platforms. Opportunities provide leverage, and generate additional leverage across the Internet, including through your platforms.

Getting leverage, then, is the fundamental difference in the public arena between a successful and a failed creative project. Often, I receive emails about tools rather than leverage, however. For example, a question like "Should I do a video promo for my book?" Or, "is a podcast a good idea?" My first question in reply is usually, "Who is going to host it and how are you going to guarantee an audience for it?"

The fact is, you can create any number of wondrous promotional tools for your project, but if you can't find a way to bring people to "it" or take "it" to the people, you might as well not have bothered — unless you're getting some kind of creative satisfaction out of it that is its own reward. *The existence of a creative object or artifact does not guarantee an audience for "it."*

The humorist Charlie Hills puts it nicely: "*If you build it, they will come* is not a proverb that applies to writing, music, art, or any other creative object or artifact. I believe at one point or another, to some extent or another, every creative person falls into this trap. We come up with a brilliantly creative idea. We work on it, feed it, nurture it. When complete, we announce it to the world and hope (or even expect) people will immediately line up around the block to see it. 'It's brilliant!' we tell ourselves. 'Why *wouldn't* people flock to it?'"

The situation reminds me of times back in the day, when I was running a literary press that mostly focused on poetry. For the first few issues of the magazine *Chimera Connections*, and even the first couple of chapbooks, we'd get it printed, send it out to what subscribers we had, and then...well, then, we'd relax for a couple of months. With big boxes of magazines in the living room. But it's worse now, because as Hills says, "People have about two thousand other things to think about, people to talk to, and places to visit. If you don't appear along any of those paths, you are invisible. Which is technically the same as not existing at all."

The great thing about the Internet is also the bad thing: it's a crowded arena, in which more and more people have access to cheap tools that allow them to be creative, along with the ability to also make them public cheaply (a different thing than making them public to a large number of people). From an artistic standpoint, this is wonderful. From the standpoint of getting the word out, it's a problem.

◼ Successful Example: "The Situation"

How can you leverage even a small project into something longer? I've got a good example. In 2008, PS Publishing in the United Kingdom planned on bringing out my novelette "The Situation" as a limited edition book. They planned to print five hundred copies and make review copies available via PDF. The story — like a combination of Dilbert and New Gothic in its mix of the surreal and contemporary office drama — had been blurbed by Kevin Brockmeier and others. Having a story released in book form, no matter what the print run, can guarantee more review attention than appearing in a magazine, under the right conditions.

At the time of publication I was also being interviewed by WIRED.COM's GeekDad blog. Since GeekDad gets about thirty thousand visitors a week, I asked my contact Brad Moon if they'd like to run a PDF of "The Situation" as a free download for their readers. When they said yes, I did two things at the same time: I contacted the huge pop-culture blogsite Boing Boing to ask if this was the kind of thing they'd mention and also made the case to PS Publishing about why having a free download of the book would be a good thing.

When Boing Boing said they'd probably do a short feature that included the link to the GeekDad feature, PS Publishing agreed to the free download. As a result, a book with a print run of five hundred was downloaded by an additional twenty thousand readers. Because Boing Boing linked to the feature, many other online media outlets also linked to it. This increased the impact of the story, the visibility of my own blog, enhanced my reputation as a writer, and in general turned a single story into a powerful part of my web presence in 2008. It also helped PS Publishing sell out much more quickly than they would have otherwise.

However, the connectivity continued past that point. In part because the GeekDad feature received so much coverage, "The Situation" is now being turned into an e-comic for another major website. Not only has that led to the story generating extra revenue and, in time, additional attention, it means I will be learning how to write for the comics. It may even lead to a book deal. Thus, what started out as an effort to get a little extra attention for my story in book form has ended up feeding back into my personal creative growth.

What's the secret to this entire cycle of events? It's simple: I spent a lot of time writing a good story that people enjoyed when they encountered it. If I hadn't focused first and foremost on the creative side nothing else I did would have mattered. The publicity would have stalled out or even backfired, resulting in a magnified negative effect.

▶▶ Creating a PR Plan

How you combine tools, opportunities, and platforms to create leverage will be unique to your book, your personal commitment, your publisher's commitment, and the competition for attention in your area of emphasis, among other factors. Many writers choose to think tactically and use tools for leverage or use opportunities for leverage, but they don't create a strategic *plan*. Sometimes, this is because they are working in concert with their publicist, who creates the strategic plan. Other times, it's because the writer doesn't have the time to do more than be proactive in one area and reactive in most others.

What does this mean in real-world terms? Here are two scenarios based on real-world anecdotes.

Writer A has an event that draws one hundred people to a library in Minneapolis, Minnesota. The writer did a lot of the legwork and made sure that the people he knew who lived in the area got information about the event. The library itself handled getting a listing in the local papers and online guides. The writer sells thirty-five books at the event, blogs about her experience, and travels to the next gig.

Writer B has an event that draws twenty people to a bookstore in Asheville, North Carolina. She didn't do much legwork and relied on the fact the reading was part of a series that attracts a regular crowd. The bookstore managed to get not just a listing but a sidebar with her photograph in the local paper. She sells five copies, signs stock for the bookstore manager, blogs about her experience, and travels to the next gig.

Which writer had the more valuable gig in terms of her career, Writer A or Writer B? On the face of it, Writer A had the more successful event. She sold more books. But the truth is more complex. For example, it would depend on knowing the details of the individual plans each writer had created for their book. Five books sold with a small feature in the local newspaper might mean more in terms of Writer A's plan than thirty-five books and no feature might mean in terms of Writer B's plan. Writer B's blog audience might be much larger than Writer A's blog audience. Writer B's plan might have included inviting a writer from some national media outlet — and if that one person came, a gig that netted five copies sold might in time turn out to be much more valuable. Maybe Writer B also managed to get attention from a major news site because her plan specifically stated that she wouldn't do readings from her book but instead a unique presentation based on its subject matter that then would be videotaped and posted on YouTube.

I've raised a lot of hypotheticals in defense of Writer B only selling five books, but what I'm trying to do is make clear the value of planning in not only having a clear vision for your efforts but also a way of measuring your success.

Doing only what you can because of other commitments or because you don't *want* to do more is a legitimate reasons for sticking to a largely tactical battle plan. *You should not feel pressure to put yourself in situations that will result in failure.*

However, if you decide to coordinate your efforts and look at them holistically, you should create actual planning documents. These documents should consist of a high-level plan, followed by a more detailed plan that fleshes out details, opportunities, and other tactical elements.

■ Your High-Level Plan

A high-level plan should include all possible elements you plan to leverage, as well as the standard elements of any plan from your publisher's point of view. Make sure the reach of your plan exceeds its grasp. Don't put limitations on yourself. You want your plan to be bigger than the potential success of the book, so if the book is very successful your plan already anticipates that success. And, unlike the plan you may present to a publisher's marketing department (see the example in the appendices), the audience for this high-level plan is *you*. Referring back to this plan should allow you to maintain balance and focus throughout a book campaign.

The high-level plan should have a simple, easy-to-follow structure. I like to organize mine chronologically:

• **PRE-PUBLICATION.** This section pertains to everything that needs to *happen* before publication, in the order in which it should occur. For example, soliciting blurbs, finding early adopters, and sending out advance copies. It should include specifics where possible, including the names of potential "blurbers." A section on advance copies should include any special considerations regarding format and the accompanying press release.

• ON/AFTER PUBLICATION. This section pertains to everything that will be made visible to the public on and after publication, acknowledging that the due dates for creating or organizing elements of these artifacts, objects, and events must occur, in some cases, well in advance of publication. Everything from disposition of published copies of the book and book release parties to bookstore events and anything special, such as a soundtrack or book trailer, should be included in this section. Include an "Additional Leverage" section as a catch-all for information that applies across multiple elements; this section will be useful when creating your detailed plan.

• OTHER IDEAS. The first two sections of your plan should include only those elements that you have established through preliminary communication with your publisher (or, in the case of self-publication, any collaborators or helpers) that are feasible and you're ninety percent sure will be implemented in the service of your book's release. However, a third section titled "Other Ideas" should be used to document elements that seem less possible because they require additional resources of money, time, or labor that have not been acquired or allocated by you or the publisher. In some cases, these other ideas may become possible later — either for the current book or a future book.

Your high-level plan more or less gives you an idea of the disposition of the resources at your disposal, and some preliminary ideas of how you might deploy them. Depending on your personality and your particular book, you may find other ways to structure such a plan. The plan will also not be complete until you finalize details with the publisher, getting their input on every aspect of the plan. (Please refer to the example of a high-level plan in the appendices, which also includes the initial back-and-forth communication between me and my publisher.)

Your Detailed Plan

Once you've finalized your high-level plan, you can create your detailed plan. Please note that if the high-level plan for your book includes several complex elements, you may need to create more than one detailed plan, each covering a few of those (related) elements.

The document or documents should consist of the following:

- A brief statement of how your PR effort feeds into your overall mission statement and goals for your Public Booklife.
- A list of all resources available for the project, including opportunities, tools, platforms, and contacts.
  - o Your opportunities should be matched with the tools you plan to use for leverage.
  - o Your platforms should be matched with the appropriate opportunities and tools you plan to leverage through them.
- A timeline across which tasks or actions occur with regard to opportunities, tools, and platforms. The timeline should include:
  - o A start-date and end-date for the effort.
  - o Specific dates for completion of tasks and actions to occur, along with who is performing the task. Typically, you, your publicist, and gatekeepers who have agreed to give you an opportunity complete the tasks. (Some of these actions will be things that are beyond your control, like a review appearing in the *Washington Post*. However, in this example if a review hasn't appeared within a month of the book's publication it will probably never appear).
  - o If you have created multiple PR artifacts or other variables, you may need to break out separate timelines to create specificity of detail.
- A list of people associated with the timeline, including you, and under each name the tasks/actions, with deadlines, that each one is expected to perform for the plan to be a success. Add your own tasks to the weekly task list you use in support of your goals.
- A list of open issues — which consists of queries concerning any problems, obstacles, or unresolved questions — with what you need to find answers, along with a deadline.
- A series of "If-Then" statements to anticipate acquiring additional leverage.

I can't stress the importance of "If-Then" statements enough, *in a plan created before you have to actually implement them*. Once you get into the flow of a detailed PR plan, with the book actually out, you're going to be re-active, not pro-active. There just won't be time, and new requests/opportunities will overload you.

What do I mean by "If-Then" statements? There are thousands of connections between your contacts and the different elements in your plan. As your plan progresses, as the reviews and successes accumulate, your plan as written cannot possibly foresee all the possible permutations and cross-pollination created by your efforts. But you can foresee the initial ramifications of certain types of success. Therefore, If-Then statements act as predictors that allow you to more easily ride the wave.

Also, some actions or tasks are not worth expending energy on if certain other things don't happen first. To give a couple of mundane examples, "If so-and-so blurbs it, then I can send it to Stephen King, a friend of so-and-so," or "If I get a reading at Borders, then I can set up a feature with the local newspaper."

Of course, at a certain point — a point that usually resonates in an instinctual way — it will be time to take your foot off the gas, and just let things happen. The reason for this is that because of the DIY, everyone-is-a-content-provider nature of the Internet, you will reach a point at which being proactive will be seen as intrusive. The secret behind viral videos, for example, is that after the initial push, they become viral because of electronic word of mouth, not because of nudges from someone in a PR campaign.

There's also an element of self confidence involved — you have to believe that the book is going to do well, and act accordingly. It's like an actor who pretty much becomes his character and lives it for months, becomes another person. If you act "successful," the gap between acting and being successful may eventually close completely. Just make sure you don't mistake "acting successful" for "acting arrogant" or you'll soon be "acting contrite."

▶▶ Five Minimum Elements for Success

What if you don't have time, money, or inclination to do any of what I've mentioned? You've slogged through the entire Building and Communicating Your Booklife sections with a growing sense of numbness and horror. If this continues to be your reaction after absorbing all of *Booklife*, then you may want to put in what I'd call the minimum effort to have a shot at success. What are those elements?

- Create a nexus for information and updates about the book, preferably a blog or as an adjunct to your existing blog.
- Approach your favorite writers in advance of publication to blurb the book, and use their endorsement and efforts to help you.
- Inform all of your public and private contacts about the book through a simple email, making sure to use the "BLIND CC" feature so you don't reveal contact information to others.
- Buy a limited number of extra copies and send them, personalized, to your most high-powered personal contacts with a note asking if they'd be willing to talk about your book on their public platform.
- Make your email address and telephone number available and prominent on your blog or website so that gatekeepers can easily reach you for more information or to set up an interview.

If you have the budget or time for it, add a sixth element:

- Find someone to design a banner ad for you, and send the relevant information to any of your contacts with blogs or websites who might run it for free. Make sure that the banner ad points to your preferred online listing for the book.

Two additional essentials should be covered by your publisher, but if you have an unconventional publisher or no publisher at all, you will need to address them yourself. First, you must get your book listed on AMAZON.COM, INDIEBOUND, and on BARNESANDNOBLE.COM, including a cover image. Although online instructions on how to accomplish this are convoluted, you just have to clench your teeth and work through it. Second, you will also need to try to get coverage in one or more of the library journals that influence book sales: *Publishers Weekly, Library Journal, Kirkus Reviews,* and *Booklist.* These publications provide the advance blurbs from media outlets you see on the actual book, since most other reviews come out around the time of the book's release. The library journals are important because a single library system buyer might be acquiring fifty copies for their area. You can conceivably sell thousands of copies just through library sales. Again, refer to instructions on the websites of the library journals. Unfortunately, if you've self-published your book such coverage may be impossible.

Chapter 3
Maintaining Your Booklife

►► Transparency

WHAT IS PUBLIC transparency for a writer? It's whatever you choose to divulge of your private and professional life in a public forum. Maybe you're transparent about your writing process. Maybe, instead, you're transparent about the details of your career. Either way, once you become transparent about a subject, your readers may expect you to continue being transparent. Sometimes that will mean giving up a strategic or tactical advantage, possibly to set an example or to actively warn others about a bad situation.

In a positive way, *Booklife* is an example of giving up advantage in favor of transparency: I'm divulging everything I've learned over the past twenty years. At the same time, on my blog I rarely share personal anecdotes not connected to the writing life. Why? It's simple. Because this would remove the distance between me and my audience that I need to be happy. (The section of *Booklife* on blogging and personal space covers this issue in depth.)

Another example — negative, but still necessary — would be using your blog to provide the details of a continuing pattern of a media outlet or person bilking people out of money or in other ways acting unprofessionally. As a freelancer, I've come across these situations more than once, and sometimes, as a last resort, this is the only way to stop or hinder behavior that is hurtful to the writing community.

However, your approach to transparency on the Internet comes down to a personal decision, because there's little consensus on the subject.

The Portland-based writer Jay Lake says, "I am a pretty transparent writer in the sense that I openly discuss process, story marketing, successes, and failures."

Lake isn't alone in this — over the past year I can think of two novelists who let their fans get close in potentially uncomfortable ways. Sarah Monette revealed that her publisher had dropped her and Caitlín R. Kiernan admitted that she needed donations or direct book sales to cover a health care issue. Both writers made themselves vulnerable by being transparent about private matters.

Kiernan's actions gave her the results she desired and allowed her to continue to protect her Private Booklife. The cost? She may have desensitized her readers to future, more urgent requests and perhaps slightly reduced her status among those gatekeepers and readers who equate salary or money with success.

Monette, however, risked much more by being transparent. Although publishing often has aspects of a shell game — authors often imply inflated sales numbers or at least don't correct assumptions by their readers — there's a tacit agreement for the most part to act as if everything is going well. An admission of weakness, while brave, can sometimes turn off readers and galvanize gossips and enemies to drive the knife in deeper. Admitting weakness can also sometimes have tangible negative effects by making it less likely a writer will be given opportunities for paid guest speaker or teaching gigs.

In Monette's case, she used the disclosure to start a discussion of how publishers market a series. The vast majority of those who commented expressed sympathy for Monette and there is no indication that the manner in which she introduced the information created any potential problems for her with other publishers. Clearly, too, the admission helped her on a personal level. Sometimes you do need reassurance, and transparency is another way of seeking out community and fellowship.

It may be a personal decision, but there are definite limits and boundaries for every kind of transparency. For example, in the past year one editor of an online publication decided to post emails from writers and some of his rejections of their submissions. It proved to be a very popular feature, and gained the editor many readers. This is a form of transparency, but does it also transgress by violating someone else's privacy? What, also, is the end result of such transparency? Can it be anticipated in advance? In the editor's case, he eventually left the publication and the publisher hurriedly replaced him with someone who didn't engage in this practice. In the long run, the editor's actions had made him the focus of attention rather than the publication, and many writers stopped submitting to the publication out of fear that not only would their work be rejected, but their correspondence posted on the Internet.

In another case, a writer posted a rejection letter that he believed included a racist slur against a minority character in his story. As a result, a flame war spread across the Internet, both condemning the writer for sharing private correspondence and condemning the editor for his perceived racism. The consequences of this one blog post on a backwater of the Internet forever ruined the editor's reputation and put the online publication out of business. Is this an example of transparency working on the side of the just or, again, an invasion of privacy? What was the overall effect on the writer who posted the rejection initially?

If these situations involve the possibility of too much transparency, then another example proved that lack of transparency can be crippling. An anthology editor had run into trouble on the blogosphere when the first volume listed only one woman writer's name on the cover, even though the book included an equal mix of men and women. The resulting heated discussion led to the publisher making a statement at a feminist convention that the second volume would have a number of women in it, as a kind of acknowledgment that perhaps the approach on the first volume had been shortsighted. However, when the anthology's editor announced the table of contents, only one woman had been included in the anthology.

As it turned out, several women writers had not sent in promised stories. In addition, the publisher had told the editor to focus more on one particular type of story from a genre dominated by men, making it harder to solicit stories from women.

The editor hadn't mentioned any of this on his well-trafficked blog, so when the news of the table of contents broke out, a second firestorm of controversy spread across the Internet. The editor hadn't actually hidden anything — he just hadn't proactively engaged in public disclosure by mentioning any of this on his blog. Combined with the publisher's misleading statement, his table of contents looked like it was founded on a breach of trust. If he had been transparent during the process of compiling the anthology, he probably wouldn't have had such a problem. As it stands, although the anthology series continues, the editor and publisher have crippled themselves with one potential section of their readership through a crucial misunderstanding of transparency on the Internet.

Other types of transparency are not so easily identified as "good" or "bad." For example, because of an acceptance on the Internet of a free flow of ideas and information, writers have begun posting detailed information about their book deals and their yearly income.

Is this helpful or harmful? When I first noticed this phenomenon, as exemplified by a post on John Scalzi's first generation blog, Whatever, I posted about it in a puzzled way, unsure of the value or the potential harm.

Expressing the positive angle, writer Steve Buchheit provided this response: "Coming from another creative endeavor (graphic design) I can tell you that having some salary surveys have helped bring equality of pay into that realm... There are still many unfair practices out there in the market. Talking honestly about money, in my opinion, is a good thing."

Kameron Hurley, a writer with a three-book deal at Bantam, made another good point: "I do think that, as young writers, our expectations are really, really high. All you ever hear about in the media are the great bazillion dollar deals (which are usually crap books, coincidentally). Sure, we've all read the 'averages,' but we never expect that to be *us* or *our friends*. Hearing somebody's personal account, for me, is a lot more powerful than averages."

This is true, but most writers with commercial publishers have agents who already know all of this information and will share general statistics with you. Also, you can view the interesting results of an anonymous survey conducted by Tobias Buckell on his website. The statistics there, without attributing specific amounts of advances to particular writers give an accurate, useful snapshot of life for a mid-list writer.

Nor, given the state of publishing today, is it necessarily true, following up on Buchheit's point, that large publishers are bilking writers out of anything. The numbers for a successful trade paperback for a mid-list writer hover between eight thousand and fifteen thousand copies sold, for example. But beyond my personal interest level in the subject, the larger issue is whether or not people you don't know having that information is a good thing.

I can't answer that question for you — or many of the others I've posed about transparency. You will have to establish your own protocols. Just remember that while you have no obligation to be transparent, a lack of transparency in some situations will be seen as a form of dishonesty in our new media age. Your decisions will affect your ability to maintain your Public Booklife. More importantly, be prepared to accept the consequences of your decisions, be they personal and emotional or public and involving raging flame wars.

▶▶ Branding

Most writers are surprised to be thrust into a position where they think of writing as a career, whether they have a full-time job or not. Few of us have the time or perspective to step back from that point of impact when we made our first major story sale or sold our first book to think about how we want to be perceived as a writer and as a person. But once you've been through some version of beginning to build your Booklife, it's a good idea to spend some time on personal branding.

It may not be possible to have total control over your image, over what people think about your creative work, or even the distance between you and your fans. But you can exercise some control by making decisions about your behavior and the positioning of your projects in the public eye.

■ Personal

Remember your short- and long-term goals document? You can create a separate list of your character traits and distill that into behavior goals expressed as statements. You then place these statements at the head of your goals document. The behavior statements inform all of your goals.

It can seem like an exercise in egotism, but if you're honest — which can be hard and uncomfortable — it becomes an exercise in self-improvement.

Here's my list of character traits:

- Positives (desirable)
  - o very creative
  - o creatively diverse
  - o funny/humorous
  - o strong advocate of other creators
  - o passionate about fiction
  - o gets things done
  - o hard working
  - o generous

o has integrity
o calls things like he sees them
- Negatives (things to de-emphasize)
    o arrogant
    o combative
    o brash
    o paranoid
    o impulsive
    o blunt
    o quick to anger or take offense

Because your actions define your character and your reactions to stimuli create positive or negative impressions of your reputation, taking this list and making behavior statements can lead to making fewer mistakes and becoming a better human being.

Here are my behavior statements based on my character traits. These statements are aimed at curtailing my negative actions and reinforcing my positive actions.

- Stay professional
- Don't overreact
- Curb impulsiveness
- Be strong but flexible
- Remain publicly positive
- Be proactive
- Convey a sense of humor

All of these personal decisions about character feed into your public persona. Other decisions influence how you position yourself as a writer.

■ Public

Many different factors determine your public brand in terms of a Booklife. Every publisher, every book cover, every online forum, every interview request you accept helps define you as a writer. Early in his career, Jonathan Lethem wrote science fiction. Now this award-winning author is seen as part of the "literary mainstream." He would retain that designation even if he wrote a novel with science fiction elements. Lethem made this transition by more or less abandoning the genre subculture and gatekeepers for a time. The decision by his publisher to package his books according to a more mainstream aesthetic also helped with the transition. In other words, whether aided by his publisher, his agent, or his publicist, Lethem made a conscious decision to be perceived as a different kind of writer. Many other writers have not been able to make that leap. *The content you produce plays a role in labeling, but not as much as you might think.*

Reviewers, critics, publicists, even your agent will define you as a writer too. However, you can have an important role in shaping your destiny by what labels you accept through your actions and what labels you reject through your actions.

If you're interested in being proactive in this area, a quick way to evaluate your current situation is to ask yourself a series of questions, the answers to which require research on the Internet.

How do my readers perceive me and my work?

A simple Google search should answer this question, especially if you take the time to thoroughly read all entries across the web, categorize each mention as about you or about your work, make a determination as to the influence each forum, blog, LiveJournal, website, or other online entity exerts, and then build a composite picture of both yourself and your work from that research. Other questions you might ask in this context include:

- What do the covers or other design aspects of my creative projects convey to readers?
- How does the reputation or slant of my publisher (or other gatekeeper) affect how I am perceived?
- Which authors am I most often compared to — by reviewers, consumers, and my own publisher? (Do these authors correspond to my own desired parallels?)

What does my blog/website tell people about my work?

Usually, blog subject patterns are very revealing. No matter how you might *want* to be a different kind of writer, your blog eventually tells you who you really are by revealing what interests you and moves you to write. Many times I have seen bloggers try to re-imagine themselves by either archiving or deleting an old blog and starting a new one, with a fresh emphasis. Most of the time, the new blog starts looking like the old blog within five or six months, in terms of the type of content presented there.

You can also understand better how you are perceived by figuring out the average profile of those who visit your blog, some of which you can determine by checking out the blogs or other online platforms of the people who comment. You will also find that any website or blog service offers powerful tracking data that may be of use in this context.

WHAT WEBSITES AND BLOGS HAVE I ADDED TO MY FAVORITES IN MY WEB BROWSER, AND DOES READING THEM SUPPORT MY EFFORTS AT BRANDING?

You're shaped in part by the content you digest. If you aspire to be a mystery writer but the geek/reader part of you has decided to visit mostly fantasy or pop culture sites, you are absorbing content that isn't directly supporting your writing goals. While there's nothing wrong with diversity or using part of your day to play, just be aware that in doing so you are making a *choice*. Indeed, you may be telling yourself you don't want to write mysteries after all.

WHAT DOES THE ONLINE TRAIL OF MY DOPPELGÄNGER LOOK LIKE?

Never underestimate the power of mimicry. If you have a writer you admire who you feel a kinship with — their writing is similar to yours in some way and their career has the trajectory you want for your own, use the Advanced Search options at Google to map out their online presence on both blogs and websites. You will find out where the writer you want to emulate has and hasn't been reviewed and interviewed, where they've been welcomed and where shut out. You can then determine at least two things by implication: a general outline of that writer's tactical decisions (roughly, what they said yes to) and the perception of that writer and his or her work on the Internet. Comparing that perception to the perception of your own persona and work helps to define the gap between where you are and where you need to be. (It also performs the useful service of uncovering possible opportunities and contacts.)

■ Managing Perception

Once you have an idea of how you're perceived, you can decide if you like that perception or if you don't. If you don't, and your personal branding statements, along with your goals, truly support a different perception, work hard to become a different writer in the public eye. Identify the gap between the reality and the ideal. Close the gap by running all of your decisions through two questions: *Does this decision support my personal branding statements and does this decision support how I want to be perceived as a writer?*

If you re-evaluate where you are in six months and the gap hasn't closed at all, your brain is lying to you about what you really want and who you really are. It requires *effort* to re-brand yourself. It requires breaking old patterns forever. At one conference I remember two science fiction writers bemoaning their inability to sell fiction to the prestigious literary magazines — the literary world was ignoring them. Someone asked them how often they submitted to literary magazines. After some hemming and hawing, they both admitted that they rarely submitted to such publications. Later on, one even admitted that he wouldn't submit to most literary magazines because genre magazines paid better. Their brains told them they wanted a certain kind of validation represented by the term "literary magazines," but they weren't willing to make the abstract a reality by putting in the required effort. Much like the bloggers I mentioned above, the schism wasn't between who they were and who they could be, but between who they were and the received perception that they had to be someone else.

Another, centuries-old manifestation of this disease is the literary writer who envies the commercial writer's sales, and the commercial writer who envies the literary writer's critical acclaim. Neither could be anything but what they've always been, but each longs for the impossible. *Make sure in your career and in your branding that you don't look for something that you can't hold onto if you find it.*

Taking the long view, you should ask yourself one final branding question as your creative life begins to unfold across years and then decades. This question cannot be asked if you've done one or two creative projects because you don't yet have a sense of your limits and true range of interests.

The question is: *Do I want continuity or flexibility?* Another way to ask this question is, *Do I want to be Picasso or Chagall?* The mercurial, ever-curious Picasso was always changing his style, while Chagall used one style and perfected it throughout his career. Each approach to creativity requires a different approach to branding. In short, do you need to concentrate your branding efforts broadly across a career of similar creative projects or do you need to concentrate your branding efforts on individual creative projects that may vary wildly in their category or even their taxonomy?

In the former case, you have clear, concise objectives. In the latter case you must allow your personal branding to drive your overall career and use your public branding in a more tactical way, to drive the success of individual projects. Accomplishing this is tricky, takes time, and requires applying branding standards from other professions (whole books have been written about this one subject). However, the rewards of diversity can be great in the new media age — an age of multiple platforms and unparalleled mutations of connectivity and cross-pollination.

▶▶ The Importance of Persistence

You can control only so much in this life. You can set yourself up for the *possibility* of a successful career by creating something wonderful and then presenting it to the public in an imaginative, organized way. But even so, you will encounter roadblocks, reversals, time-sinks for no purpose, and people who passively or actively wish you ill. Sometimes you will have a sense as you monitor the Internet and converse with gatekeepers that everything is going south, despite your well-laid plans.

Such times are a test of your endurance and your toughness — and your ability to maintain a successful Booklife. Persistence, not giving up, is often the main difference between success and failure. Sheer determination to stick to your course, combined with hard work, can close that crucial gap in many cases. My entire career may just have been a vast tangle of anecdotal evidence aimed at proving that point.

I've had publishers who wanted to change the settings of my books or change characters to fit cover art. One publisher took advance order money I'd raised and used it to either go on his honeymoon or check into a sanatorium — I never did get the full story.

My big break actually came when a small publisher called Prime green-lighted my mosaic novel *City of Saints & Madmen* and let me have complete control over the process. Since Prime used print-on-demand technology, we had to work within certain constraints when it came to quality, even though the book had been imagined as lavishly illustrated and adorned (including a cover meant to look like a modern version of an illuminated manuscript). Pre-production took about eight months as we experimented with different ideas on how to reproduce images and photographs in an acceptable way.

When we finally managed to find solutions and get the book printed — a process that would have been impossible without the Internet because I was working with dozens of artists and designers from around the world — there was the additional stress and responsibility of guiding the project toward success by overcoming the objections of gatekeepers to something that looked (and was) so different from just about any book being published at the time. We also had to overcome the fact that the book wasn't available through brick-and-mortar bookstores. But, somehow, we managed to overcome all of these potential crippling problems.

City of Saints & Madmen went on to define my career. It sold many thousands of copies from Prime, became a finalist for many awards, and has to date been printed in fourteen languages. Pan McMillan in the United Kingdom and Bantam in the United States reprinted the book. The U.K. edition has sold out and the U.S. edition has sold well past its initial sales cycle. I still get emails every month from new fans of the book.

Many of the strategies I share in this book came out of the persistence it took to complete, find a publisher for, and then promote *City of Saints & Madmen*. At any one of dozens of key points it would have been easy to just give up, to turn away from the project and move on to something else. But not giving in to that easy temptation eventually resulted in success.

I also learned the limits of persistence. I can't claim that my level of commitment to the book didn't hurt my personal life or take time away from more important things. But I did learn a lot about why you should persist and what form persistence should take — the constraints of persistence. Here's a partial list:

- Know what you can and can't do if you do have limited resources.
- Only fight against the constraint of limited resources when the goal is worth it.
- Be prepared for a war of attrition on some projects, and don't let it rattle you.

- Be prepared to have to follow-through against elements you couldn't have predicted would be a problem going in.
- Understand that the journey toward the completion of a project may not always be the joyful part — sometimes the journey is horrible but the end result is heaven.
- Fight for creative elements you know are right — even in a PR context.

More generally, in the context of the many projects I've brought to a successful completion, remember that:

- New media breeds a sense of swift entitlement and accomplishment. Be careful not to abandon a strategy or tactic too soon because of unrealistic ideas about how *fast* something should be happening.
- Setbacks are opportunities for personal and professional growth.
- Reaching your goals too easily can be detrimental to your career.
- See the entire shape or form of your plan when making tactical decisions so that you don't act out of an impulse at odds with your goals.
- Because of the fluidity of the Internet, situations that seem to box you in or appear intolerable and permanent often turn out to be swept away in a matter of weeks or months, and the paradigm reset.
- Sometimes waiting out a situation is better than giving in to the temptation to take precipitous action.

Although new media and the Internet project a sense of rapid evolution and constant change, the needs and cycles of the physical world often still trump the electronic world.

▶▶ Paying it Forward/Community

The Internet has created a new sense of community, with a new set of rules. Many of the ways you can pay things forward will come through your blog or your comments on other forums — or in other ways visible via the Internet. Remember these four points when trying to be a responsible member of not just the community of writers, but the wider world as well. These points also often pertain to interactions in the physical world.

▉ Only link to things that you think are worth promoting

Let's take a very selfish but important example: book reviews. The fact is, anyone can post a book review on their blog. Linking to every single one of them lends legitimacy to much that's little more than a public diary of stray thoughts. If a blog gets maybe two hundred visitors a week (you can check through TECHNORATI.COM, which rates blogs by their popularity) and that blogger trashes your novel *The Living Spleen of Prudence Boulevard*, you're under no obligation to post about it. If your blog gets thousands of visitors and you do that, all you are doing is strengthening the enemy, so to speak. (If you're publishing a book you don't believe in one hundred percent, I can't help you here.) The hard lesson to learn is that just because something related to your work pops up on the blogosphere does not mean it should be linked to. Of course, if there's something in a negative review that you find interesting and want to blog about — other than saying "this guy sucks" — that's different. Sometimes a review can provide fodder for engaged and illuminating discussion.

▉ Contribute to factual accuracy

The Internet is a lovely place but it is also easier, because of the immediate nature of the medium, to post something that contains inaccuracies. Making the Internet a more accurate place is a positive thing. Under the rules of the new transparency, correcting errors of fact pertaining to you personally is also a proactive way of protecting your reputation. In such cases, you need to be open, polite, and non-combative. Humor will also help. (Even better, have a friend do the dirty work for you.) Remember that the Internet shouldn't be a battleground for competing interests that change the facts to fit their position. Sadly, even Wikipedia, which has provided such a great source of information to Internet users, tends to fall prey to this mentality. If you have a Wikipedia entry, you may need to monitor it for "fiddling" by others.

■ Be helpful to others and contribute to the unimpeded flow of information

Now more than ever paying it forward is not only the right thing to do, it is the *smart* thing to do. Information itself is no longer important in such a mega-world — it's how you leverage that information. There is also nothing new that will not, *within days sometimes*, become old. Building connectivity is much more important. Within five years, this will become increasingly obvious. Take, for example, the idea of "traditional media gatekeepers." Right now, they are dams across a river (the word "dam" is not used here with any positive *or* pejorative weight). Soon, they will be rocks around which the river flows. The ones who recognize this new paradigm will adapt and continue to be valuable both as mentors and as resources. Those who don't will simply control smaller and smaller islands in that river. Eventually, no one will remember who they are or why they were once important. However, don't be naive — there are trolls lurking out there, and people who suck, but you have to try to ignore them and listen to your better angels.

■ Defend what's worth defending

Internet flame wars are generally pointless to contribute to, in part because few minds are ever changed and the communal mind of the Internet forgets the substance of the argument within a few days or a few weeks. However, if you feel strongly about an issue and you can articulate your feelings in a logical way that does not constitute a personal attack, you should stand up for what you believe in. This, too, is a potent way of contributing to, and protecting, the integrity of online communities. (Also refer to related advice in the Public Platform Example: Blogs section of *Booklife*.)

▶▶ Against Trends

As I write these words, releasing your book as a PDF through Creative Commons — either at the same time as its physical release or at some point thereafter — is the "in" thing to do. In terms of types of content, Young Adult fiction is hot. Many writers are harnessing both trends, one as a tactic and the other as a strategy. Taken together, they represent two powerful ideas that, because they are trends, should be looked at with suspicion by a writer seeing them from my vantage point of early 2009.

By the time something has been recognized as a trend much of the initial energy and impetus has gone out of it. While some trends develop into something more permanent, most do not. In almost all cases, the spoils of trends go to the early adopters. For example, every YA writer, no matter how successful, toils in the shadow of a dozen iconic trendsetters, from J. K. Rowling to Stephenie Meyer, the author of the Twilight books. You can certainly still have a lucrative career in YA, but you will find that you are one of a pack. And if you talk to agents right now, they're getting so many YA submissions that it's now harder than ever to sell in that market.

Similarly, releasing your book (or novella or story) in electronic form on the Internet a year from now isn't going to be a unique event unless you're Neil Gaiman or Salman Rushdie — writers who already have the leverage to create a unique event. (In fact, as I write these words, I've learned that Gaiman has released his children's book *Coraline* in a free online format...just in time for the movie — and coincidentally just after having won the Newbery Award. He's thus chosen the best possible time to leverage a free download.)

The point is: repetition devalues an idea until it's like chewing a piece of gum that's lost all flavor. Further, as Thoreau famously said, "What everybody echoes or in silence passes by as true today may turn out to be falsehood tomorrow, mere smoke of opinion, which some had trusted for a cloud that would sprinkle fertilizing rains on their fields."

For these reasons, it's extremely important to think about why you are doing something in support of your career, not just do it because everyone else is doing it. If you can't find a unique angle or a good reason from a leveraging point of view to do it, maybe it's a waste of time. At the very least, it may not be something on which you want to spend too much time.

By the time you read these words, for example, releasing your book online for free will still be something you may want to do, to help hardcopy sales, but very possibly not near the top of your list of tasks. At the very least, try to find (1) the best time to leverage such an action and (2) a twist or slant that makes your effort different. The lovely independent Small Beer Press created an interesting variation by offering a free electronic download of Kelly Link's first short story collection during the month they published her second collection in hardcopy. The free download was only offered for a limited period of time. Thus, they used a trend as a tactic to drive sales and author awareness, but altered the formula in an effective way.

Although approaches to your writing are addressed in Private Booklife, it's worth noting here that strategic decisions — like whether or not to write YA — must be driven by your creative side. A good rule to remember: *Always try to work on what you most love, so that when you do have to present it to the public, you are one hundred percent sincere in your passion for it.* Write what moves you, what you must write, if you have the choice, before letting someone else's preconception/waking dream of *market* and *professional* influence you. A writer separated from his or her work is a lost soul. It matters not what Giant Best-selling Rabbit Head Author is doing — although you may be best-selling, you will never be Giant Rabbit Head Author, not with those antlers of yours.

▶▶ Positive Survival Strategies

▩ Multi-purposing the Public for the Private

Part of working smarter not just harder is to anticipate connectivity between your public and your private booklives. You should be able to find ways to enhance both at the same time. I've called this process multi-purposing, but it's a little more organic than that. Let me explain using a couple of examples.

Recently I embarked on a somewhat arduous task that served multiple purposes: reviewing one of the Penguin Great Ideas books each day and sharing my impressions of it on my blog the next day. The Great Ideas books are paperback abridgments of the work of great thinkers and iconoclasts, from Virginia Woolf to Jonathan Swift, Seneca to David Hume. I called this feature the "60 in 60," and it enhanced my Public Booklife in many ways. The blog was named the *Guardian*'s booksite of the week, which drove thousands of new visitors my way. Penguin's blog and the Harvard University Press also did features, and the very nature of titling each post with the author's name and the title of the book brought readers doing Google searches on those subjects.

This was the primary public advantage, because I had just come back from a period of not blogging and needed to do something dramatic to retain and grow my audience. But it wasn't even the main benefit in the long run, with regard to my Private Booklife. In addition to getting a set of sixty books free from Penguin, I had the opportunity to encounter startling and wonderful thoughts from thousands of years of great minds — something that will influence my writing for years to come. On a more practical level, I knew I would be writing *Booklife* while reading the Great Ideas books, and that being exposed to so many different thoughts on creativity and so many approaches to narrative would enhance this book. I also expected to include quotes from those authors in *Booklife* in support of various arguments.

I could have just let it affect my Public Booklife, or I could have bought the books myself and read them without blogging about them, which would have meant the activity would only have benefited my Private Booklife. Instead, I thought about ways to leverage the 60 in 60 feature to get the most possible benefit out of it.

But "multitasking" in this way can be a long-term thing as well. For years I reviewed books for *Publishers Weekly*, and I specifically asked to review mysteries and thrillers. On one level I did this just to make money while reading authors I might not otherwise encounter, and to become a specialist for *PW* and thus continue to receive assignments. On another level, I knew I would eventually be writing a detective novel, and focusing on these types of books for my reviews would force me to do extensive research without even really thinking about it. When I wrote that novel, *Finch*, in 2008, all those years of reviewing for *Publishers Weekly* meant I had a near-encyclopedic knowledge of mystery/thriller tropes and situations. This proved invaluable in completing the novel. In a related type of multi-purposing, I signed a contract to write a media tie-in novel in 2007 not only for the income, but also for the experience of writing a thriller in a "controlled" environment. This, too, benefited *Finch* in extraordinary ways.

The point here is: try to consider the advantages to your Private Booklife of performing a particular task or action in your Public Booklife. The more connectivity you can create, the more you will enhance both aspects of your life.

▋ Using Personification

I use a technique I call "personification" any time I'm feeling frustrated because of roadblocks or overwhelmed because of the intensity of effort still before me.

Personification is a subset of visualization, a process by which you imagine your goal — in the case of a *Booklife*, a book in any of its many modern manifestations — and use that image as a carrot. Visualization can be a powerful way to energize yourself in all of your tasks. It's not just about imagining your in-progress book or other project completed and polished. It's also not about seeing that book or project on the shelves at the local bookstore or up on the Internet. The fact is, you can use visualization in the context of *any* day's work for your public Booklife. Even a blog entry that's giving you trouble becomes more doable if you can imagine the reaction of your core readers, or the reaction of others in the blogosphere. Visualization can also be a great way to anticipate possible problems. (Just make sure you don't let the thought of negative possibilities discourage you.)

Personification, then, is a *proactive and immersive* type of visualization that requires conjuring up images of relevant personal heroes, engaged in an activity that parallels your own. My three role models are: the tennis players Thomas Muster and Stefan Edberg, and the boxer Lennox Lewis.

TENACITY

Thomas Muster, an Austrian tennis clay-court specialist, was a tenacious competitor who broke his leg in an automobile accident and yet came back to briefly become the number one player in the world. His trademarks were strength, resilience, and a kind of transcendent toughness that not only result-ed in that number one ranking, but also a stunning undefeated run through most of the major clay court tournaments in his best year. Whenever I need these qualities, I think of Muster — "If he could do it, I can do it" — and redouble my efforts, grinding out whatever needs to be done. (That Muster had a quirky sense of humor and was often considered an eccentric in the ten-nis world doesn't hurt, as in some of his qualities he seems perfectly aligned with most writers I know.)

PROBLEM-SOLVING

Stefan Edberg, by contrast, was a serve-and-volleyer from Sweden, equally comfortable on all surfaces. Edberg had a kind of natural grace, and an imaginative, often inspired knack for shot selection. Watching Edberg, you forgot you were watching tennis — he seemed to glide around the court. Whenever I need to think outside of the box, or to approach a problem from some other perspective, I conjure up Edberg and think "If this were a tennis problem, how would Edberg have solved it?" Sometimes remembering another's effortlessness is enough to make effortlessness part of your style, too.

DEALING WITH ADVERSITY

Lennox Lewis, one of my favorite boxers, avenged three knock-out defeats by devastating the same opponents in rematches. He could also brawl or jab and box from the outside, adapting his style to best defeat his opponent. The highlight reel of his best fights includes stunning knock-outs that lifted his opponents off their feet and brilliant tactical matches in which he neutralized his adversary's strengths and exploited their weaknesses for twelve rounds. Whenever I feel like I've been knocked down, and I'm not getting back up, I remember Lewis and tell myself there will be a rematch someday, and I'll be ready. And whenever I'm facing an opponent — often not a person but a situation — that seems unsolvable, I try to re-evaluate it.

I'm a huge sports nut, so it's natural for my better angels to take the form of sports stars — those physical manifestations of effort, forward movement, and endurance really capture my imagination. Your own role models may be very different, but it helps if you use personifications from beyond of the field of writing. Using positive examples that come from a different context help you to see situations, problems, and other issues from outside of yourself and your experience. Being able to imagine the actual movement or actions of those examples is more helpful to me than more inert versions of visualization.

BOOKLIFE GUT-CHECK
TOWARD PEACE OF MIND

▶▶ The Search for Balance

BOOKLIFE IS AS much about balance as anything else. Balance between your Public and Private Booklife — working smarter and more imaginatively for greater creative satisfaction and gain. Losing balance means losing perspective. When you lose perspective you no longer understand the real value of the elements in your Booklife. You distort the importance of promotion weighed against the actual writing. You rationalize web surfing as "research." You tell yourself that all you need is one more push and you'll be over the hill. You respond to email as it appears in your inbox rather than developing a protocol for response.

In all things, you are completely *reactive* to stimuli. This is one consequence of a modern Booklife that has *drifted*, because our platforms, opportunities, and tools create a false sense of control. By simply responding to information that comes to you from conduits, you feel you're closer to achieving goals. But there's the nagging sense behind it all that instead all you're doing is treading water. The goal's still on the horizon, and you're expending a lot of useless energy.

Consequently, too, you're probably not spending a lot of time in the physical world. A balance between the physical and electronic worlds is crucial here. My personal sense of balance requires at least a few hours of walking in the woods every week to truly reset my fragmented, overstimulated mind. As writers, we don't enhance our skills of observation and intuitiveness by sitting in front of a screen 24–7, and so an hour in the woods or out among people is about a hundred times more valuable to me than an extra hour for networking or other work situated on the "intertubes." As the writer Brendan Connell wrote on his blog, "I plan all my writing while walking…usually in some natural setting. I once read that Dickens would plan his novels while walking also. I think movement and seeing things outside is very beneficial for the mind."

However, everyone is different. You might have another approach to achieving balance. Many of my friends find peace by going to church or synagogue, for example. Others prefer meditation. A few hang out in bars or coffee houses just to recharge by soak up some atmosphere; stimulation of the senses can be a powerful way to regain balance.

The sedentary, insular nature of a writing career is exacerbated because most writers have full or part-time jobs. This means that your average work week, including the writing, might run anywhere from sixty to eighty hours. In this kind of situation, you will quickly lose track of family, friends, and your spirituality. The house will fall into disrepair. At times, I must confess my office has looked like a storage room, or like a pigsty — even though I work at home and theoretically should have the time to clean up.

So I'm certainly no stranger to a lack of balance — you strive for the ideal and you always fail. Sometimes you must sacrifice balance to achieve your goals, but you have to be aware of that sacrifice and realize that you will need to "reset" at some point. You'll need to do so not just for your sanity but for the sanity of the people around you.

▶▶ Your Health

◾ Positive Choices

If you want to live a complete and fulfilling Booklife, you should think about your diet and getting enough exercise. Any profession that requires a human being to sit for long hours in front of a screen typing *must* contain the antidote to that lack of activity. The benefits of eating healthy food and making sure you move your body every day are immeasurable but very real. For every hour of exercise I put in, I receive back hours and hours of increased energy. For every day I cut back on bad carbohydrates and avoid desserts and soft drinks, I gain at least four days of clarity in my thoughts.

Should you be skeptical that a writer needs to be in good shape, just look at professional golf for a moment. Although golf requires extreme concentration and walking around a golf course all day, many if not most professional golfers only recently started taking care of their bodies. Players like the talented but obese Craig Stadler could win tournaments because few opponents put that much extra effort into their health. Tiger Woods revolutionized golf not just by a combination of practice and talent but by *protecting* his talent. Woods follows a strict diet regime, especially during the season, and has used weight training to gain a strength advantage over his opponents. Although those opponents have a spotty record in their attempts to match Woods' commitment to physical fitness, the lesson is clear: even though golf isn't the toughest of sports in terms of its physical demands, golfers benefit from adopting wise diet and exercise plans.

Writing is no different than golf in this respect. You not only protect your own long-term career by eating right and exercising, you also gain an advantage over your competition. More energy equals greater productivity. You will also retain mental acuity and endurance long after many of your colleagues have receded into silence. The demands of public appearances will not be as severe, either.

I offer this advice not to castigate writers who are out of shape. I was obese until I cut out soft drinks, processed foods, sugar, and simple carbohydrates.

After taking up weight training and increasing my time spent on the exercise bike or jogging, I lost more than eighty pounds and put on over twenty pounds of muscle. I know what it's like to be fat — how uncomfortable, how distracting, and how debilitating when it came to being able to sustain long-term creativity. And without long-term creativity, you cannot sustain a writing career.

Still, being healthy is *not* about losing weight. It's about engaging in a series of behaviors that support a healthy lifestyle conducive to living a productive Booklife. If daily choices regarding diet and exercise result in a boost to your energy level, then it doesn't matter if you lose a single pound. Concentrating on losing weight rather than making healthy decisions not only dooms diets but can put a writer, especially a writer on a deadline, in a bad mental space because of too much pressure from all sides.

As in all things related to your Booklife, make sure you form-fit your health decisions to your particular circumstances. If you enjoy jogging, jog. If you enjoy yoga, do yoga. Take the path of least resistance in terms of the type of exercise you decide to take up. Your method of exercise has to be addictive enough or relaxing enough that you'll want to do it every day — and miss it when you don't. As for finding the time, even a thirty-minute workout is highly beneficial, and if you count up the number of minutes you spend surfing the Internet each day, I'm sure you'll be able to make time in your schedule.

◼ Avoiding the Negative

Eating healthy and exercising are positive steps you can take to ensure a productive Booklife. Other decisions, like not self-medicating, using illegal drugs, or abusing alcohol, constitute rejecting the negative. I once had a good friend who had amazing potential as a writer. But he began to use ever more powerful drugs, which affected his work in a terrible way. Instead of writing novellas and short stories, he began to produce short-shorts. Then, he began to write one paragraph stories and told me he had created a new art form. In actual fact, he had simply lost the ability to concentrate on anything for too long.

Every person reacts differently to stimulants and depressants. Every person has a different tolerance and a different threshold for addiction. Whether a drug is legal like alcohol or illegal like cocaine matters situationally, in terms of the legal consequences of using it, but in terms of your Booklife the effect of each is equal. Any diminishment in your mental acuity or your physical endurance that persists over time will make it less possible for you to achieve your career goals, because your creative abilities will eventually deteriorate.

However, writers in particular seem to have a bad relationship with alcohol. I surmise this is in part because writers, as observers, tend to be too cautious to venture into the illegal, but also because alcohol has a long and pseudo-romantic association with creativity by now.

Part of networking often requires drinking, or participating in social circles where drinking is widespread, and anything done in moderation can be fun and relaxing. But writers tend to be both obsessive and addictive, so it's important to monitor yourself and pull back as necessary. Don't allow yourself to spiral into patterns you will later find hard to break out of.

Are there exceptions to this rule? Sure. I once heard a possibly apocryphal story about a writer whose brain was so hyperactive that he would write for stretches of twenty-four hours at a time. Without access to pot, he would burn himself out. Pot allowed him to only write for ten hours a day. The truth of this so consumed his world that he agreed to a verbal contract for one book, the terms being that the publisher pay for his apartment during those three months of writing and deliver pot to him twice a week.

Please note that even if this story is true, it's unlikely that you are such a writer...

▶▶ Multitasking and Fragmentation

◼ White Noise and Dark

One thing I enjoy about working on a novel is that it forces me to disconnect from the Internet and everything else that causes fragmentation. We're told to multitask, but no one can multitask forever without suffering the consequences. Without that time away, the lack of solitude can eat away at your center. In some writers, it can shorten attention span, and make it difficult to get into that deep, submerged place that your power comes from. Instead of allowing things to come into you, you are continually projecting things *out* from you. It will seem as if you are in a sense accumulating more power, but in fact you are diminished because nothing is flowing into you. It creates fatigue, a hollow feeling, and, over time, resentment.

Over the years, even as I have gained more perspective and more balance, I am no wiser about the amount of what people call "white noise" I allow to accumulate around me as a result. Except it's not really white noise in aggregate — it's more of a dark noise, a noise with a substance and texture like an electric shock or sandpaper. It's a barrage of, among other things, positive reviews, negative reviews, good vibes from a contact made, bad vibes from a contact made, anger and irritation and satisfaction and fondness and love originating from a hundred glimpsed or participated-in electronic conversations. Taken separately, it's harmless enough, but all bundled together it equates to thousands of received ideas trying to get into your skull.

◼ Managing Open Channels

I'm clearly not the only one to think about such issues in relation to creativity and career. When I wrote about white and dark noise on my blog, my good friends Dan Read and Tessa Kum, both writers who often move effortlessly through new media, shared some interesting and extremely sobering thoughts on the subject. Dan sees dark noise as "coming from everywhere, and it has an element of randomness to it." Whereas "white noise" comes from "channels" you open or allow to be opened. His theory is worth quoting at length:

> I have experienced an overload of what you call dark noise. It was followed by a depression, actually. Instead of the dark noise metaphor, though, I've thought of it as having a finite ability to handle a limited number of "open channels." Mostly the idea of a "channel" centers around a communication medium: a blog one writes, a site where one participates in comment threads regularly, an email account (each conversation is a sub-channel), a collaboration on a project — but a channel could be any relationship, really, though I think particularly an online one, because the other side of the channel is not feeding back into you directly, if at all.
>
> One thing that's tricky is that the channel stays open in your consciousness even when you're not paying attention to it. In fact, the fact that you're not paying attention to it at any given moment creates an extra stress. I've started training myself to be careful of opening new channels. And online, I've found myself becoming more of a passive consumer of online channels that don't know I'm "listening." Connected to this topic for me was an overload of too much attention spent in the virtual world of the Internet, and also mass media in general, particularly TV. The "real world" became more foreign to me, and that took a toll.

More than once Dan went over his limit, experienced burn-out, and "ended up letting some people down by over-committing." But Dan's situation isn't unique: most of us keep too many channels open, resulting in a kind of continual, amorphous stress. Relief from that stress may require a general retreat from *all* open channels. At the very least, it's important to recognize that too many channels are open *before* a fuse blows. If you push too hard you run the risk of not just burning out, but finding it hard to regain whatever it is that keeps the imagination continuously putting out ideas and images and stories.

It's particularly astute of Dan to observe that "the channel stays open in your consciousness even when you're not paying attention to it. In fact, the fact that you're not paying attention to it at any given moment creates an extra stress." Even a dormant open channel can become a problem. This is why some people don't just abandon their blogs or Facebook accounts — they actually delete them.

Just as you may feel you have to be "on" all the time when you do a series of presentations or fulfill obligations like a string of business lunches or dinner parties, you can begin to feel as if you have to be "on" because you've created an online presence that requires an element of performance and acknowledgment of an audience.

But open channels don't just occur in the electronic world; they also manifest in the physical world. "Real world" channels can be even harder to close, as Tessa points out:

> I have no stamina with any sort of interaction, and no matter how much I may enjoy a person's company, there's no relief greater than saying "goodbye." If there are loud conversations around me in the office, I have trouble. It doesn't affect my ability to work at all, but the fact that I can't escape these voices stresses me to no end — that would be an overloaded open channel at work, I assume. The same is true of situations in which I'm not required to do anything, conversations around me on the train, or being in the vicinity of loud music, for instance. I can't keep my surroundings out of my head. It feels like an invasion. I don't think I'm capable of actually closing a channel.

Some people need that stimuli, but many others don't. I've already recommended finding peaceful space in the real world to combat fatigue and stress originating from the online world. But what if, as with Tessa, these kinds of stressors come from the real world, too? Especially in big cities, the sheer rigors of daily commutes can wear you down. These rigors can be similar in effect to daily "commutes" through the possibilities of the Internet.

Unfortunately, there's less you can do to block out the real world. Solutions include meditation and noise-reducing headphones — as well as, ironically enough, blogging to let off steam, thus relieving real-world stress and freeing yourself up to write again. As Tessa says, "it's been a vital tool for keeping myself sane when I'm cracking up, and I honestly have no idea what I'd replace it with [for that purpose]."

As in all things, self-awareness equals power, no matter the source of the interference, the open channels, the dark noise, in your own life. Just remember that you can at the very least try to figure out how many channels any particular project is going to open, and whether that's a price you're willing to pay.

■ Tolerance for Channels

The good news is that, depending on your personality, you may have more tolerance for open channels. Dan suggests that an introvert can be energized and rejuvenated by alone time, while time spent with people almost always drains energy. An extrovert in this context "means that one takes *in* energy from the company of others, and alone time is draining."

Still, the problem for most writers is that wanting to sit in a room by yourself and write requires a tendency toward being an introvert, while everything else about being a writer these days requires being an extrovert — or at least pretending to be one.

Tessa again: "Being alone isn't restricted to saying nothing, but *needing to have nothing said in return*. Hence, anything even remotely creative happens in quiet. In solitude as well, as even if another person is being quiet, they're a sitting mass of potential interaction, and the tension is another stress."

Thus, a return to the idea of generous selfishness: to be creative, most people need their brains turned inward, toward the task at hand. You may play music or not while you write (I do). You may or may not need a calming view (I do). It just depends on what your brain categorizes as an open channel as opposed to an element that aids focus. The only mistake you can make is not to be proactive in protecting and preserving your ability to create.

All of this discussion feeds into the idea of a constant push and pull to the rhythms of your life, made more powerful by new media and manifesting more negatively because of the constant call to multitask. In discussing this book with Dan, he wrote:

> There is [a] cyclical nature to things — to every season, etc. It's natural and normal to sometimes be in a state of taking in, sometimes of putting out, sometimes producing, sometimes incubating. These cycles are baked into nature itself. It seems to me that some of your techniques [for *Booklife*] are designed to harness these natural cycles in order to keep a constant flow of some kind going. Art is very much a craft at that point, and in some ways like the process of an endurance athlete.

This speaks to the challenge of finding balance: often balance is a pendulum that glides back and forth: you hope that most of your endeavors will fall into the middle of that arc, rather than the extreme ends.

Often, total immersion in a novel helps me to get into a positive cycle for awhile. During such times I'll be off the Internet in the mornings and have no access to my phone. I'll use afternoons for nonfiction. I'll use evenings for edits to the novel and to read books I had to set aside while writing fiction... but, inevitably, one day I'll look up from what I'm doing and find I'm just as fragmented as I was before, and I need to reset again (a refrain throughout *Booklife*).

Another challenge for me personally? As a full-time freelancer for the last few years, I have both more and less freedom. On the one hand, I am writing all the time. On the other, *I am writing all the time.* So I need to find new and unique ways to recharge and relax — and I rely more and more on what would seem from the outside like a straitjacket of a schedule. But that rigidity allows me to keep going, because as Dan says:

> The product of your energy is not just a burst, but rather the result of a deliberate discipline. Your physical and mental ability to keep up a steady output are also based on your discipline. But when what you do requires inspiration as well (controlled bursts?), not just perspiration, you've got to design things into your process to let the inspiration in while you keep the wheel spinning.

Dan concludes that "without the dark noise, and some open channels, we have no raw material for either life or art" while Tessa reaches for an older explanation: "Mostly, I think all artists are mad, and follow no sane pattern."

Dan's conclusion is reasonable, but Tessa's speaks to an uncomfortable truth: *because writing isn't a balanced, sane pursuit — it requires giving of yourself in many different and often uncomfortable ways.* Even a book like this one, no matter how it focuses on balance and creativity can add to your stress. One problem with discussion about any aspect of a sustainable creative career is that if you separate out any particular subject, especially approaches to new media, the results can seem both more artificial and, oddly enough, more daunting, not less so. That means you will in part achieve balance by evaluating how useful and how useless parts of *Booklife* are to you personally.

Why? Because perhaps the most important result of balance should be peace of mind. Yes, you will be busy. Yes, you will be stressed at times. What you need to do to make a dream your reality can be incredibly tough. But: Are you contented in the present moment while still hungry for the future? This is an ideal state that recognizes the value of hard work and artistic ambition.

In our tightly wound, information-saturated world, we often forget the important things. If you need to slow down or to opt out, it's often a sign of an underlying sanity. It doesn't mean you're a failure or that you need to feel like you've failed.

As Tessa puts it, "Because I know my interaction saturation point is so very, very low, I don't tend to have many channels of any sort in existence at any one time, and I've burned myself so often I'm a lot less reluctant about shutting everything down."

For this reason, you need to ask yourself a series of questions every couple of months:

- Am I centered and calm?
- If not, is there an end in sight?
- Is that end a true end or a false vision?
- Am I not just professionally fulfilled but personally and spiritually fulfilled?
- Do I love my Booklife or do I merely tolerate it?

Confront these questions honestly to avoid opting out for the wrong reasons, but more importantly to avoid doing yourself serious harm, possibly even temporarily or permanently blowing out the circuits that allow you to be creative.

If your answers add up to unhappiness, stress, and worse, then you will need to make a decision. Both Dan and Tessa are wonderful, creative people, but both of them can disappear down the rabbit hole for months at a time. And perhaps that's the only way to retain your peace of mind. You can never tell when another channel is going to open up.

Always opt out in favor of your Private Booklife. Nothing else is as important.

II. PRIVATE BOOKLIFE

Chapter 1
Living Your Booklife

▶▶ The Pillars of Your Private Booklife

YOUR PRIVATE BOOKLIFE constitutes your core activities: the engine that drives your creative life. It has several essential pillars, or qualities. Try to encourage these qualities in yourself and others. Draw them out into the open if necessary, and in some cases allowing yourself to *indulge* in them. In all ways be generous to yourself so that you can be generous in your work. Although several of these pillars are useful to your Public Booklife, nowhere are they more necessary than in your Private Booklife.

• CURIOSITY. Nothing is more essential to a writer than an inquisitive nature — being curious about the world and the people in it. Curiosity reflects a willingness to be disappointed and an urge to understand the world. It sends out a series of queries that exist for their own sake, and gathers back into itself anything it finds, transforming it in the process. The truly curious reject received ideas and try to see everything as freshly as a child with an adult's mind. This "gathering" of information and texture through your senses, through your questioning nature, should be non-judgmental, finding pleasure in seemingly disparate, often contradictory elements. From the fusion of these elements comes an essential aspect of creativity. Curiosity is in a sense allied with qualities such as cleverness, and thus can be impersonal — like a pack rat that accumulates buttons and bottle caps and scraps of paper without caring about the provenance of such items.

• RECEPTIVITY. Openness and empathy spring from being receptive to the world and the people in it, not just being curious about them. Receptivity means allowing more than just information to come in over the transom. Eliminating barriers to other people's emotions, predicaments, tragedies, and other aspects of the human condition is crucial to a writer, even when it hurts. You must allow yourself to be a raw nerve end that internalizes whatever it experiences in life. When you do this, you not only create a well-spring for stories, novels, and nonfiction, you also retain a sense of empathy for your fellow human beings. Putting up walls to avoid being hurt may temporarily solve problems in your life, but it may also shut you off from the source of your creativity. (The only caveat, in this age of acute connectivity? An excess of "open channels" can result in you becoming too wrapped up in the issues of other people, the weight of this overload damaging to your creativity and your sense of self.)

• **PASSION.** Cynics find it hard to be passionate about anything, and therefore passion is linked to retaining your idealism, which is in turn linked to retaining your receptivity. First you lose your curiosity, which turns off your receptivity, and then you lose your passion. If you are not passionate about what you write, no amount of effort can revive your work. It will remain inert, waiting for an infusion of new life. Passion is the blood that fills the veins of your creative self; it provides the circulatory system that allows your imagination to breathe.

• **IMAGINATION.** The imagination moves beyond passion: it is a lifelong relationship with the world that transforms both the world and the writer. All of the best fiction hums and purrs and sighs with the imagination, and in this way fiction mirrors the best of life. But no imagination can long survive without recourse to curiosity and receptivity as well. It needs all of this as fuel for both its serious and deeply unserious aspects. On the one hand, it is the most visible manifestation of a "soul" and on the other a quality that allows us to express the most absurd and silly aspects of play. During Medieval times, the imagination was often associated with the senses and thus thought to be one of the links between human beings and the animals. Only with the Renaissance was the imagination firmly linked to creativity and thus the intellect. The imagination defies easy measurement, even though we "know it when we see it." It brings yet another level of uncertainty to an endeavor already supersaturated with the subjective — and yet that uncertainty is a kind of blessing. (Is it true that imagination cannot be taught? Yes. It is a brutal truth, too. But one with an escape clause. A latent imagination can be drawn out of its shell. A change of topic, focus, or even setting can also reveal in a writer an imagination not previously in evidence.)

• DISCIPLINE. Without discipline, the imagination would float off, untethered, into the sky. While imagination is the ultimate expression of idealism — curious, receptive, and passionate — discipline grounds the imagination in pragmatism and structure. At the center of the essential tension between these two qualities exists the perfect writer.

• ENDURANCE. Endurance is toughness projected over time, and the perfect writer in motion rather than inert: the potential for work expressed through work. Imagination and discipline create endurance by continually replenishing creativity and giving it form.

Taken together, these pillars allow you to reach toward the perfect Private Booklife. Think of them often. They ghost through and infiltrate almost every subject set out below.

Why do we write? The reasons may not be legion, but they are many, including: to express ourselves, to tell a story, to entertain, to explore the human condition, to be well-known, to be known well, to be wealthy. Foucault said that he wrote "To be loved." George Orwell in his famous essay "Why I Write" gave not one reason but four:

1. Sheer egoism.
2. Aesthetic enthusiasm.
3. Historical impulse.
4. Political purpose.

The last two reasons made Orwell great, inspiring him to bring transparency to the language of deception by learning to be transparent and straightforward in his prose.

Unlike some, Orwell doesn't squirm while discussing egoism, or try to pass judgment. Instead, he regards egoism as largely inherent to "the minority of gifted, willful people who are determined to live their own lives to the end," as opposed to some who "abandon the sense of being individuals at all" by the age of thirty or "are simply smothered by drudgery." Can wanting to satisfy the self be a noble reason to write, then? Is writing a way of retaining one's core consciousness as long as possible?

Young Adult author Meredith Ann Pierce says "I write because I can't not write," which satisfies me, even though many of you may think, *That doesn't really answer the question.* Michael Phillips, who runs the Lithium Creations blog and has his own unique life story as documented on Showtime/NPR's *This American Life,* says, "I love the thrill of creating something new — taking something bizarre and bringing it to life." But what are we creating? How can it have life independent of us? And is the question still unanswered?

One reader of my blog, Andy, says he finds writing "a very therapeutic experience. Most of the time it makes no sense. All I do is start writing and I go where my writing leads. Much of it is unpublishable, but that is not the reason why I write. I guess it is therapy to me, like long walks or getting drunk is to other people."

Others, like Florida writer Bill Ectric, get a sense of continuity and tradition from writing:

> I have always loved creative writing. Maybe, in part, because my father let me sit at his desk and use his typewriter when I was a little kid, or that my mother taught me how to take different passages from the encyclopedia and synthesize them into my own words.

Terry Weyna writes reviews, essays, criticism, and scholarly work:

> Why do I write those things? To share my enthusiasms — to evangelize — as my way of thrusting something I love beneath the nose of another and saying, "Read this!" or "Look at the cool way these things relate to one another!"

Natania Barron, author of the Aldersgate Cycle, believes in something close to a communal reason to write:

> I tend to think that storytelling, all forms of fiction, is an art that's ingrained in the DNA of our species, as a way for our oversized brains to cope with the world around us.... Not that we ever really get it, but it's something like an ongoing exploration, with every generation taking on the next stanza, adding their own melodies and harmonies to the song.

Into the midst of this uncertainty, then, creeps the thought: *Are we all, then, just contributing to some as yet unfinished act of creativity, each finishing some small strand of an unfathomably enormous masterwork?* That explanation, too, strikes me as fiction.

Any honest answer is perfectly legitimate — indeed, many of these have been codified by writers down through the centuries. But if some of them fall short of feeling satisfactory, it might be that the simplest and most direct answer concerns the act of creation itself. It's a little more personal or revelatory, and therefore perhaps more embarrassing to talk about than other aspects of your Private Booklife: it's that moment while writing when you feel as if you are outside your body yet more intensely inside your body than ever before. This nameless spark, or shock, makes endless days of slogging through pages worthwhile.

In exploring your Private Booklife, it may or may not improve or focus your writing to make a list of reasons why you write. *Why* you do something doesn't necessarily affect the *quality* of what you do — hundreds of writers who said they wrote for money produced amazing work — but it does help define you as a person.

Of course, Orwell also wrote that "All writers are vain, selfish, and lazy, and at the very bottom of their motives there lies a *mystery*." What is that mystery? Perhaps that the animating impulse behind our need to write often eludes us — that in a sense we not only make up stories, we make up stories about why we write.

▶▶ Attitude and Creativity

Even as we leverage the Internet and new media, we're often told that certain types of writing, like fiction, don't mean anything beyond entertainment (a term that, like happiness, continually changes depending on the eye of the beholder) and we should shut up about anything more serious. There's often a kind of anti-intellectual streak to the discussion, a kind of "let's beat the crap out of the smartest kid in the room" mentality. But "entertainment," in all of its many permutations, doesn't cover the full range of possibilities open to the fiction writer. And, ultimately, if you're not writing for yourself and because you believe that what you're doing is in some way of use — that it *means something* — then just don't do it. There are easier ways to make money.

What you decide to write about doesn't matter, but your attitude does matter. A writer who specializes in space operas like Iain M. Banks can and should be as careful and passionate in his work as a writer like Ian McEwan with a mainstream literary novel like *Atonement*. In my continuum, both writers bring equally unique and valuable strengths to their fiction. Both — one working in a genre often disrespected and the other in a genre expected to be about Art — can achieve greatness. Fiction *does* mean something and it is important. It's only when we cynically tell ourselves it doesn't that we make a much more depressing reality come true.

This is not to claim anything unspeakably *pretentious* for the form, but it has, like any art — yes, it is a form of art, like sculpture or painting — huge potential in certain unique areas. Whatever the actual results, perfection being unattainable and perhaps undesirable, I want my novels to have every chance to be, yes, entertaining, but also immersive, specific, and resonant in their details, emotional (in the positive sense of the word), character-driven, and to get as close to their full potential (whatever that is for a particular project) as possible. In part, this is because achieving something different, whether it's a renovation or an innovation, and *doing something well that's difficult* is its own reward. In part, as the English writer Angela Carter famously said in an interview for the *Paris Review*, "I always want my reach to exceed my grasp." By which she meant that if you're ambitious creatively, even if you fail you'll have more success than if you tried for a lesser goal.

In that context, your attitude as a writer matters a great deal. In addition to not abandoning what makes you unique, you should strive for a unique mixture of arrogance and humility. Does that sound contradictory? It shouldn't. A good writer requires both qualities in equal measure. To survive the countless rejections you will receive from editors — I have over five thousand since 1987 — you need to have the arrogance to say, "Even if what I've created is flawed or broken, only I could have written it. I have something unique to share." Simultaneously, you need the humility to open yourself up to any and all criticism. Examine it and think about it. Don't immediately reject criticism, even if internalizing it hurts you. Then, dispassionately, use what resonates with you and discard the rest.

Even established writers, even writers near the ends of their careers, will, if they're smart, display this mixture of two extremes. It's the best way to protect your self while continuing to grow as a writer. It may never get easier, but it becomes more familiar.

■ Acknowledging the Passion

> Every detail on the sidewalk, from a rage of red-orange leaves to a green
> meandering crack in the concrete, took on a binocular significance. It
> was a forethought of the awareness that overtook him when he wrote:
> the premonition of something moving through him and onto the page,
> the pen in hand become a blur and the heart so full, limbs aflame, body
> with fever. Like sparks burrowing into you until, finally conquered, you
> become vessel, container not contained — trapped and free — and all
> the little hairs on your arms rise, and you feel as if your own skin has
> been painlessly flayed back to reveal, beneath the perfect diagram of
> veins and arteries, the beauty and horror of the world the words like tiny
> mysteries and the combinations of words solutions to those mysteries,
> and yet more mysterious for the revelation...

The quote above is from one of my short stories. It may employ somewhat lush
language, but it's the best way I know to describe what inspiration feels like
when I'm in the middle of it. I'll be honest. I've never understood writers who
find the actual physical act of writing painful. To me, there's nothing more
pleasurable than writing. There's nothing more insanely self-indulgent and
wonderful than sitting down to write — either longhand or on the computer
— and finding that your fingers are outrunning your brain. To be so inspired
that you're not thinking as you write, that you're just the vessel, the receptacle,
for the words, which are pouring out as if they were your life's blood.

Still, as I mentioned in "Reasons to Write," writers rarely talk about this
aspect of their craft. Writers talk instead about technique. They talk about
perspiration, endurance, and practice. They talk about the long slog. And
maybe there's some truth to speaking about the slow slog rather than moments
of inspiration. A lot of your days are spent slogging through, of just making
the forced march necessary to complete a story/novella/novel. You can't be
inspired every day just like you can't be madly, deeply, insanely in love every

day. It's just not possible. No one can sustain that. Your relationship over time with words, with stories, with characters, has to be deeper than that first rush of emotion.

But also, at base, that rush is what it's all about — about the almost sensual pressure of your fingers on the keyboard or the press of the pen against the notepad, the point at which you stop thinking and you're channeling something through your fingers and you almost don't know how you got to that point.

I'm not suggesting that what you produce during blind inspiration/infatuation is superior to what you produce during the slow slog. Everyone knows the deep disappointment of being unable to make the vision on the paper match the vision in one's head.

But there's an important relationship between slogging and inspiration on my blog recently, as exemplified by a comment made by writer Jonathan Wood:

> There's been a lot of slogging for me lately. Mostly because I've been in editing mode. But then I was just finishing up a short the other day on the train home and I had one of those moments, when you're just desperately trying to channel it before it escapes you. I had to sit in my car for five minutes typing before I went home just so I wouldn't lose it. And that, right there, is definitely my crack juice. I've got to imagine that it's a little like lucid dreaming. That's the only thing I can possibly compare it to. Because I'm right there and I wish I knew shorthand because it's happening before my eyes, and I'm feeling it, and I just desperately want to capture it, crystallize it, just get it on paper so other people can see just how exciting that moment is. Of course, then I re-read it and, well…but in the moment: yes. Definitely yes.

You can't be madly in love all of the time. But if you're not in love some of the time, how do you continue? Why do you write if not for that moment when you're opened up to the point where there's nothing of you left but the story and the characters and the words? Why waste your time doing something you don't get pleasure from? Even expressing angst and frustration and despair in fiction are forms of pleasure-seeking, or at the very least pain-avoidance, because they provide catharsis or a kind of informal therapy.

Recognizing moments of inspiration as a powerful argument for writing is only part of living a fulfilling Booklife. As Faulkner once said: "I only write when I'm inspired. Fortunately, I'm inspired at 9 o'clock every morning." The reality is, sometimes you have to write even if you're not inspired, as part of a productive creative routine. Sometimes you have to jump-start inspiration.

On a high level, you can stimulate inspiration by first identifying what works for you as a writer, and then leaning toward those approaches. Here are a few entry-points into writing that can help you become more inspired in your writing:

• **WRITE WHAT INTERESTS YOU**. The received wisdom in most books and online articles is to write what you know. The problem with this advice is that what you know may not interest you, just as what you're talented at may not interest you as a career. A writer often has to be a kind of benevolent liar, to convince the reader he or she is an expert in the absence of real expertise. You can always find out what you do not know, but you can't fake that spark of curiosity that comes from being *interested* in something. Writing what interests you engages more than your imagination — it ensures that you can reconcile your writing and non-writing lives. Besides, sometimes the mind needs to come at things sideways. If you write what interests you, you may find a way to write your way toward the things you know as well.

• **WRITE WHAT'S PERSONAL**. If you feel compelled to write what you know, let what you know be personal. There's great cathartic power, and thus ample room for inspiration, in taking the events of your life and finding ways to fictionalize them. Writing what's personal is different from writing what you know because it emphasizes your stake in the fiction. If you're not being inspired by what interests you, perhaps it's because you're not being personal enough in thinking about entry points into your writing. At the same time, recognize that confessional or deeply personal writing often requires time to gestate — that trying to write about events that you're still too close to may block inspiration.

• **WRITE WHAT'S UNCOMFORTABLE**. Subjects that interest you on a personal or non-personal level may also trouble you. Either you shy away from a subject or approach because you can't believe anything worthwhile can be written from that perspective, or because in writing about the subject you will reveal something you want to be a secret to the world. The problem, then, is not with inspiration, but with your perception of audience. Here's the good news: you don't need to share what you write with *anyone*. Emily Dickinson didn't, and she's become immortal. If you are drawn to write what's uncomfortable, it may help to recognize that you are allowed to write *for yourself*, and that any decisions about seeking publication are separate from that first, fundamental decision (and freedom). Denying your attraction to the uncomfortable may result in thwarting inspiration.

• **Write What's Random.** Some writers require chaos to find inspiration. Your path to inspiration might not be through writing what's interesting to you, or personal, or uncomfortable. You might be someone who needs a jolt to the system — who needs to tell yourself, on seeing a duck wearing a sun hat, being led on a leash by a child, "I need to write about that duck, that hat, that child." You don't require anything more than surprise and the unexpected moment for inspiration. That sudden shock — that introduction of chaos into the world — serves as the catalyst back into writing what's interesting, personal, or uncomfortable.

• **Write from Prompts.** Some writers require order in the form of prompts to find inspiration. What are prompts? Suggestions not from the world but from editors or other gatekeepers. The writer finds inspiration from contemplating an idea *another person* has put into the writer's head. For example, I know one amazing, award-winning writer who works best when he receives a request to write a story for a theme anthology. He can write original stories without a prompt, but he gains some essential element from the constraint of being told to "write about this" that inspires him — perhaps because it challenges his storytelling chops.

All of these approaches are connected — each is an entry point into the others, like a kind of honeycomb of interconnected tunnels. The mental trick for the writer is to consider how each entry point affects his or her ability to be inspired to write.

Beyond that entry point you'll find you still have every possibility at your disposal, but that the way you perceive those possibilities has changed from indifferent or negative to inspired and fully engaged. Over time, you may need to mix your approaches, because lack of inspiration often means your subconscious mind is bored — it needs a challenge, much like your muscles, if subjected to the same routine of exercise over months and years, require a change of routine to make gains in strength and endurance.

Being aware of the wellspring of your inspiration, and nurturing it, is important not only to the quality of your writing but also to your peace of mind in your Private Booklife.

▶▶ Being Receptive

■ The Subjectivity of Taste

In your Private Booklife it's always good to remember a fact that's about a lack of facts: there's little objective reality to writing. That which was out of fashion in one generation is lauded as genius by the next. That which was popular is now seen as shallow or silly, or both. Sometimes, this happens within a few months or a year rather than a decade due to the rapid cycling of our modern society. In a way, such subjectivity seems ideally suited to our times: the amount of data available about any given topic makes it hard to reach a consensus not just on *what happened*, but what's *important* about what happened.

Contemporary readers and critics, blinded by the speed of our world, must step back even farther from the point of creation/publication to really understand what is classic and what is not. Meanwhile, the blogosphere, by erasing certain forms of hierarchy, has contributed to confusion about what opinions do matter and which *should* matter. Mere experience is no longer an attribute given much authority by our online selves.

This debate over standards and what constitutes good writing, or good art of any kind, has been going on for centuries. In the 1800s, David Hume in his essay "On the Standard of Taste" discussed the subjectivity of applied standards, and how sometimes we value a work despite certain deformities in it — that in praising the whole, we also praise the defect. Yet, he also determined that "Many of the beauties of poetry, and even of eloquence, are founded on falsehood and fiction, on hyperboles, metaphors, and an abuse or perversion of terms from their natural meanings." Therefore, "To check the sallies of the imagination, and to reduce every expression to geometric truth and exactness, would be the most contrary to the laws of criticism."

Hume ultimately believed you *can* establish a standard of taste, but puts a lot of the onus of doing so on readers and critics being educated, careful, patient, and nuanced in their exploration of a particular piece of writing. In re-reading his complex, back-and-forth argument, I am reminded of conversations just as complex that have raged online since the beginning of public access to the Internet. The fact is, even if a standard of taste could be created — no matter the ultimate value of Hume's conclusions — you cannot control other people's tastes, and taste does not conform to the rational. The Internet demonstrates this daily with the aggregate insanity of the weight of conflicting opinions pouring into our brains through our browsers.

Why is any of this important to you as a writer?

Because there is always more than one way.

■ Mastery as Uncertainty

One of the more audacious novels of the past few years, *Light* by M. John Harrison, contains its own comment on being open to possibilities. Whether Harrison intended it or not, the following passage speaks to the craft and art of creating fiction better than almost anything in a book of writing advice:

> Every race [humankind] met on their way through the Core had a star drive based on a different theory. All those theories worked, even when they ruled out one another's basic assumptions. You could travel between the stars, it began to seem, by assuming anything. If your theory gave you a foamy space to work with — if you had to catch a wave — that didn't preclude some other engine, running on a perfectly smooth Einsteinian surface, from surfing from the same tranche of empty space. It was even possible to build drives on the basis of super-string-style theories, which, despite their promise four hundred years ago had never really worked at all.

The same idea applies to fiction, in that you can use an almost infinite number of approaches to achieve the same or similar effects. It illuminates the frightening thing about fiction — that you have so many choices, so many ways of getting from point A to point B (or in some cases, point C to point A, or point A to point 5).

The irony is that the broader your skill-set and the more mastery you gain, the more you will find yourself starting from scratch with each new book or story. The more choices, the more chances you will choose incorrectly. So mastery actually equals uncertainty. The more mastery you achieve, the less confident you become, although I don't really mean "confidence" and "uncertainty" in the strict dictionary definitions of the words. I'm referring to a good kind of uncertainty, and a bad kind of confidence. Because you are uncertain, despite having mastery, you know that your writing is still alive, that you are not simply doomed to repeat the same path you chose so many times before. Because you feel once again as if you are writing your first book, you know that writing is still meaningful to you. As Sun Tzu said many centuries ago in *The Art of War*, be flexible rather than rigid, "formlessness" as he called it, being a defense against "the most devious spy" and the plotting of your enemies.

Part of remaining receptive, and therefore open, in your Private Booklife is the ability to have sympathy for multiple theories of what constitutes good writing. Read two writing books with differing viewpoints, or the welter of contradictory opinions on a blog's comments thread. If you can appreciate the worth of opposing viewpoints, even if you don't ultimately agree, then you will strengthen your imagination and uncover new approaches in your own work.

■ The Tactics of Prose

Another manifestation of seeing the worth of opposing viewpoints pertains to style. In your Private Booklife, the prose you use in your writing constitutes a kind of *tactic* in support of a *strategy* or *story*. Perform a Google search for basic writing advice and you will find hundreds of entries saying that you should write invisible or "transparent" prose that won't take the reader out of the story, while dismissing other ways of writing fiction.

Our current preoccupation with invisible prose — and inability to recognize that "invisible" differs for every reader — is in part cyclical in nature, but also stems in part from the context of online communications, which increasingly dominate our lives. Transparency often equals necessity. Yet one mistake we make when we embrace new media is that we assume that the limited containers used, for example, to say "I just made some new coffee for my co-workers" on Twitter, which tend to favor invisible prose because of the need for brevity, can work equally well for all of our creative projects.

Consider also that "style" has many different functions across sentences, paragraphs, and pages. For example, your style simultaneously conveys, at minimum, the following:

- Narrator's voice/character perceptions
- External character context
- Specific events in real-time
- Subtext
- Elements of a believable setting

Precisely because your style must perform so many different functions, "purple prose," as a minimalist would typify a lush style, is therefore underrated in this day and age. By "purple" I really mean dense or layered, sometimes or even often in a pleasing or playful way — or a way that explains exactly why we'd sometimes rather read a novel than a menu or an airline magazine or a Facebook status message or the side of a cereal box.

Expressing this opinion on my blog — which is, after all, a stalwart example of new-ish media — seemed potentially perilous. Yet when I did so, I was surprised to find that most of those who commented shared my views.

For example, Alistair Mather wrote:

The power of dense or difficult or different prose [is that it] forces us to reassess how we ourselves describe the world in which we live. And if you ever need to convince someone in a hurry, I suggest merely reading the opening paragraphs of Nabokov's *Lolita* to the unbeliever, and watch how quickly the language of obsession is recognized by any who have ever lost a lover.

The power to make the unfamiliar universal is not just a strength of writing tactics that draw no attention to themselves. Nor is invisible prose able to accomplish certain strategic objectives.

"Good prose is like a window pane," Orwell stated in "Why I Write," even as there's a lingering echo in his essay that longs for a richer style of prose that he was incapable of doing well.

Good prose *is* a window pane, but sometimes the pane is dirty or cracked, and sometimes it has the reflective qualities of a mirror, or even a hint of soft green fungus growing in the gutter between glass and wood. We need our Salman Rushdies and our Michael Chabons, our Ursula K. Le Guins and Margaret Atwoods, as much as we need our John Cheevers and our Ernest Hemingways.

There's nothing wrong with invisible prose, any more than there is anything wrong with a more layered approach. But there *is* something wrong with your prose if it's transparent or invisible because you haven't explored all of the options.

As Nick Summit put it, "There is a venerable tradition...for the laconic and the direct. But not enough at present seem to know the difference between the Emperor's new clothes and the Hemingway-esque: Sparse yet with a definite point of view and voice and tone."

If you read an Elmore Leonard novel or a Ken Bruen novel, you'll find exactly what Nick describes: a sparseness that still creates a muscular voice and tone. Leonard will make dialogue do what description does for other writers. Bruen will take one detail and set a whole scene with it. That's an "invisible" style worthy of the name.

However, simply writing featureless prose, being unable to do the basic blocking necessary to set a scene, having no ability to work in senses other than sight and hearing, and thinking that having your characters basically move from empty room to empty room in a brisk fashion constitutes plot... well, that's bad writing, not an invisible style.

This subject is important because it's all too possible today for a beginning writer to mistake simplicity for mastery, without experimenting or honing their craft. In fact it is much easier for a writer with an invisible style to tread water because the defects in a lush style, by contrast, stand out from a mile away. This tends to affect feedback in a way that emphasizes stylistic problems in flamboyant prose while neglecting style problems in invisible prose.

Nick said it best: "It is not about being willfully obscure, it is acknowledging that text, fiction, is not life. It is like life, but it is not [the thing itself]; fiction is a world unto itself and that world is multi-dimensional, or layered. Very often it is crucial for words or phrases to draw attention to themselves to enhance meaning — and most importantly, the story — not get in the way of it."

In short, the problem with championing one approach over the other as a writer rather than thinking of them as part of a range of tactics you should deploy is that you limit your range of options. *Voice* is something intrinsic to a writer and his or her world view. *Style* is something malleable that, in any writer willing to receptive, should be fluid: more or less invisible, more or less lush, depending on the needs of the story or novel. To rob yourself of that flexibility is to limit the kinds of stories you can tell.

Any kind of flexibility in this regard will enhance your work and make your Private Booklife as rich as your Public Booklife, with its multiple platforms and myriad opportunities.

Put another way: *Do you want to accept advice from sources that tell you there is only one path or sources that tell you there are multiple paths?*

▶▶ **Room to Think**

■ Recognizing the Nature of Distraction

> It is not that we have a short space of time, but that we waste much of it. Life is long enough, and it has been given in sufficiently generous measure to allow the accomplishment of the very greatest things if the whole of it is well invested. But when it is squandered...when it is devoted to no good end, forced at last by the ultimate necessity we perceive that it has passed away before we were aware that it was passing. So it is — the life we receive is not short, but we make it so, nor do we have any lack of it, but are wasteful of it. Just as great and princely wealth is scattered in a moment when it comes into the hands of a bad owner, while wealth however limited, if it is entrusted to a good guardian, increases by use, so our life is amply long for him who orders it properly.
> —Seneca

For most of human history we've found ways to distract ourselves from the essential, unsolvable joke of our own eventual mortality. So perhaps it's never been easy for some of us to find the mental space necessary to really concentrate on a book — we're so busy avoiding the future anyway. But novel writing in particular is like some kind of three-dimensional chess game in terms of how you break down and build up the connections, and how everything around you plays into the writing. As Orwell wrote, no matter how enjoyable individual writing sessions might be, the overall process of writing a book "is a horrible, exhausting struggle, like a long bout of painful illness."

Modern distractions don't help make it any less of a forced march. Being on the computer too much is a terrible thing for me during novel writing — it fragments the brain, sets the mind to racing, saturating it with information that's often trivial and almost always purely visual. A novel needs spurs to the writer's imagination from all the senses to induce inspiration. A novel also takes a great deal of uninterrupted thought, not to mention uninterrupted writing time. In my opinion, anything that distracts from this directly affects quality and depth. Therefore, the sustained effort required by a novel should not include multitasking, if you have the option. Even if the open channels mentioned earlier don't stress you out, you need as few channels as possible while writing.

Work on my last novel, *Finch*, went well because every morning my long-suffering yet often amused wife Ann hid the Internet router box and my cell phone (it has Internet access on it). I would get up around seven in the morning, have my breakfast, and watch something innocuous like BBC News or the sitcom *Frasier* for about half an hour, and then get down to work. Around noon I would take a break for lunch, then get back to it, usually at that point editing or organizing notes. Around three in the afternoon, I would call Ann on our land line. She would tell me where she'd hidden the router box and the cell phone so I could finish up the afternoon with necessary emails and other work before going to the gym.

Ten years ago no one would've had to worry about this kind of intrusion. In fact, I remember writing parts of one novel in an apartment that didn't even have electricity — or any furniture, really. I got up around dawn, went to my day job, and then came back and wrote until it got dark. Sometimes I'd go to a coffee shop so I could write longer.

The point is, certain incarnations of modern technology can be dangerous to sustained creativity, and cool tools should not control you. Sometimes in workshops my wife Ann and I will force students to write longhand just to cut them off from their laptops and all the distractions that pop up on the screen. Some hate it. Some realize what they've been missing. Many become converts to "de-frag" as I sometimes call it, and find themselves much happier

Another pressure on the modern writer looking for a little peace and quiet is that more and more people believe they have a right to inhabit your personal space, electronically, whenever they want to. That's why I try to be online only during times that are not disruptive to novel writing and thinking about the novel. Yet, while I was writing *Finch*, a fairly large number of people expressed irritation of varying degrees because I guided them to Ann or told them I wouldn't be in touch until after my deadline.

Why? Because in this case one rule of my Public Booklife — to make myself accessible and available — had run up against a vital requirement of my Private Booklife: to be largely inaccessible.

A certain inconsistency also began to manifest itself. When I have a great day of writing, I am more likely to be Internet-sociable at night. When I have a slow day, I'm more likely to cut myself off from the world and think things through. So in one sense I can understand the frustration of my fans, friends, and colleagues. My patterns of interaction seemed unpredictable and erratic to the outside observer, even though those patterns actually demonstrated the constantly shifting *logic of creativity*. It's not a science. It's not some kind of quantifiable paint-by-numbers process.

For this reason, it may be important to set up, on your most visible platform, rules of public engagement while working on a novel. These rules should be conveyed with humor and apologies, acknowledge the fact you're going to be inconsistent, and be general where they need to be and specific where you can make them specific. (For example, don't say "most email will still be answered within two weeks" unless you can back up that statement.) However, as necessary you may need to be ruthless to individuals who just don't get it.

■ The Other You

It may not be obvious after reading the advice in Public Booklife, but I am not the kind of person whose book promotion/Internet brain is interwoven with my creative brain. The two are separate. To summon one I must banish the other. To go from being in the moment while writing in the morning to this *other thing* in the mid-afternoons — this person who fields requests for interviews, fan mail, production questions on forthcoming books, and all of the other things a writer or other creative person deals with outside of the writing — to do this I must make a transition. I cross the border into another land, assume another identity. Because, for me at least, I am becoming someone else entirely.

The writer me is monosyllabic, doesn't care if his beard grows down to his ankles, scribbles notes on little bits of paper, takes long walks in the woods mumbling to himself, maps out character positions in rooms and notes where the light is coming from, doesn't answer the phone, and isn't fond of talking to people.

The other me is, in general, chatty, sociable, likes talking to people and putting people in contact with one another, and uses the Internet to make friends, advance projects, and communicate a love of books. And, yes, this other me also sometimes gets involved in online flame wars, arguments, can be caustic and sarcastic and moody, but is still always what you'd call *engaged*.

In becoming this other me, I deliberately choose to erase the space between myself and others. I allow myself to be *accessible*. And, then, as noted, some people forget about my other, more introverted self. They don't see the writing — the longhand journals, the print-outs, the notes strewn across the table. They forget, I think, the point of all of this, and that it isn't a miraculous, instantaneous conception, churned out like Twitter entries or Facebook status updates.

Right now I'm finishing up *Booklife*. When I'm done, I'll come up for air. I'll be available and accessible and social. A part of me, even right now, is thinking that maybe I'll be a little more wary this time. That maybe I won't wind up being on email 24–7 between projects. Maybe I'll make myself a little harder to reach.

And yet I know I probably won't have that much discipline — until I have to, for the next creative project. I'll know when the time comes. The router box and the cell phone will find their way to the strangest places. I'll turn from the page I'm scrawling, in the grip of an emotion I can't identify but that tightens my throat, makes me somehow vulnerable, and February will have become May and the weather outside the window will seethe with storm clouds, and I won't know where the time went, or where the stack of manuscript pages came from, or even what they might mean, to anyone.

▶▶ Relinquishing All Fetishes

Here's an incomplete list of things I've given up over the years so I wouldn't have excuses not to write:

- Special notebooks.
- Favorite pens.
- Particular times of day (or night).
- Comfortable desks and chairs.
- A dedicated office space.
- Specific mental exercises.
- Nostalgic typewriters.
- Impressive laptops.

These days, I don't care where I am when I write, who I'm with, or if it's midnight or noon. I don't care if I scribble on a piece of toilet paper or in some fancy goatskin-lined tome. If I don't have a pen, I'll as easily type a phrase or scene fragment into my Palm Centro and send it to my email account as try to write a note on paper.

I'm for whatever creates the least distance between thought and capturing the thought, that provides the least friction between "eureka!" and writing down "eureka!" before it becomes "What the heck was that brilliant phrase I was just thinking of a second ago and now have forgotten?"

My younger self didn't understand this truth. My younger self kept putting obstacles between me and the act of writing. Every minute spent fetishizing the process instead of simplifying it cost me moments of creativity. I also wasted money on all of the accoutrements we see in our mind's eyes as belonging to the writer's craft.

In addition, my younger self didn't understand that there's not always a link between improved technology and greater efficiency. There have been times that my computer, with all of its distractions, with its Word that failed on me, became a much greater hindrance to my creativity than finding that special artist's paper, that particular brand of smooth roller pen.

On long projects, my favorite notebook now is actually the simplest possible invention: the lined notecard. I write one thought or sequence or phrase per card, shove a bunch of blank ones in my back pocket wherever I go. It has made novel writing a lot easier for me. Nothing's more annoying than having to take all of your random novel notes in a notebook and put them into sequential order. With note cards, just sequence them in minutes. *Voila!* Low-tech, DIY innovation. No software in the world can provide that kind of organization.

On a writing panel at a convention in Helsinki, a Finnish writer related the story about how the younger generation of writers in Finland was now advocating radical new approaches. These young writers had discovered that writing their drafts in longhand made them more productive and their writing stronger. The Finnish writer could barely contain his laughter as he told the story, and I was reminded of my stepdaughter telling me about this great Puff Daddy song that turned out to be a cover of a song by The Police.

That said — and while I play the old-school curmudgeon here to make a point — many writers I admire use sophisticated new tools to be efficient and make it easier to produce word count. Scrivener or other programs that help with chapter organization may be of use. John McCarthy, a writer and graphic design artist for the Museum of Comic Book Arts in New York City notes, for example, that "Speaking strictly as an amateur writer — whose schedule and work habits are fractured — Scrivener has been like found gold. I've made it part of my workflow and I'm quite confident endorsing it." Still, for me, these tools make work *too* easy — word count is a hollow goal unless they're the right words — and also impose templates that guard against the unexpected mistake, the moment when human error creates something wonderful. Thus, I find Scrivener an insidious kind of fetish or crutch — performing functions I want my brain to engage in directly.

But regardless of what you think of writing longhand or using Scrivener, I hope my point is obvious by now. In pursuing productivity, don't abandon old technology in favor of what's shiny and new just because everyone else is doing it. And don't hold onto the old just because you've always done it that way. If you can accomplish that goal, you will be liberated in your Private Booklife from a multitude of decisions that have nothing to do with writing.

▶▶ Writing and Revision

■ Testing Your Work

Booklife was never intended as a book on writing per se, even though some subjects in Private Booklife help you by encouraging inspiration, ensuring there are no unnecessary roadblocks between you and the blank page, and helping to recharge your imagination. As for the act of writing, that's a transaction between you and your imagination, although some of the resources listed below will be of use, both for creation and revision.

However, I can help you here with approaches to revision. If creation often has a *Wuthering Heights*, "oh Heathcliff I am overcome" quality to it—as if you've just emerged from a raging thunderstorm onto moors that look like the English Romantic landscape artist J. M. W. Turner painted them—then revision has more of a surgical, scientific aspect to it.

Or should, because you can indeed test the rough draft or second draft (or third) in a logical manner. This analytical process can consist of the few basic steps set out below, but I am providing just one example of a systematic approach to revision. You should incorporate my suggestions into an overall strategy for revision suited to your particular temperament and writing style. (I also highly recommend applying the questions set out in David Madden's *Revising Fiction*.)

■ Poking the Structure with a Stick

First, examine the structure of your story or novel. Doing so is akin to the "reverse outlining" described later on in Revitalizing Your Creativity, but on a more intimate level.

- List each scene.
- List every action or act that occurs in each scene—not anything that occurs "off-stage." ("Sally sticks the fork in Emma's eye." "Emma faints." "Sally runs away." "Emma's pet poodle calls the police.")
- Ask yourself a series of questions based on your list.

o Is there true cause-and-effect displayed on the page, for every action or act?

o Is every necessary action or act within a scene dramatized on the page?

o Are actions or acts included that are unnecessary to the scene or should be airlifted out into some other part of the story or novel?

o Is there true cause-and-effect *between* scenes? (Another way of putting this is: Are your progressions sound? For example, you might have a flashback scene in the wrong place, or you might jump three weeks forward and realize that's too jolting a gap in the narrative.)

o Are there unnecessary scenes? (If there are scenes in which nothing happens, is this "nothing" necessary to the characters or narrative?")

The simplest reason for this kind of testing? To determine whether there is any confusion in the surface of your story — places where the reader will have a bumpy reading experience because of lack of clarity on your part. More than once, I've made an assumption or a leap between actions or scenes that I couldn't actually justify when I went back and tested it. I've also found opportunities for strengthening elements that appeared sound but could still be made better.

The effectiveness of this process depends in part on the kind of story you're telling, although even a surreal dream of a tale requires some kind of logic — perhaps an even more rigid logic than a conventional approach. Performing this series of actions should dredge up all kinds of valuable intel in the context of your overall revision process.

▪ Interrogating Your Characters

However, stress-testing your story by structure will only get you so far. You also need to examine the interactions between characters, because, on some level, characterization *is* plot. To that end:

• Write out the names of your characters in a circle on a piece of paper.
   o Draw lines connecting the characters that have some relationship to one another.
   o Write the relationship or relationships between two characters on the line you've drawn between them (whether "mother/son" or "friend" or whatever).

o Take a good look at characters who do not seem that connected to other characters and make sure that is a strength in the story, not a weakness. Consider whether there are connections you haven't thought of, and how those connections might change your narrative.

- With your diagram of character relationships in hand, look again at your list of scenes broken down by action and act.
- Examine each interaction between characters set out on the list. Ask yourself the following questions:
  o Why does X act or react this way? Is there another way they might have reacted? How does that change in reaction affect the rest of the narrative?
  o Is there a history or past between these two (or more) characters that I haven't considered that might drive their actions or speech in this scene?

You'll find that this kind of testing helps to create depth and layering, but you're also largely determining whether you've made things *too easy* in your story.

For example, at one workshop I applied this form of interrogation to a scene in which the main character acquiesces to a demand by the antagonist. I asked the writer, "What if X says 'no' to Y instead? Isn't that more in keeping with X's character anyway, and how does that change the story?" It turned out the writer hadn't thought about the possibility of X saying no, but that saying no immediately turned scenes that plodded along into totally different scenes with much more subtext and dramatic potential. The initial "yes" had just been the writer's knee-jerk way of moving onto the next scene, and the next.

I then asked a second question. "Are you sure that X doesn't already know Y before this scene?" This possibility also had never occurred to the writer, but creating a past between X and Y immediately opened up additional opportunities for character development. It also added many layers to the scene in question, and again fundamentally altered the rest of the story. The writer found that X's mistress had a connection to Y as a result of this testing, and suddenly what had been a simple A-to-B story with little tension had a three-dimensional quality to it.

Does this process seem too artificial, or too simplistic? Perhaps, and it's just one starting point for your revision process, but sometimes being mechanical is good because it relieves you of the burden of coming up with a spark during revision — the process jump-starts that spark, and helps you to see the story with fresh eyes.

■ Reconciling Feedback

Some writers have at least one more step in their approach to revision, because they share their rough drafts with a writing group or selected first readers. Thus, their revision process includes the opinions of others. Especially when developing your voice and your style, consider processing comments in a systematic way. Why? To get the most out of those comments and to better weed out irrelevant comments without losing anything valuable to you.

An approach that has worked for me, and which I still sometimes use, involves assimilation and prioritization.

- Read and absorb all comments, no matter how absurd you initially find them — in short, internalize them all before rejecting any.
- Once you've had a chance to think about each comment, separate out the ones that you think apply across most or all of your fiction. After further thought, make a list of the most useful ones that denote both strengths and weaknesses. Use that list to improve your writing in general.
- Before continuing further, make sure you know what you want the novel or story to do (what it's about thematically and what you want it to accomplish), perhaps even using the structure/character testing discussed above.
- Make a list of all the specific comments that support your vision.
- Make a list of all the specific comments that don't support that vision.
- Explain to yourself why you're not using comments that don't support your vision of the story. (For example, "This comment isn't applicable because my novel is not really about colonialism in India but more about the friendship between two soldiers.")
- Use all remaining comments to improve your story.

This kind of systematic approach will allow you to get the most out of feedback in the same way that an expert butcher wastes not a bit of the meat on a carcass.

One final note: Regardless of your process in revision, try to separate out levels of edit. For example, you could reserve one round of revision for only making line edits to your work, while you take care of re-imagining problematic scenes during another round of revision. Otherwise, you may get lost in the bloody mess that your manuscript should resemble after having marked up the rough draft, whether with a pen or through revision tracking on a computer.

▰ Resources

Part of living a fulfilling Private Booklife requires using the experience of others to shorten your learning curve. Really good books on writing are few and far between. Most of them are not worth the paper they're printed on — you're much better off reading ancient and contemporary classics and dissecting their technique yourself. However, I *do* highly recommend the following texts to help both your writing and your ability to revise your writing.

• **THE ART OF SUBTEXT: BEYOND PLOT BY CHARLES BAXTER**. This book discusses hidden subtextual overtones and undertones. While that might sound dry, it's actually a marvelous and exciting exploration of how writers create visible and invisible detail in their work, using examples from modern and classic writers.

• **NARRATIVE DESIGN: WORKING WITH IMAGINATION, CRAFT, AND FORM BY MADISON SMARTT BELL**. Bell examines twelve stories written by his students and by well-known writers, analyzing their use of time, plot, character, and other elements of fiction. In this workshop-in-print-form, Bell deconstructs elements of the stories to show what works and what doesn't. It's a masterful performance, but you may want to buy two copies, since the relevance of each chapter's end notes to the overall effect means you'll otherwise constantly be flipping between pages.

• **THE PASSIONATE, ACCURATE STORY BY CAROL BLY**. Bly discusses the role of the imagination, ethics, and your characters, and many other topics not dealt with by most writing books. Her observations pertain in the best possible way not just to technique but to very human aspects of the writing life.

• **WRITING FICTION, A GUIDE TO NARRATIVE CRAFT BY JANET BURROWAY**. This book is the closest thing to a semester-long creative writing course you'll find, probably because Burroway uses it as the foundation of her creative writing classes. Invaluable for beginners and intermediate writers alike.

• **About Writing: Seven Essays, Four Letters, & Five Interviews by Samuel Delany.** This thoughtful perspective from an underrated giant of literature features a few reprints from books like The *Jewel-Hinged Jaw*, but mostly collects previously uncollected nonfiction about writing. The letters, which I thought would be slight, turn out to be insightful, focused, and consistently fascinating. The interviews are sometimes a little long, a little too detail oriented, but still wonderful to read. The essays are, of course, magnificent.

• **The Art of Fiction: Notes on Craft for Young Writers by John Gardner.** An eccentric genius as a fiction writer, Gardner's writing book aimed at beginning writers discusses theory as well as the craft of writing. It contains a mixture of practical, specific advice, along with graceful observations about the writer's life.

• **Creating Short Fiction: The Classic Guide to Writing Short Fiction by Damon Knight.** Knight was known for his science fiction writing, but this guide is much more universal than that and steeped in the wisdom of fifty years of writing fiction. Perhaps more importantly, Knight includes diagrams of various plot structures. Early on, this helped me visualize my plots as diagrams and sometimes enabled me to spot structural problems as a result. His thoughts on "form" are also useful to beginning and intermediate writers.

• **Revising Fiction by David Madden.** Madden breaks fiction down into its components (like character, theme, setting, etc.) and then creates subcategories of possible problems you may be having in your work. He uses examples of these problems from the drafts of books and stories by famous writers, and then shows you how the writer fixed the problem in the final draft. Just being able to see an early paragraph from *The Great Gatsby* and compare it to the published version is invaluable, but Madden's advice and commentary make this my favorite writing book of all time.

• **Word Work: Surviving and Thriving as a Writer by Bruce Holland Rogers.** Much of Rogers' advice is for published writers, and in some cases published writers with books out. However, certain sections are relevant in terms of the psychology of dealing with rejection and the difficulties of the writing life. I much prefer Rogers' approach to these topics than some of the more New-Agey writing books that seem to value mysticism over commonsense.

• **How To Suppress Women's Writing by Joanna Russ.** A sharp jab at the ways in which women's writing has been marginalized by men and by society. Chapters include "The Double Standard of Content," "False Categorization," "Isolation" and "Lack of Models."

• **Writing the Other: A Practical Approach by Nisi Shawl and Cynthia Ward.** A guide to writing about people who are not of your ethnicity, gender, economic class, etc. The book discusses basic aspects of characterization and offers elementary techniques, practical exercises, and examples for helping writers create richer and more accurate characters.

• **Maps of the Imagination: The Writer as Cartographer by Peter Turchi.** This brilliant exploration of creative writing through the metaphor of the map makes you see craft and form from a different perspective. Chapters like "Projections and Conventions" and "A Rigorous Geometry" provide insightful analysis of various short stories and novels in the context of topography.

• **How to Write Killer Fiction by Carolyn Wheat.** This unassuming book provides a great breakdown of the tropes and expectations of thriller and mystery fiction. While acknowledging commercial requirements for the two genres, it also provides ample space for individuality and the art of fiction. Even if you don't write mysteries or thrillers, Wheat's advice applies more generally to pacing, story, and plot.

The value of any of these books is that as you consult them multiple times during your career they will change because you have changed as a writer. It's one way to measure your growth, and to keep learning. (For additional resources, including websites, visit BOOKLIFENOW.COM.)

▶▶ Work Schedule

I discussed daily/weekly task lists in the setting goals section of Public Booklife. However, your daily work schedule requires explanation in the context of your Private Booklife. Whether you're a full-time or part-time writer, nothing has a greater effect on your ability to create a routine that allows you to write on a regular basis. A work schedule is really about killing distractions by giving yourself space to write by adhering to a set structure. Any schedule has to be realistic or you won't follow it and the guilt will negatively impact your planning ability in the future.

■ For Part-Time Writers

Until two years ago, I had a full-time day job working on educational materials for school children. That job robbed me of at least forty hours a week, usually more. Despite this, I finished novels, edited anthologies, wrote short stories, and in general managed to get a lot done. How? In part by taking advantage of any available time. This was my general schedule:

Weekdays
7:00 to 7:30: Exercise bike (excellent opportunity to read books)
7:30 to 8:00: Shower, then breakfast
8:00 to 8:30: Travel to the day job, and getting settled.
8:30 to 11:30: Tasks associated with the day job.
11:30 to 1:00: Writing and editing of my fiction, in addition to eating a quick lunch.
1:00 to 3:30: Tasks associated with the day job.
3:30 to 3:45: Break, during which I would either relax or write.
I usually assigned myself a finite task, like writing a character description or a few paragraphs about a setting.
3:45 to 6:45: Tasks associated with the day job.
6:45 on: Home two nights a week, gym three nights a week.
Followed by watching TV, reading, responding to emails including

tasks related to the day job, or editing fiction. To bed by 11:30.

> Write at least 4 hours Saturday morning, with Sunday morning
> off. Additional editing and other writing-related tasks on-and-off
> throughout the weekend.

Adding up the hours, I had at least one hour each weekday to work on my writing. I had at least four hours during the weekend (although I often wrote for more hours). That's nine hours a week to write, not including time spent on editing what I'd written. I used my lunch and breaks. Sometimes I'd take a much longer lunch and stay late at the day job, so let's say for the sake of argument that I averaged ten hours a week on my writing.

That's five hundred twenty hours a year. Let's round that down to five hundred hours, factoring in vacations and other distractions but also times when I was more productive. That's thirty thousand minutes. I type about one hundred twenty words a minute, but let's assume I was working at a lower pace — that I wasn't typing every second — and averaged half of that, sixty words a minute. That's a potential three hundred thousand words despite holding down a full-time job. You could take two hundred thousand words off of that estimate and still have a full novel draft completed in a year.

My point is this: If you want to write, you'll find the time, whether you have a day job or not. Time is not the issue: *the will to write* is the issue. The ability to will yourself to write is enhanced when you have a schedule. Your schedule might look entirely different from mine. You might love to write in the morning enough to get up an hour early to write before going to work. Or you might prefer to work through lunch and go home early and write in the evenings. Honoré de Balzac used to write on the train ride to and from work, and on breaks during his fifteen-hour shifts — and that's not an unusual story. You'll find extraordinary tales of almost supernatural commitment by writers throughout history.

Admittedly, not every day job allows equal flexibility in terms of your schedule. Also, other parts of your life, like raising a family, can be an obstacle to having the energy to work and to write. Just recognize that even fifteen minutes of writing per day is progress toward your Private Booklife goals.

◼ For Full-Time Writers (Bowing to Reality)

Shortly after I became a full-time writer, I joyfully posted my schedule on my blog. I was joyful because, for the first time in my life, at the age of thirty-eight, I could devote myself more fully to the work I was best suited for: writing fiction. Here is that posted schedule, with accompanying notes:

Weekdays:
7:15 to 7:45: Exercise bike (an excellent opportunity to read books *for review*)
8:00: Breakfast.
8:30 to 11:30: Writing of first-draft fiction in longhand, sometimes at a coffee shop, with some book review writing on the tail end of that time if I run out of fiction inspiration.
11:30 to 12:30: Brisk walk (for brainstorming) and check email. Also includes lunch.
12:30 to 3:00: Typing up of first draft fiction and writing of first-draft book review, other nonfiction material, sometimes career stuff; nutritious, energizing snack.
3:00 to 4:00: Nap, watch TV, or follow up on email, PR, etc.
4:00 to 6:00: Gym or exercise at home.
6:00 to 7:00: Dinner.
7:00 to 8:30: Outer limit for continuing work on responding to email, finishing off reviews, etc.
8:30 to 11:00: Time off to relax.
11:00 to 7:15: Sleep.

And repeat. Weekends are more leisure-oriented, in that I don't push myself to finish fiction. Usually a long walk on Sundays, racquetball on Saturday. I do a lot of my book review reading and prep for blog posts on weekends.

Now, that's best-case. Sometimes it doesn't happen exactly like that, but that's the goal. Every weekday. Sometimes we goof off more in the evening or have some wine, or whatever. But I strive to meet that optimum schedule. I'd say I hit it about seventy-five to eighty-five percent of the time, which is enough to be efficient.

The thing that has really had to change with more fiction deadlines, though, is how I access my email and the Internet. I no longer turn on my computer until lunchtime and I try to turn it off by around 7 or 8 PM, tops. I find myself allocating more blocks of time to answer email, rather than just answering when I get an email. This has given me much more peace of mind and I find my brain is less fractured and fragmented. I think it's a lot healthier to do it this way.

This all sounds wonderful, and at times it is still wonderful. But here's the reality of being a working full-time writer who isn't on the *New York Times* bestseller list: your schedule soon becomes more fragmented than this, and you find that too much discipline can drive you insane.

Writer J. T. Glover began to get at part of the truth when he posted this comment: "Do you find that it's easy to hold to a rigorous schedule, or does the work inspire its own devotion in the end stages?"

That question suggests a few different answers. First, yes, the work does inspire its own devotion in the end stages. The extent of that devotion can render you house-bound and reclusive, but that is the price you pay for the luxury of spending most of your time on an activity you love but that doesn't provide the same kind of remuneration as being a lawyer or a doctor. By the time I had finished *Finch*, I hadn't left the house in two weeks. I worked out at home and had become completely lost in the maze of the novel. Some part of me didn't want to come back from that to the real world.

The second answer? I am now, after two years of freelancing, convinced that no human being on Earth can stick to this rigorous a schedule. The part-time writer schedule might seem tougher, but the hours devoted to the day job contained their own kind of peace — full of activities that included socializing with co-workers and taking little breaks.

When you are your own boss, especially when you rely on a series of small "jackpots" in the form of advances, royalties, and checks for piecework like book reviews, you have less of a safety net — and less of a comfort level in goofing off. There's also a tendency to take on any and all work, against your better judgment. Thus, even while working on *Finch*, I had other commitments. Thus, despite my optimistic statement above, I counted it a good week when I wasn't on the Internet in the morning more than two weekdays. I also thought myself lucky if I got to the gym twice a week.

After experiencing the intensity of this kind of life, I'm convinced that the schedule of a freelancer has to be reset every few months, to try to get back to that rhythm in which your creative life takes priority over everything else. The very diversity of "bosses" that makes you less susceptible to the misfortunes of the economy can fracture your attention span. So, periodically, I try to get back to a better creative schedule, as when I posted this entry on my blog in the first quarter of 2008:

> May through September, excepting public appearances and prior non-fiction commitments, are reserved for finishing *Finch*. I've archived my email, deleted all of my links to blogs other than news blogs, and stopped taking on new commitments. I've instituted a strict diet and exercise regime. All weekday mornings will be spent on the novel. Afternoons will see limited Internet connectivity for business communications, but will most often be reserved for typing up rough draft material or working on anthology commitments. Evenings will be for reading and relaxing and some blogging — replenishing the mind for the next morning's work. Weekends will be the main time I do nonfiction as it's less taxing.
>
> The rigorous schedule is the goal, and one reason to post about it is to help me visualize being successful with the schedule. The thing most likely to happen is, in the later stages of working on the novel, my exercise rate will fall off and I will be pretty much entirely working on the novel morning, noon, and night. I'm hoping to be more disciplined than that because I hate getting out of balance.

However, by July I had fallen off the wagon and had to get back on again. My novel was hopelessly delayed, and this book you're holding in your hands, which was supposed to be published in May 2009, was pushed back to October 2009, because I hadn't yet finished writing it. (Indeed, the first thing I am going to do after finishing this book is re-read the section on "Peace of Mind" and apply it once again to my own life.)

There are a few lessons you can pull from this example. First, I had unrealistic expectations of myself. Second, as a new full-time writer I misjudged the amount of time it would take me to perform certain tasks. Because I had always fit writing in around other things, I didn't realize that being full-time wouldn't increase my work rate exponentially. I still needed time to think about what I was writing. As a part-time writer, that time, or that buffer, had been provided by the day job, which gave me distance from my fiction. But that buffer doesn't exist in my life as a full-time writer. Third, visualization and publicly telling people what you are going to do won't always carry you through a busy period.

In your Private Booklife, try to keep my example in mind — and use it to either avoid the mistakes I made or to anticipate them and find other solutions. More importantly, recognize in your own endeavors that no one's perfect. All any of us can do is start out each day with a blank slate, a fresh start, and try to make smart, honest decisions.

▶▶ Habit versus Process

■ Do You Know the Difference?

A habit is not a process. Just because you have always sacrificed a goat and three hamsters and then completed a novel doesn't mean there is no better way. It's easy to say that "I prefer to write on a laptop" or "I prefer to write in the mornings" or "I write best when I polish a page and move on, rather than writing a full rough draft" or "I'm really best at writing thrillers," but until you test your habits scientifically, with an open mind, you really don't know if you're doing something in a particular way out of habit or because it really is the *best* way — for you.

You see this in business all the time when a project is successful. The participants in that success tend to assume *every aspect* of what they did, except for obvious tactical failures, contributed to that success. Then they repeat all of those elements, even the ones that didn't actually contribute to success. Eventually, they come across a situation in which it becomes obvious that some of their process is actually habit, and that habit gets them into trouble. In business, the results of misjudging the paradigm can be utter ruin, whereas the results of not analyzing your habits as a writer are less severe: inefficiency and, possibly, not leveraging your imagination or talent across your writing as well as you might.

This gap between habit and process in writing occurs in the same way as in business, only more so. You develop a routine as a beginning writer — sometimes in your teens — when you don't necessarily understand your motivation or your craft, and by the time you have acquired some mastery of techniques, habit is codified as process, usually in a vacuum.

However, there's a further complication. In the arts, unlike in business, *efficiency* isn't always the goal. I even have processes that *include* inefficiency as an element of creating a better piece of fiction. Which is to say, having tried using computer programs for organization and for brainstorming, I need instead the messiness of little notes and scrawled charts because my inefficiency leads to further inspiration. A word I can't read on a note card may actually become a springboard to further invention in the text. Having to reorganize scraps of paper may suggest a better ordering of events, in a very organic way.

If my process, or anyone's process, seems ridiculous to you, make sure you've tried and discarded it first. Also recognize that your response to various processes changes over the years as your writing changes. If you're stuck on a creative project, it might have nothing to do with having written yourself into a corner. Instead, you might need to change your process. You might even find the solution in a process change you rejected five years before that now works perfectly for you.

For these reasons and more, the idea of process in writing is murkier than in other fields. There is no template that fits every writer. This is also, understandably, why we tend to confuse habit and process in our daily lives as writers. Still, that doesn't mean you shouldn't be systematic in your exploration of process versus habit.

■ A Novel Example

In my own Private Booklife, I recently changed my entire process for writing a novel. My standard modus operandi meant I never started out with a detailed outline. I just knew something about the characters and situations. I also knew the ending, in a general way, even if it often changed by the time I got there.

However, while writing a recent novel, which has a more action-oriented plot, I used an outline the whole time. It's a very crude outline, in that I took the description in the synopsis and slotted it into a series of chapters, which correspond to the alternating points-of-view of four characters or five characters.

The first parts of the outline and the last parts contained the most detail. When I reached the beginning of the middle portion, I realized I had to flesh out the outline before could I continue, because I was getting good results writing that way.

I've thought about why this approach worked, and it has to do with the shift in emphasis. Yes, I knew what I was going to write about in a chapter ahead of time, so there was less process of discovery in terms of what was going to *happen*. However, I found I could give more thought to *how* and *why* things happened because I already had this outline in place — on some level, I focused more on each scene, and how the scenes fit together. In the process, it changed my thoughts and theories about how to put a novel together.

Having gone through that process, I find that there's relief and a great calming effect in knowing that I can extrapolate ahead of time on the macro level, fill in a certain level of detail, and still find the writing and the actual scene-writing vibrant and exciting. In fact, I used this technique situationally on another novel, applying an outline structure to problem areas.

It's not that I didn't think about all these issues while writing a novel using my old process. However, I do believe that if I can be more organized in advance, without losing that spark of inspiration and the ability to layer in complexity, that there will great benefit to the work I do going forward. Will it be better fiction? Who knows, but the process to get there will be different, and that will make things more interesting. It may also make it easier for me to write, in that I may do even more organized thinking ahead about the writing instead of combining that process with a kind of stop-start on the actual drafting.

Oddly, too, this experience made me think more about the character motivation on the micro level, with the possibility of creating more character variation. Plotwise, it was helpful inasmuch as I find myself thinking even more heavily than before about the character interactions, which is, after all, the point of plot and story. I'm also finding dialogue easier.

Without abandoning my normal process, I would never have entered into this journey of self-discovery. For you, that journey may be the complete opposite: for example, abandoning outlines in favor of something more free-form. Just make sure you try something new from time to time, to make sure you're getting the most out of your processes.

▶▶ Permission to Fail

The eighteenth-century artist and essayist John Ruskin is one of my favorite writers. In particular, I enjoy his defense of ambition and audacity in art, which I read as an admiration for these qualities in creative work generally. Ruskin loves a risk-taker, understands in his gut that perfection can be a signal of a lack of imagination. We have but one life — why devote that life to the attainment of a stifling standard about as exciting as mentally noting a mile marker when we drive by it?

To be great, we must attempt so much that we not only are in danger of forever failing, but that we *do* fail, and in the failure create something greater than if we had set our sights lower. Otherwise, we become what the philosopher Arthur Schopenhauer called creators who "shine moreover only with a borrowed light, and their sphere of influence is limited to their own fellow travelers." As Ruskin writes:

> In the work of man, those which are more perfect in their kind are always inferior to those which are, in their nature, liable to more faults and shortcomings. For the finer the nature, the more flaws it will show through the clearness of it; and it is a law of this universe, that the best things shall be seldomest seen in their best form...

Ruskin came to mind as I sat in the audience a couple of years ago watching my brother Francois graduate from high school. I was thinking about advice, especially during the speeches given by members of the graduating class. These speeches had the ingredients one would expect: hope for great accomplishments in the future, pride at the accomplishments of the past, a gung-ho attitude. Every so often, these platitudes would be infiltrated by advice on dealing with college and the job market. It made me think about what advice I would have wanted as a graduating high school senior.

The term "permission to fail" kept running through my head. Yes, that's what I would have liked coming out of high school. I would have liked permission to fail. In fact, I think it's great advice for writers in general, sometimes even more for intermediate writers who have gained a certain level of success and public praise. (Samuel Beckett: "Fail better.")

J. T. Glover pointed out on my blog that sometimes this advice has mammoth ramifications:

> Lately I've been thinking about Elizabeth Kostova's *The Historian*, which took years to write, is dense and neo-Victorian, and is something that I think very few writers would feel encouraged to try for their first novel, largely for fear of failure. The same thing could be said of Susanna Clarke's *Jonathan Strange & Mr. Norrell*. Both were big, ambitious books, and from a fearful-of-failure standpoint horribly risky. What happens if you spend ten years on a novel, only to find it doesn't work?

All I could think of is how much Kostova and Clarke *learned* while writing those novels — how at times, for whole years, their lives must have revolved around work on their respective novels, and much of everything they did had some relationship to those novels. The risk factor is incredible, and yet even if those two books had never been published, I find it unlikely that either novelist would have said they'd *failed*. The failure would have come from never attempting what had appeared in their imaginations. The failure would have come from thinking *what if I had tried?*

Sometimes you might not have the skill or mastery of technique to pull off certain effects. You might be of a more cautious temperament than other writers so it might take you longer. But that doesn't mean you can't get there. I can only go by reader and reviewer response, but every single time I've had the patience and bravado to jump over the edge into someplace initially terrifying, I've provided people with a read that draws them in, that brings them a unique experience.

One of the things I always loved about the brilliant English writer Angela Carter was her fearlessness. I think she always gave herself permission to fail, and she didn't care. She wouldn't have cared if she'd written ten stories that never saw publication if that got her to a place where she'd be able to write one truly extraordinary piece. Lack of nerve is often the only thing separating talent from its full potential.

In part, having nerve or daring is a matter of simply not limiting your options. (That mad stray thought you immediately put out of your head; that typo that had all kinds of psychological complications before you decided to correct it.) Of not pre-editing yourself into not writing a particular story because you don't think you can pull it off. Of not shying away when it comes to putting painful or personal things into your stories. Of not shying away from the true implications of your scenes and situations.

You know perfectly well when you're not willing to go to the places necessary to make a story truly complete or perfect. It's the kind of "niceness" that makes so many Hollywood movies that start out well end so poorly — the endings don't do justice to the set-up.

It's not a matter of using more daring technique or being shocking just to shock — most definitely not. It's about seeing how far you can go in so many different ways. It's testing your stories and novels by asking yourself: Is that what would have really happened? Might it have gone even farther if you'd let it? It's about giving yourself over to the characters and storyline so that even if you have to write something uncomfortable, you still do it. And all the while, not thinking about the fact that you might completely screw it up — not worrying about your readers or reviewers or anything other than the story.

I would have said to those high school students: Whatever you do from now on, don't feel that it has to always be successful. To be successful, to be as good as you can possibly be in whatever field you choose, you need to feel like you can bungee jump out to the edge of success and into that space where the ropes might break. If you don't, you won't take risks, you won't get out there, to that place with a night sky full of unfamiliar stars where "success" might become either something extraordinary or utter failure...because utter failure and extraordinary accomplishment are conjoined twins most of the time.

Or, put another way, the space between a "publishable" story or novel and a "good" story or novel can be a chasm. This chasm becomes even wider and deeper given the proliferation of online venues for content. Do you want to be good enough or great? Many elements of your journey through a Private Booklife may be beyond your control, but you can make sure you always pushed, hard, for perfection...by being willing to fall flat on your face.

Chapter 2
Protecting Your Booklife

▶▶ Addiction

BOOKLIFE IS NOT a general time management book, but time management, if you haven't guessed already, is a crucial part of having a sustainable career and sustainable creativity. You can function for awhile being inefficient, but you'll never fully capitalize on any success or realize your potential without better organization and prioritizing. Personal technology like cell phones and computers, coupled with Internet addiction and more traditional distractions like television programs and videogames, has created a serious problem of fragmentation because we have so many more ways to distract ourselves than in the past. The same Internet that provides knowledge also obscures or falsifies it, makes all information oddly equal, and further allows others to waste our time for us. As Seneca wrote so long ago:

> The minds of the engrossed, just as if weighted by a yoke, cannot turn and look behind. And so their life vanishes into an abyss; and as it does no good, no matter how much water you pour into a vessel, if there is no bottom to receive and hold it, so with time — it makes no difference how much is given; if there is nothing for it to settle upon, it passes out through the chinks and holes of the mind.

Negative aspects of the Internet and our electronic lives include: being trained in Pavlovian fashion to check our email every five seconds, having our instant messenger up all day, spending hours recording our most minute thoughts on

Facebook or Twitter, and writing on computers where we can be interrupted at any moment. Some of these aspects of a (post)modern life affect our attention span. Others turn perfectly viable *tactics* into an unsupportable and detrimental overall *strategy*.

As a writer, I feel the greatest dangers of the Internet are (1) equating the constant appearance of new information and new correspondence with a requirement to immediately reply/be instantly available and (2) the constant, daily loss of uninterrupted time not only to write but to think about writing. Many writers and others who depend on the Internet find themselves *controlled by* their involvement with the electronic world, without even realizing it. They still think they are in charge, but they are not: their tactics have become their strategy. The electronic world also sucks up time when we, as writers, could be observing the physical world. As Brendan Connell wrote to me in an email recently:

> I think the Internet is in many ways very fun and useful. But for a writer it can be really dangerous. Particularly regarding creative thought, since every moment spent here is one spent away from the creative world. Because the real creative world is one of introspection, reading, seeing things in real life. At least that is the creative world I am interested in. The Internet magnifies in a sense the petty, and I often don't pay enough attention to the amazing things going on in the real world, because we are confined by the digital.

The majority of the ideas, characters, and experiences in our writing come from the real world — it's only our connectivity that comes mostly from the Internet.

Here are some specific symptoms of Internet addiction:

- You sit down to write, and thirty minutes later you find that you're surfing the Internet on your laptop instead of writing.
- You respond instantly, at all hours, to email.
- You tend to treat all demands on your time with the same weight.
- You become irritable and fidgety if you don't have a way to check your email or the Internet.

If this addiction were an addiction to, for example, alcohol, the results would be obvious and the reaction of friends and society corrective. But when it comes to the Internet, we're nearly *all* addicted, and we receive so much instant gratification without understanding or monitoring the attendant dangers that we often do not even realize what we may have lost. If you grew up with the Internet, you may not understand this position, but before you dismiss it, try going a week without being online. See what you gain and what you lose. You might be surprised to find that nothing much happened in the electronic world while you were gone.

Books provide a surprisingly effective antidote to this addiction. The ability to focus on a long, complex book not only provides evidence that your attention span hasn't become too fragmented, but also helps to wean you off your dependency. Other strategies to finding balance include saving non-creative activities for non-peak times and writing in longhand at a location outside your home to avoid the distractions provided by your computer.

In extreme situations, as mentioned previously, my wife Ann had to hide the Internet router box. But my current favorite strategy in my own life is to disconnect my computer from the Internet but still have my cell phone available. I have the Internet and email through the phone, but by separating out the tool I use to write from the one I use to monitor the electronic world, it creates the necessary division for me to get writing done. I leave the phone in the bedroom, work in my office, and even if I wind up checking my email five or six times a day, I have to physically walk from one end of the house to the other. Although this might seem like an artificial solution, it somehow works on a psychological level by the simple act of compartmentalization.

Sometimes, too, the Internet isn't the problem, as the real world provides distractions enough for those who seek them. No matter what the context, you need a certain amount of discipline. Periodically taking stock of whether you've let things slip and become enslaved again to some frivolous meat- or virtual-world master should be part of protecting your Private Booklife.

No one wants a life devoid of fun, though. Recognize that a certain amount of interruption and break-taking helps to keep you sane while you're writing. Just make sure that those interruptions aren't actually *addictions* destroying your Private Booklife.

►► Rejection

You generate rejection from your efforts to live a productive Public Booklife, but rejection pertains to what you produce in your Private Booklife. Rejection thus affects your Private Booklife much more than your Public Booklife, in that I have known writers to stop writing from rejection but never a writer who kept writing but stopped promoting their work because of rejection.

Rejection is a necessary and important part of the process of improving your writing and of toughening you up for a long-term career. I have accumulated over five thousand rejections from editors over the last twenty years. Many of those rejections were painful, but I'm still here. In addition to those rejections, I've won awards, had books out from major publishers, been published extensively overseas, and in general created a space for myself as a mid-list writer of note.

However, rejection takes many forms. I've also been rejected by other writers and by reviewers. A nasty email from a writer you admire or a bad notice from a reader are both a kind of rejection. The hurt from both can feel the same as the more standard definition of rejection as originating from an editor or other gatekeeper.

Some writers can put all of this rejection into perspective and others cannot. Unique individuals like Alan Thomas, have a different take entirely:

> I think one needs rejection (writers included) to remind him/her that the lens through which one sees the world is singularly unique, and therefore not always understood by others. This is precisely why one should tirelessly continue to explore his/her perspective, and to make an effort to express this perspective through some form of creative articulation. To do this effectively is to construct a bridge that can unite two seemingly disparate realms of perception.

I'd never thought of rejection in those terms before, and I find the analysis and distance in Thomas' point of view admirable. Still, few of us, being human and thus subject to a thousand insecurities and foibles, will be able to remain this contented in the face of rejection. Here, then, are a few things to remember when trying to put rejection in perspective.

■ From Other Writers

Despite the inroads of new media on traditional hierarchies, writers still think in terms of pecking order. A new writer approached by someone higher up in that order may feel the need to puff out his or her chest. A writer approached by a peer may feel territorial and perhaps even threatened by the perceived success of the other. An older, well-established writer may be on the downswing and bitter about it, or simply impatient with greenhorns.

In contacting the writer you may have violated some protocol of professional communication — or made some assumption or given some unintentional insult. The writer may simply be very busy. You may have caught him or her at a bad time. Their personal life might be falling apart. They might have received terrible news minutes before replying to your letter or email.

There are many reasons to forgive rudeness and rejection from a fellow writer. It's important to try to forgive because *you* may one day be in the same position.

Although most people won't admit it, the main reason that new writers seek out established writers they look up to is for external validation. Surface reasons like "I really want a blurb" may be legitimate, but they're not usually the whole truth. Sadly, though, this kind of validation doesn't exist, and even if it did would be meaningless. But, in this context just about any comment from the writer being contacted that isn't entirely positive can cause pain in the recipient.

Sometimes, too, the person you're contacting is just a bastard. One of my first contacts with a writer came through email. I contacted one of my heroes and asked if he'd consider blurbing my first book. He wrote back that based on the title of my book all I was doing was copying his own work and to come back in twenty years when I'd established my own identity.

What I should have done is laughed at the rudeness and the presumption. What I did instead is fall to pieces. I shouldn't have given him the satisfaction. I should have recognized that this response reflected either an underlying meanness or some kind of situational stress. Indeed, in later years, I've corresponded with this person several times. While we're not best friends, we are at least cordial to one another.

If you can recognize that the ranks of writers are filled with cranks, curmudgeons, and the mentally insane it will go a long way toward dulling the sting when a writer you admire turns on you like a rogue bull elephant.

◼ From Editors

Editors are overworked and underpaid, for the most part. They spend long hours reading crappy manuscripts from people they don't know, and it is some of the most mind-numbing work in the world. If this makes them cranky every once in awhile, that's understandable. If they misdiagnose in their rejections, this too is understandable.

Having been an editor on and off for two decades, I can tell you something else as well: an editor is a gatekeeper to a form of publication, not your personal creative writing instructor. Rejection from an editor tells you that a particular person at a particular publishing house, magazine, website, blog, or other platform could not use your work. Even if a rejection is particularly vicious, this still holds true. The only way in which a rejection speaks to a wider problem with your story or novel is if you have received more than thirty or forty rejections with no positive news in any of them. At that point, you may want to consider revision or more drastic measures. (Keeping in mind that some of the world's most famous manuscripts suffered hundreds of rejections.)

You *will* receive some good information from editors in rejection, and there is no greater gift to a writer than a personal rejection containing commonsense advice from a source that has otherwise only given rote responses. However, this is still a rare occurrence.

A rejection is also a way of overcoming inertia. Receiving a rejection is an editor's way of giving their blessing for you to send your writing elsewhere. Now it can re-enter the flow of manuscripts being sent to editors all over the world. I say this somewhat tongue-in-cheek, but also in recognition that the only thing worse than a rejection is an editor holding onto a story for six months or a year and *then* rejecting it.

If you can hold yourself far enough above the fray to take editorial rejection as a kind of closure that liberates you for the next opportunity, you will be a much happier person. Still, if you continue to be unduly affected by types of editorial rejection, seriously consider having people like your partner, your agent, or other third-party help shield you from it whenever possible.

■ From Reviewers

You'd think that once your book or other creative project has made it out into the world it would be accorded the respect you think it deserves. Alas, the opposite is often true. If editors are overworked and underpaid, then reviewers are often in even worse shape: overwhelmed by torrents of books, paid little, accorded less respect, and sometimes outright reviled by the very people they tend to love (although it's not always clear, that would be *writers*). Reviewers, being human, have all of the same foibles as the rest of us. Reviewing is also like every other field, including writing: ninety percent of professionals are mediocre at what they do. That you may also be mediocre is beside the point in this context.

You will definitely receive bad reviews during your career. You will receive stupid reviews by people who like the book (some of them might even be by me). You will receive reviews meant to stick a knife through your ribs. You will receive reviews that passively-aggressively take you apart while seeming to praise. You will receive reviews by frustrated writers who are looking to make their own reputation on the back of yours. (A book about reviewing by reviewers would probably have a different point of view...)

At various lucky times in your career, you will also be blessed with a multitude of reviews by people who understand what you were trying to do *and* appreciate it. Cherish those reviews and those reviewers. Understand, too, that words of praise are as ephemeral and soon forgotten as words of blame. Many a book or other project has been lambasted and torn apart upon its first appearance on the stage, only to take its final bow to thunderous applause. (For more on book reviewing, refer to the appendices.)

Still, you may need tools to help you bear the sting of a bad review. In such cases, I recommend Jonathan Swift's radical and hilarious *A Tale of a Tub,* the best part of which is "A Digression Concerning Critics," every word of which applies to our modern world, especially in this frontier age of "intertubes," "blogospheres," and both the softening and roughening of published opinion.

Swift identifies several kinds of critic, their uses, and their associations down through the ages. One amazing description after another creeps up on the reader in this bestiary, including that of the critic as a serpent "that wants teeth, and consequently cannot bite; but if its vomit, to which it is much addicted, happens to fall upon anything, a certain rottenness or corruption ensues; these serpents are generally found among the mountains where jewels grow, and they frequently emit a poisonous juice: whereof whoever drinks, that person's brains fly out of his nostrils."

By the time Swift had reached a rhetorical crescendo dealing with asses, I quite frankly had lost all semblance of analytical reading and was cackling: "whereas all other ASSES wanted a gall, these horned ones were so redundant in that part, that their flesh was not to be eaten, because of its extreme bitterness."

I keep those quotes near my desk and read them whenever I need a laugh — and especially whenever I've suffered a rejection. Not only does it soothe the sting, but it usually stops me from responding to the reviewer or commenting publicly about the review on my blog or elsewhere.

Generally, any response to a review is a mistake. However, a blanket no-response rule may also be a mistake in our current era of transparency and degenerating hierarchies. You may, for example, want to respond if a reviewer has made an error of fact, in keeping with the idea of promoting accuracy on the Internet, as discussed in Public Booklife. You may even ask a friend to perform this function for you, as a correction by a third-party makes the point without exposing you to criticism.

■ ■ ■

In all of these scenarios, there's little to do except to keep busy if you're hit hard by a particular type of rejection. Work, with its promise of acceptance, is a strong antidote. Knowing you're not alone, and that every writer has experienced these forms of rejection, should help, too. I can also confirm that the person you think is a roadblock or adversary today might be your friend tomorrow. A negative, somewhat searing review I once wrote resulted in a friendship that lasts to this day.

Finally, no one can tell you that you won't accumulate scar tissue in pursuing a productive Private Booklife, but I can tell you it becomes less and less important over time.

▶▶ Envy

Envy is a subject of intense interest to writers (or, really, driven, creative people in any profession) because it has been known to curdle careers and twist older creators into a kind of rigor mortis of bitterness. Thoughts of *might-have-beens* cross-pollinate with a sense of entitlement, and suddenly anyone getting more attention is a creep, a thug, a soul-sucking light-stealer leaving you in shadow. And, just as electronic media have made it possible to access a blinding stream of information in seconds, so too these tools have left writers more susceptible to envy. Today you can easily discover the unpardonable triumphs of your colleagues, across platforms, across tools, across time.

■ The Many Faces of Envy

To anyone in the position of being envious, I highly recommend the eighteenth-century philosopher Francis Bacon's thoughts on the subject in his essay "Of Envy." In a short space he manages to analyze envy from many different angles.

Bacon allies envy with love — "love and envy do make a man pine" — using the following argument: "They both have vehement wishes; they frame themselves readily into imaginations and suggestions; and they come easily to the eye, especially upon the presence of the objects: which are the points that conduce to fascination, if any such thing there be."

I especially like how Bacon continues this exploration of envy and the eye, noting that in scripture envy is called an evil eye, and that astrologers call "the evil influence of the stars evil aspects, so that still there seemeth to be acknowledged, in the act of envy, an ejaculation or irradiation of the eye." It's not much of a leap, then, to think of envy as a kind of vanity: what we most want to be is embodied in others, whom we would love as if kin, if only they *were* us. Envy is an evil that seems to feast upon others, but instead feasts upon the one who envies, much like vanity.

Another good point made by Bacon concerns those of us who are jacks-of-all-trades (because most of us have to be): "They that excel in too many matters...are ever envious. For they cannot want work, it being impossible, but many in some one of those things should surpass them." Thus, the book reviewer working on a novel who envies the full-on novelist. Or the novelist who dabbles in short stories and reviews and cannot understand why the attention for each is not equal. Or the short story writer who, with a titanic effort, manages a novel every ten years and in the interim grumbles about how the short story is underappreciated in the current literary climate. And so on and so forth, all with an undercurrent, an implied *subject*: "Except for *that person,* who gets all the attention."

Bacon also explores the effects of time on envy: "It is to be noted that unworthy persons are most envied at their first coming in, and afterwards overcome it better; whereas, contrariwise, persons of worth and merit are most envied when their fortune continueth long. For by that time, though their virtue be the same, yet it hath not the same lustre, for fresh men grow up that darken it."

Because of new media, this process of establishing and fortifying a career can occur in weeks or months, exacerbating the situation. Even though this is just a side effect of having easy access to information, that doesn't mean that the psychological reaction of gatekeepers and other stakeholders has kept pace with this kind of acceleration. Besides, in any context, appreciation for an intruder who appears not to have paid his/her dues or who simply, in the opinion of the observing eye, does not have talent equal to the praise given to it is unlikely (and yet, precisely because information travels so fast these days, we have more of both types).

For this reason, however, the longer this "unworthy person" retains the public eye, so too does the "envy" expressed toward the person begin to falter — in part because, as with love and lust, it cannot be sustained; in part because a new outlier will soon enough come along; and in part because the subject of this scrutiny does, because he or she gains experience, become more worthy. Perceived envy is sometimes simply an expression of an honest eye that cannot tolerate the unfairness of life.

Envy is like a great dysfunctional circle of life among those who cannot overcome their attraction to this debased emotion. The elder eyes with distrust the greenhorn and the greenhorn wants now what cannot be until later. Unchecked, envy will feast upon your Private Booklife like a kind of fungus, manifesting in your Public Booklife in unseemly ways.

But envy isn't just projected *out*, it's also projected *toward*. As you become more successful, you will find others envying you. To blunt that evil eye upon you, Bacon gives good advice, counseling that the wise man will ever bemoan "what a life they lead, chanting a *quanta patimur* [how many things we suffer!]. Not that they feel it so, but only to abate the edge of envy." Bacon further observes that "…nothing increaseth envy more than an unnecessary and ambitious engrossing of business. And nothing doth extinguish envy more than for a great person to preserve all other inferior officers in their full rights and pre-eminences of their places. For by that means there be so many screens between him and envy." Note that Bacon in no way places blame for envy upon the *recipient* of envy, only advises that those in the public eye make provisions for dulling, blunting, or deflecting it, inasmuch as it may *harm* the recipient.

■ Difficult Solutions

Like the open channels mentioned in the Gut-Check section, envy is hard to close down. Bacon writes, "…there is no other cure of envy but the cure of witchcraft; and that is, to remove the lot (as they call it) and to lay it upon another. For which purpose, the wiser sort of great persons bring in ever upon the stage somebody upon whom to derive the envy that would come upon themselves." Envy is like a sliver, driven deep. Better, then, as in certain types of voodoo, to transport that curse to another. Make a kind of scarecrow née figurehead: something sturdy that might better withstand the scrutiny, and leave the object of envy free of it.

But Bacon is also saying envy expresses a perverse feeling of helplessness: an acknowledgment of our inability to control what we could never control anyway. The only true balm is to tend to our own work, our own business, and to be as sound and honest in it as we can be — and as for others, to treat them with love and affection, recognizing that what we may see of them in our eye, they too may see of us in theirs. Recognizing that the fortunes of our fellow travelers rise and fall as do our own — knowing that we are bound in a brotherhood and sisterhood of envy — may remove the sting of the sliver when it enters, and when it exits.

But to truly protect against envy, I must suggest a corrective that may seem to contradict advice elsewhere in *Booklife*: the busy and inquisitive would be well advised to create blinders for themselves while online: shut down instant messenger, delete your blog favorites list, do not Google yourself, and most definitely *do not* Google those whom you envy. Otherwise, the reflection upon your eye may be like a nascent tumor that will only grow, dilating outward until there is nothing that you see of the world not tinged by envy. "For envy is a gadding passion," Bacon notes, "and walketh the streets, and doth not keep home." Nor does envy "take holidays." However, if you take a holiday from media that drive you nuts by emphasizing the successes of others, you can escape envy for awhile. Otherwise, you may end up living in the final dark night of the soul for the envious: actively rooting for the misery of others, and monitoring it online!

▶▶ Despair

Despair is a companion who keeps coming back to you no matter how far you've traveled along the path toward a sustainable Booklife. Things go wrong. What you have visualized does not come to pass. That opportunity you thought you had turns to dust. This is most difficult for beginning writers. If you have not yet held your own book in your hands, despair over the here-and-now can seem like it will last an eternity. You walk into the bookstore and your book is not there, will never be there, no matter how much you want it to be there. (Cue: violins and videos of endless rain.)

But it's important to know that even widely published writers experience despair, too. The setback that threatens a whole career. The sense of being so close to something major, which then recedes, like some amazing deep-sea creature glimpsed for just a moment through the murk. Granted, a writer with a few published books has perspective. That writer knows, if they think about it, that the despair one feels today can turn to triumph in a month or a year or a decade. Sometimes, too, it is more satisfying when it comes to you later. Sometimes, despair is the vanguard of great success.

A former student and a fine writer, Catherine Cheek, has this to say about despair:

> Me and despair are old drinking buddies, seeing as how I'm working on my twelfth novel manuscript and still trying to sell the first one. Every once in a while I start to wonder why the heck I'm wasting my time writing books no one will read.

Catherine is still writing, and having success, but sometimes that wondering turns into something bleaker. Last year, a friend — a writer with novels out from major publishers and with excellent reviews in, among others, *The New Yorker* — decided to pack it in and stop writing because of poor sales and problems with an agent.

This writer withdrew their latest novel from consideration by an agent (and, really, a publisher) and in essence said, "I relinquish my career." This is not exactly the same as giving up. It is, instead, *giving in*. I say this because a career is something that requires constant maintenance and attention, so when you acknowledge the prevailing inertia — which is almost always working against you — and simply stop doing the things required to have a career, it is more like giving in than giving up.

What do you say to a person in this kind of situation? Nothing external will really carry enough weight. Everyone's breaking point is different, and when someone does reach a breaking point, sometimes you have to respect it. I've had my heart broken many times, including early in my career when my first short story collection never saw print for a number of bizarre reasons. Sometimes that sense of success being taken away just as you're about to taste it is worse than never having gotten close at all.

Jim Hines, a humorous fantasist, related to me that:

> The worst despair moment for me was having an offer on the table from a major publisher back in 2005 then having the publisher withdraw the offer. That book eventually found a home, as you know, but that episode knocked me down hard.

The fact is that although a fair percentage of writers whine about the hardships they encounter, most whine in the same way one does about cafeteria food while in college: with a hint of secret satisfaction. You're living the life you want to live, and any deprivation involved is as much a sign and symbol of your choice as is success.

But the writing life *is* hard, and it *is* a constant struggle to keep the engine running, to make progress, often in the face of random cruelty, stupidity, incompetence, and indifference. You get scar tissue. You get paranoid at times. You forget that the deal you think is make-or-break important, the situation that must go your way, is only part of the journey. (Usually, there's another deal, another break, out there.)

Above all, you make yourself vulnerable in many different ways, even if you don't show this to many other people. Letting go of all of this can be a relief or a release, even if it means giving in, or, even, giving up something, or part of something, that you love.

For those who weren't born into the writing life — like my friend — it's even tougher. If you grow up writing and you start submitting in your teens, you develop a very thick skin. You are still vulnerable and you are still susceptible to the same frustrations, paranoia, envy, and everything else that comes with the territory. But you tend to bounce back faster.

If you only come to the writing life later, you don't have that protection. You don't have that extra layer of resilience, in that context. This also applies to many of what I term "fast risers" — the kind of writer whose first book or first series of stories achieves a kind of critical mass in reviewers' and/or readers' minds. Some of these writers, too, have problems later on, if they find themselves in any kind of difficulty. They just aren't at first mentally prepared for it. Some of these people could climb mountains or hike thirty miles through thigh-high snow without blinking an eye, but in the context of the writer's life still do not have the necessary armor. The situation has a somewhat similar boxing parallel: Mike Tyson, who had never had any tough fights in his initial string of knockout victories, was never the same after he finally faced adversity against Buster Douglas, one fateful night in Japan.

Anyway, my writer friend clearly needed a break, and took it. At first, I had a hard time with this decision, and probably added to the problem by trying to find solutions that didn't address the central question of why this person wanted out. Eventually, I stopped and thought about what I was doing, and I finally figured out *why* I had taken it so personally: because I was afraid I might come to a similar crossroads, and that I might make the same decision. Once I realized that, I was able to forgive my friend and be more constructively supportive.

Another important point, which came up in conversation with Tessa Kum, whom I've quoted elsewhere in this book, concerns the fact that, as she puts it, "Despair is not clean. Returning to writing is not necessarily a happy ending. Discovering what is right for you is a better ending." A tumultuous relationship with writing doesn't mean you shouldn't be a writer, but if the decision "not to write gives you exactly no regret, then so be it. You tried, and now you know for sure."

For Tessa, as for many others, wrestling with this issue speaks to a question of identity:

I despaired once so hard I decided I wasn't a writer and I wasn't going to write anymore. Which made the situation worse, because I didn't know what else I was, and could think of nothing else to turn myself into. Because writing isn't a label, it's the same as having a kidney — it just is. Having confronted that, I'm more comfortable.

Thus the echo of "writers can't not write," and thus many stories of despair have happy endings one way or the other: either you recognize you really have no choice and you continue, or you find relief and purpose in abandoning that which wasn't as central to your life as you thought.

As for my friend the novelist who had given up — she couldn't really get away from writing in the end. Even after saying she wasn't going to write anymore, she started working on nonfiction and short stories. Eventually, she found herself working on and completing a new novel, for which she has found a publisher.

Jim's story, meanwhile, turned from despair into career success:

I'm sure the business will kick my butt again over the years, but...it helps a lot once you finally get a book or three out there. For me, it provides a certain level of validation that wasn't there before. No matter what happens, I know now that I can write a publishable book and sell it. Even if I have to reboot my career as Happy J. Bobswaggler, I still know I can do this.

As for Catherine, who now has an agent and has sold several short stories to prominent publications, she knows why she keeps writing:

This weekend I reread some of my old stuff and spent three days in a click trance poring over novels I finished in '06 and '07. It was so great to spend time with old friends that I feel recharged. It was like, "Oh yeah, that's why I started doing this. Because it's fun!"

Although not always easy, the writing life usually *does* reward talent and perseverance to some degree. But, at core, especially if everything goes to hell career-wise, you have to ask yourself one question that speaks directly to despair: *Is my Private Booklife about my expectations of success or is it about the work?*

▶▶ Revitalizing Creativity

Sometimes, no matter your best efforts, you'll find yourself stuck in a rut, bored with your work and yourself. At such times, here are a few techniques that may nudge or jolt you out of that mood.

• REVERSE OUTLINING. Many writers hate the idea of using outlines for novels or other books. The reasoning is that, yes, you need to know where you're going, but if you know too much, it's not interesting to write, and you are too bound by what you've written in the outline. Although I do outlines for some novels, I came to novels by an organic process of writing longer and longer stories, and it felt like to maintain a natural writing method I should continue to leap off into the unknown. Still, even back then I outlined every novel: I just waited until I'd finished the rough draft. At that point, I created an outline from what I had on the page, and you can do the same. Wherever there's a rib missing, I know there's something missing. Wherever there's a second tail or a fifth leg, I know I've kept something in that needs to be amputated. Eventually, through reverse outlining you come to know the true shape of the creature that is your novel. (Sometimes you'll actually keep that second tail.)

• CONSCIOUS INPUT FOR SUBCONSCIOUS OUTPUT. If you're stuck on your latest creative project, consider putting it aside for a day. Do nothing creative on that day, but prime your mind for the answer by thinking about every aspect of the problem. At the same time, even though it sounds counterintuitive, keep trying to distract yourself from the answer by living in the moment. Physical activities, including hiking, are great for this purpose — anything that requires your full attention. Then, right before you go to bed, tell yourself you'll have the answer in the morning. While it doesn't always work, you'll be surprised at how many times you wake up with the answer in your head.

• RE-IMAGINE THE CONTEXT. If you need to see a particular creative project in a different way, consider re-imagining its context. There are physical ways to do this and more radical ways. For example, change the font and the font size. Read and record your writing and listen to the results. Have others read it aloud to you. Rewrite a chapter of your novel from memory and compare the two versions. If you want to be more radical, transform parts of the project into something else. If you're having problems with a character, write a version of the character as if he or she were actually an animal — a refugee from an ancient bestiary, a relic of cryptozoology. What would the person be like as an animal? Then translate the character back from animal into person. Or, take a scene and re-imagine it as the act in a stage play, forcing you to add more dialogue and take out description. Any way in which you can change the context will recharge your creativity by presenting your mind with a different problem than the one it had before.

• **INTRODUCE A CONSTRAINT.** Although similar to re-imagining the context, the introduction of a constraint has a slightly different application. It forces you to work within a boundary, and by staying within that boundary find new opportunities. For example, take a problem part of your text and ban the letter "t" or "a" from it. See if you can reconstruct the text and have it roughly mean the same without using that letter. In forcing your mind to perform this exercise, you often hit upon a new path out of your problem.

I also highly recommend any book of surrealist or Oulipo games, some of which mimic the techniques set out above. The Surrealists, with their battle cry of "beauty in the service of liberty," tried to surprise the mind into creativity through use of the unexpected, and unexpected juxtapositions. The Oulipo movement, popular in France in the 1960s, tried to use mathematical equations and limitations to get to the same place as the surrealists. Either way, getting out of your comfort zone, challenging your mind with something new, will tend to recharge the creativity in your Private Booklife.

▶▶ Success

Success can be as difficult for a writer as managing feelings of despair at not being successful. For one thing, if your goal was to publish a novel with a major commercial publisher and you've suddenly achieved that goal after years of work...what do you do next? You may not have thought past that point, and thus feel at loose ends, drifting, at the very moment when most people think you should be celebrating. Or, you may have spent so much time expecting the worst and having to push up against gatekeepers and other obstacles...that the lack of an obstacle makes you stumble. You literally don't know what to do without an obstacle in your path. It throws off your balance. Finally, success may go to your head and you may behave like a coked-up rock star for a few months, until reality hits you in the face.

One child prodigy I know had four novels out from Bantam by her early twenties but by the age of twenty-five had literally joined a circus and disappeared into Eastern Europe, never to return — as an author, at least. Another writer achieved great commercial success at the expense of mental health, ever more erratic in emails and face-to-face meetings, and eventually became a recluse. A third writer got a huge deal for three books and, with his day job as an anchor, proceeded to adopt an arrogant (can I say "dickish" in a book?) attitude, and blow almost all of the money on clothes, books, travel, and thirteen pairs of very expensive shoes.

Failure's easy — wrecking your life, not living up to your talent, can be accomplished painlessly over years, or even over the course of an afternoon if you really put your mind to it. But once you're successful, you have real problems: expectations put on you, readers who correspond with you, and responsibilities you could never even imagine while you were typing away in your tiny office, certain no one would ever read your words even as you hoped the opposite would be true.

Even a modicum of success can throw you off of your game, especially if there's an unfair niggling little voice in the back of your head saying you don't deserve it. Success is a form of praise, and praise can be hard to take, because it requires acknowledging a form of love. We're generally not good with love, or being as generous to ourselves as we're told to be to others.

Here are some of the possible untoward *results,* of success, sudden or otherwise:

- You quixotically quit your day job based on having won a lottery that you may never win again — namely, the big book advance — and run out of money within a couple of years. (Crawling back is much, much worse than never having left, or going part-time and gradually phasing out the day job once you're assured of future writing income.)
- You turn into a horrible human being, a premature midlife crisis induced by your sudden change in status, and when you wake up from this delusion, you find the wreckage of your life all around you like an airplane's burning fuselage. (In this case, you will probably have lost the affection of friends and family members, and possibly even the love of your spouse or partner.)
- You have trouble writing your second book because you're too enamored of your own work, or because you've listened too closely to book reviewers or fans, relinquishing your vision in favor of a belief in theirs.
- You never write another book because you discover you don't like everything that goes with having an actual career.

Can you avoid these outcomes? Of course — you may be the type of personality that is resistant to all the dangers of success; I don't mean to suggest these scenarios are inevitable, or even likely. But if you are susceptible, you probably won't avoid problems because of reading these words in *Booklife,* although possibly you can limit their impact.

Alas, success is an emotional rather than intellectual experience. No matter what counsel I give you, you may still get the bends trying to adjust to success. All I can advise is that when success comes, try not to make any sudden changes in your life. Try, no matter how hard it might be, to simply enjoy it and incorporate it into your existing paradigm.

As for me, I was the jerk with thirteen pairs of shoes. They still stare at me from the closet, a Greek chorus shouting "idiot!" every time I walk past them.

▶▶ Support from Your Partner

Writing is a solitary activity, but you need to have some kind of moral support or it can become a lonely activity. I'm lucky in that my wife Ann is my partner in editing projects, my first reader for books, and loves my work — yet she still has the distance to give me honest feedback. Because she isn't also a fiction writer, there's no tension between rival careers, the kind of dynamic that's especially destructive when one writer's career is going strong and the other's is entering a decaying orbit.

But support comes in many forms. It might come from friends and family instead, whether or not you're in a committed relationship. It might be less proactive, as in the case of a partner who believes in your effort and helps you find time for it. In one case, a friend's husband supported her for over fifteen years, believing in her even if he didn't always care for her work. One day, after hundreds of rejections, she not only got a book deal, she won a literary award with a huge cash prize, received offers for publication in foreign language editions, and now provides most of the income for their family. Without her husband's belief in her, she might never have gotten to that point.

Only one situation is intolerable for the health of your Private Booklife: to have a partner who either passive-aggressively or actively doesn't support you — doesn't support you or the work. I know several people in relationships like that and, inevitably, if the person is serious about pursuing their goals, they find someone else to support them emotionally (or they quit writing). In a sense, they have an emotional affair with another person — someone who better appreciates their writing and their goals.

In his book *Word Work*, award-winning writer Bruce Holland Rogers has done a great job of identifying the six main areas in which a partnership can hurt or help a writer: Identity, Work Habits, Play Habits, Audience, Blame, and Gender Roles. I haven't found any better description of the dynamics of support in a relationship between a writer and his or her partner. Here's a summary of his analysis of these six areas:

• IDENTITY. A partner can either help confirm or deny your identity as a writer. A partner who tends to agree with the view of the wider world that your dream is futile or impractical (or, worse, ridiculous) helps to erode your identity as a writer. A partner who confirms that identity helps you to create a separate reality in which you *are* a writer. This also creates a positive physical space in the home for your writing.

• **WORK HABITS.** Your partner should be respectful of your personal space — not, for example, forever tidying piles of material that may look like a mess but constitute the organic progress of a book for some people. In addition, you may have odd habits, like stopping in mid-sentence to write down a sudden idea or image. Ideally your partner will try to understand this behavior and not take it personally or think of it as rudeness. It's an essential part of many writers' process. (Nor, however, should you feign a certain amount of eccentricity to get out of responsibilities.)

• **PLAY HABITS.** A vital element of stimulating the imagination is play, which means writers can be pretty silly sometimes. A partner who doesn't engage in reciprocal play with you may actually be stifling your ability to recharge your imaginative batteries. At the very least, reacting negatively to a playful situation will make it harder for you to be creative over time — especially if that sense of play involves sex.

• **AUDIENCE.** You must be understanding of partners who do not want the role of reading and responding to your work. Although there's a great temptation to want your partner to be your first reader, not all people are suited to this job. Don't force the issue, especially in a situation where the partner is otherwise supportive.

• **BLAME.** You shouldn't blame your own creative frustration on your partner. Partners often sacrifice as much as the writer for the writer to have the space and time to be creative. Blaming your partner for your problems isn't just wrong, it's unjust.

• **GENDER ROLES.** Your relationship with a partner should acknowledge the unique stressors pursuing a creative dream can put on the division of labor in a household. Unfortunately, many homes still assign certain roles to women and other roles to men. Male writers in particular can unwittingly take advantage of that traditional division of labor to find time to be creative at the expense of their partner's time and effort. Without a frank discussion of roles within the household, and finding a realistic balance that benefits both parties, someone will eventually be simmering with resentment, and communication will deteriorate. As one female writer who wished to remain anonymous put it in an email to me:

> [The significance of sacrifice is] wrapped up for me in the stress/struggle I have as a female writer, on the losing end of gender expectations. There are a number of things I always felt like I should do: cook healthy meals, exercise, keep the house clean for me and my significant other, remember my friends' and family's birthdays, be there for my five younger siblings whenever they need me, etc. Yet I'm constantly aware of the fact that all the time I spend on those good things is time that I'm not writing. I constantly feel guilty — either guilty because I'm not writing, or guilty because I'm not keeping up with the tasks mentioned above. I think women are probably more prone to that feeling of guilt and personal failing than men, though perhaps that's just a stereotype.

This last issue, of gender roles, speaks to another issue, as well: the value of self-sufficiency. No matter how much support you receive, there's something solitary at the heart of being a writer, and you alone are responsible for making the decisions that nurture and support your creative life. There can be a liberating quality in recognizing this fact. As Tessa Kum puts it, "I'm flying solo in every sense of the word. No one does the dishes. No one requires my time. No one tells me what I can and can't do. Every good and great and kind thing a partner might do for me, I do for myself. Every harsh and horrible and crippling thing a partner might do for me, I do for myself."

▶▶ The Long View

A writer's career can last many decades, and the ephemeral quality of the current moment is exactly that. There is always the next story, the next book, the next narrative — what slips through the hands now comes back willingly later — even if we don't always believe that in our hearts. Every book also has two lives: that heat-signature descent from thought to publication and reaction, like a meteor encountering atmosphere, and a second life after the dust has settled from the impact. A wise writer will remember this, take the long view, and not sink into despair if at first their book plinks to the ground with all the raging force of a penny dropped from a torn pocket.

Remember Francis Bacon on envy? In another essay, "Of Revenge," Bacon writes, "This is certain, that a man who studieth revenge keeps his own wounds green, which otherwise would heal and do well." All of the base emotions are tied to the short view. These emotions not only keep wounds green, they also burn your time and your energy. They keep you from your work, or burrow into the work, causing great damage.

Granted, part of taking the long view is a matter of experience. I am a more patient man now than I was at twenty. Hopefully I will be more patient still at fifty. But, there's another way to approach it, too.

Whenever I'm at the end of either writing a book or a tough, long campaign for a book I've written or edited, I begin to turn away from it — it's just a husk, a skeleton, dry and brittle — and I turn toward this kind of space that is not yet filled or complete. It's dark around the edges. It might contain a horizon, or it might just be a field of stars. There's a sense of something coming down from above, from a distance, at a great speed, but so far away that even if I saw what it was it would appear to be moving slowly. I can sense the need to become receptive to what's coming. That focus on the work that's coming often allows me to pull back and look at the world with the perspective I need to make better creative decisions.

No matter how you do it, if you can somehow find the ability to zoom back and put every situation in its maximum perspective, you will find your life immeasurably enriched and you will be positioning yourself for a successful Private Booklife.

APPENDICES

▶▶ A Note on the Appendices

I have created the appendices to address issues that aren't dealt with in the main text, like choosing an agent, and topics touched on but not discussed in depth in the main text, like the difference between marketing and publicity. In several cases, including such information in the main text would have weakened or needlessly complicated the narrative.

Some of these pieces are written by other people whom I consider experts on the topic; any text not by me is so attributed in the titles. For example, I invited Matt Staggs to contribute some of his expertise with new media to give you advice tangential to the Public Booklife sections but still important to them. I've also commissioned a couple of essays on topics like "Chasing Experience" and "Luck's Child" that I think are important to your Private Booklife, but which other people were better qualified to address.

My hope is that this material helps to fill any gaps, and I foresee adding appendix material to future editions of *Booklife*.

Appendix A
Additional Information on Relevant Roles

▶▶ Agents

THE ROLE OF the agent in a writer's life is ever-changing. One day the agent is negotiating a contract for a writer. Another day the agent is providing career advice or helping to edit a manuscript.

Unfortunately, some writers view this relationship with suspicion, and enter into contract with agents already irritated that that person is taking fifteen percent (the standard percentage). Anyone who doesn't understand that having an agent allows you to get twenty to twenty-five percent more than you would otherwise doesn't understand the value of a good agent. They also don't understand that when you have a good agent, you're a team. It's both of you against the cold, cruel publishing world.

Because of the shifting nature of the agent's role combined with the fact that you are hopefully picking an agent for life, figuring out which agents to approach and which not to approach is essential to the health of your Public and Private Booklife. My current agent is Howard Morhaim, founder of the Morhaim Literary Agency. In part, what I've learned about agents has come from him and my interaction with him. For example:

- The wrong agent or a bad agent is worse than having no agent at all. Your agent is a reflection on you, and an incompetent agent makes you look like an idiot to editors and publishers. The wrong agent, by contrast, probably just won't get you a deal. Case in point: an early agent for my other ultra-violent novel *Veniss Underground*, I found out later, specialized in selling children's books!

- It's fine to look at the guides to what agents are out there, but some of the best agents don't really advertise. Even with information on the Internet, nothing beats personal testimonials. The best advice I got with regard to agents was to look around at writers whose books and careers I admired — ones who I thought I could emulate careerwise — and then ask those writers who their agents were, and if they'd recommend them.
- The qualities your agent possesses reflect on your reputation in your Public Booklife. I like Howard and consider him not just a friend but my best advisor because he always tells it to me like it is, but if I don't take his advice he still supports me to the hilt. I feel like I don't just have an agent, but I have someone whose word is his bond, someone *I'm* willing to go to bat for (and, in fact, some of Howard's current clients were referred to him by me). Four of the qualities I most value are honesty, integrity, a kind of bulldog tenacity, and the ability to get things done. Howard has all of those qualities.
- The persona projected by your agent reflects on your Public Booklife. Howard has charm and dresses nicely. If your agent looks like he's just out of high school, wears loud clothes, and puts more product in his hair than a rock band, remember, once again, that this person is your "persona" interfacing with the publisher. If that's the image you want to project, that's great. If not, then that's not the person you want.
- The talents of your agent must be the talents you personally need from him or her. If you don't want career advice, just someone to negotiate contracts, make sure the agent you sign with has that talent. If you want your agent to also be an editor of your work, make sure your agent has that talent.
- Where your agent lives and works can make a difference in his or her approach to selling your work. Your agent may or may not live in New York City. If your agent doesn't have a presence in New York City, it's not as important as before the rise of the Internet. However, in certain situations it may be important to have an agent able to sit down at a moment's notice with a potential buyer of your novel somewhere in Manhattan. On the other hand, New York agents can be out of touch with major West Coast publishers — one of my favorite agents, Sally Harding, lives in Vancouver, British Columbia.
- On a more specific but important topic: Your agent will either want to cede foreign rights to the English-language publisher or sell them directly

to foreign publishers through a network of sub-agents. Writers split on this issue, but I prefer an agent like Howard, who has an extensive network of sub-agents all over the world. Selling those rights individually rather than ceding those rights to your English-language publisher(s) is much more lucrative, and generally a more proactive situation. While your English-language publisher may have contacts overseas, they're not as likely to auction off the rights to the highest bidder as sell the rights to their "affiliate," and a lot of times they just wait for offers to come to them, rather than pursue deals. (In addition, Howard's transparency regarding foreign interest has led to subsidiary benefits in the form of short stories and other non-novel writing sold, even to foreign editors who didn't wind up acquiring rights to a book.)

To give you a wide variety of perspectives on this subject, I asked my agent and several other agents with various levels of experience and different types of clients to answer a few questions relevant to the subject. *Please note that these agents may or may not be closed to submissions.* Here's some information on each participant:

• **STEPHEN BARBARA** worked as a contracts director at the Donald Maas Literary agent before joining Foundry as a full agent in January of 2009. He represents all categories of books for young readers in addition to servicing writers for the adult market. His clients include acclaimed middle-grade novelist Lynne Jonell, noir novelist Paul Tremblay, and leading fat loss expert Tom Venuto. A graduate of the University of Chicago, where he studied literary criticism, Stephen has worked previous stints at HarperCollins publishers and The Fifi Oscard Agency.

• **SHANA COHEN** joined the Stuart Krichevsky Literary Agency in 1999, with a degree from Tufts University in English and Art History. Clients include fantasy writer Gregory Frost, Young Adult novelist and Nebula finalist David J. Schwartz, and Alina Adams, whose *Jonathan's Story* and *Oakdale Confidential* were published in conjunction with CBS daytime dramas *As The World Turns* and *Guiding Light*, respectively. She has worked as a contracts manager, rights director, technology-problem-solver-for-clients-in-distress, and also maintains a Kindle Tips blog.

• **DIANA FOX** studied English Literature and Creative Writing at Smith College, which helped shape her interest in representing fiction. Before starting her own agency in 2007, she worked at Writers House.

• **SALLY HARDING** moved to Canada in 2001 after eight years in sales and marketing, editing, and bookselling in New Zealand and Australia. She began her career as a literary agent shortly after her arrival in Vancouver, and in 2005 started her own agency, The Harding Agency. The fledgling agency's rapid growth led to merger with The Cooke Agency in 2007. She has always read widely, and that is reflected in the range of genres she represents. She is particularly drawn to books that present fresh perspectives and ask questions of their readers. She regularly travels to international book fairs and conventions, and is on the board of the British Columbia Book Prizes.

• **HOWARD MORHAIM** established his literary agency in 1979 after several years as a line editor, book doctor, and acquisitions editor at several New York publishing houses. Because of his editing background, he quickly developed a reputation as an agent who works very closely with his clients, giving detailed manuscript feedback and proposal development. At the same time, the agency also became known for representing the best of writers working in a very wide range of fiction and nonfiction. Current clients include the iconic Michael Moorcock, international bestseller Arturo Perez-Reverte, and many others.

■ What do you look for in a client besides talent?

Stephen Barbara: Aside from talent, I look for a writer who's ambitious, hard-working, and serious about his career. Anything else clients bring to the table is gravy — good looks, fame, a platform, a sense of humor, tickets to the next Mets game, a best friend who's a buyer at Barnes & Noble, and so on.

Shana Cohen: Eagerness to consider my advice (not take it unquestionably, but to think about it) is probably the first positive note. I recently reviewed an author's manuscript that had a fascinating concept and shots of brilliance, but got lost in backstory, retellings, and memories. I sent her a page or two of notes, suggesting she make a timeline for the book and see how the book's outline as it stands differs, and marked some of my problems with the characters and their interactions. Within twenty-four hours, she wrote back to say that she'd already started the exercise I'd suggested, she recognized the problems with one character's motivations, and she was eager to get started reworking the novel. This, to me, was the best sign of a great potential relationship.

Diana Fox: I think maturity and professionalism are crucial, along with the willingness to be a partner in his or her own career. As the saying goes, writing is an art, but publishing is a business: I look for authors who are good business-people in addition to being good writers. I also need my clients to communicate with me early and often, and to keep me in the loop about everything that will affect my ability to be an effective advocate for them. Finally, there is a personality component to it which can't always be quantified, but I look for clients I feel like I *click* with. It is a business relationship and we don't need to be friends, but I do have to like them as people. I think it's just human nature that we don't do our best work for people we actively dislike, and I don't feel it's fair to myself or the client to offer representation if I am not sure I will be able to give one hundred percent to them professionally.

Sally Harding: In creating a literary work and getting paid for it, the writer becomes a small (hopefully to-be-large) business. So I look not just for enormous amounts of creative talent, but those qualities that we associate with a successful business person. They are determined to be the best they can be, and are prepared to put in the hard work to get there. There is honesty and integrity in their dealings. They have a cooperative spirit and are supportive of others — book publishing is the most team-sport undertaking I've ever come across, so being a team player is very important. Finally, we all work incredibly hard in this business — authors, agents, and publishers — so it's terrific to connect with an author in a way that makes for some fun along the way!

Howard Morhaim: What I look for in a client besides natural talent is focus and the capacity to understand that real talent is about growth. All writers need an idea of where they're going with their work, both artistically and commercially, and by commercially I mean with respect to the medium of the business of publishing, without which they'll be writing only for their friends and relatives. But, without exception in my experience, the writers who feel their work is untouchable, who view intelligent suggestions as micromanaging, who know better than everyone else — these are writers who always go nowhere.

◾ What are some common misconceptions about agents?

Stephen Barbara: I think a big misconception now is that web presence correlates in some way to clout within the industry. There are a lot of these agents blogging and twittering and using the web to promote themselves, and I wonder if writers over-value that. I mean: Morton Janklow isn't blogging, Nicole Aragi isn't blogging, Molly Friedrich isn't blogging, and probably most of the best agents would be too busy to spend a lot of time updating a blog or website every day. So I think writers need to take what they read online with a grain of salt. Spend some time in a bookstore looking at different books you admire — from the acknowledgments pages you can usually see who sold what.

Shana Cohen: Most people think I sit around and read all day — and it must be heavenly! I agree, it would be fantastic to spend my days reading. The fact is, all of my reading happens on my own time — outside of the office, on evenings and weekends. During the day, I do work for my current clients, working on contracts, tracking publication processes and payments, selling subsidiary rights, maintaining relationships with editors, and keeping tabs on the publishing world.

Diana Fox: A lot of people don't understand what it is we do! They either think we are publishers, or that we mainly serve the function of lawyers and accountants. While there is a little of the latter two jobs involved with negotiating contracts and interpreting royalty statements, etc., the work of the agent encompasses so much more than that. I've also seen the attitude that agents should be glorified salespeople employed by the author, and that once a book sells and the contracts are done, our active role is over except for cutting the checks. In my opinion, nothing could be further from the truth.

Sally Harding: By writers — an agent's job is easy, because it largely involves taking phone calls, attending industry events, and going to lunch. By others — "I'd love to have a job where I could sit around and read all day."

Howard Morhaim: Probably the most common misconception is that the agent (and this carries over to ideas about the publisher, as well) is there to provide some kind of public service to all writers everywhere. Many writer hopefuls believe that agents have an obligation to read their works within a time frame that suits them, the writers, and to comment on it in a helpful and detailed way. They fail to understand that (1) successful agents are busy and have very little room on their lists or time with which to read manuscripts other than their clients' and (2) a literary agency is a business, not a public service.

▆ Who is the boss in the writer-agent relationship?

Stephen Barbara: That depends a lot on what the writer needs. Some clients are looking for guidance and leadership. Others know exactly what they're about and they may only want you to make a deal for them, or to handle the back office sort of stuff. But at the end of the day, I think everyone realizes that the agent works for the client.

Shana Cohen: Who needs a boss? It's more like a marriage — I'm better at the business side, but I wouldn't want to write; if you feel strongly about particular suggestions for edits, it's your book and you're the writer, I wouldn't insist — *if* it doesn't interfere with my ability to sell the books effectively. My job is to manage the business of publishing, so the author can do what they do best: *Write.*

Diana Fox: The ideal writer-agent relationship is a partnership. Either can fire the other, so I don't think it's a traditional hierarchal relationship; at its best it is symbiotic. Authors put a lot of power and trust in the hands of an agent, and it is the agent's responsibility to honor that, but the author also needs to trust the agent and understand that in certain situations it is in their interest to do what their agent tells them to do (regardless of who you want to say works for whom). That may sound coercive, but it isn't, because it's about having that trust.

Sally Harding: The author is the boss — no question. I can suggest a client rework Chapter Three of their manuscript, but they decide whether they'll do it, or not. I can put offers in front of them and advise on each one, but they choose which offer they will accept. I can strongly suggest they take on a promotional activity, but they decide whether they will, or won't. And don't forget, it is the author who pays the agent. However, here are a couple of things to bear in mind: The kind of boss an author is likely to be is something I think very hard on when I decide whether or not to sign with an author. And for the author, a key thing for them to consider in the author-as-boss scenario is, if they've hired someone with years of experience in the business, and are not listening to them, why have an agent?

Howard Morhaim: The writer, without question. An agent should never do something against the wishes of his or her client.

■ What are some of the main reasons a writer should use an agent?

Stephen Barbara: Well, if I were a writer I would think seriously about getting an agent. It's about maximizing potential. You've written a great novel and now you're in a position of opportunity. You want the best publisher, the best editor, the best terms you can get, whatever sub-rights deals there are to be made: audio, film/television, foreign, not to mention the support and direction a top-notch agent can provide. Probably no one can fully exploit that opportunity on his or her own. So I think you probably get an agent once you realize that you're going to have this career that needs to be taken seriously.

Shana Cohen: I can't think of any reasons against it — but I'm biased, of course. I know how hard I work for my clients, and I can't imagine how a writer could do without the knowledge, contacts, contracts, and experience that my colleagues and I bring to the table.

Diana Fox: First of all, agents have specialized knowledge of the publishing industry that most writers just don't have, and don't even know they don't have. In addition to selling books and getting the best deals for his or her clients, a good agent will advise writers on how to reach their professional goals, advocate for them with publishers, and take care of a lot of business stuff (which can be very time-consuming!), thus freeing up time for the writer to concentrate on writing. Agents also sometimes help edit and develop manuscripts to make them more salable, act as a sounding board for the writer in developing new ideas, and simply provide hand-holding when the writer needs support. Last but not least, agents can help to preserve the relationship between author and editor by acting as a buffer between the two when necessary.

Sally Harding: As the writer, ready or not, becomes the boss of their own creative business, they need a specialist adviser who can be business manager, career consultant, and cheerleader — someone who has expertise, contacts, and industry insider knowledge. Just as a writer needs an editor to provide a fresh view of their manuscript, a writer needs an agent to provide a big picture view of their career. We are in an era when more is expected of writers than ever before, and I'm not just talking foreign tax forms. The demands are a heavy burden to manage as a solo performance.

Howard Morhaim: A good agent can help a writer identify a work's strength and weaknesses prior to a submission so that a work can be read by publishers in the best possible shape it can be. He has a broader range of contacts among editors and publishing houses than a writer will and a firsthand understanding of their likes and dislikes. He serves as a buffer between the editor and the writer so that that relationship is not poisoned by the often very tough discussions about money and terms. He's able to generate competition for a writer's work among different houses in a manner quite acceptable to editors and publishers, who would take it quite personally if the writer did it. He is — or should be — a skilled negotiator, and has an active knowledge of what terms are possible to achieve in the current marketplace. He has a solid knowledge of publishing law and contracts and is able to identify important contractual issues most lawyers outside of the field would miss entirely. Finally, he's a career manager and helps writers work intelligently towards long term goals.

▧ What characteristics or traits should a good agent have?

Stephen Barbara: Agents come in all stripes, but I think most writers would be happy with someone who's enthusiastic, responsive, committed, a good negotiator, an expert in contracts, loyal to his clients, a strong advocate across the board, in essence. And at the end of the day keep in mind that a big part of what we do is sales. I remember at the agency where I first worked, they used to say, "If you bat .400 you'll go to the Hall of Fame one day." I still think about that a lot. A high sell-through ratio in a subjective and rapidly-changing business — that must be a sign of an agent who knows something, no?

Shana Cohen: Passion for books, of course — I can't sell a book that I'm not utterly enthusiastic about myself, because that enthusiasm passes through to the editor when they pick up my submissions. The ability to juggle many projects and ideas and multitask is crucial, I find, to keep all the projects in all their stages straight.

Diana Fox: Professionally a good agent should be knowledgeable about the business of publishing, both generally and specifically. They should also be able to maintain relationships with publishers and clients alike. Good taste in books and good commercial instincts help a lot, too. Personally, see above with regard to maturity and professionalism. Having good boundaries is very important, and I would also rate patience and the ability to listen highly. However, this is a difficult question to answer because the very traits and characteristics that make an agent perfect for one client may make them totally wrong for another. Some agents are great at networking, others have hugely successful blogs and are adept at publicity, others are fantastic editors, or whizzes at contracts, or whatever — and not every agent needs to have every quality in equal measure in order to be a good agent. They just need to have enough of them to a great enough degree to do their job well.

Sally Harding: If I were to seek an agent to represent me, the first thing I'd look for is integrity. Integrity brings respect, and I'd want to work with someone I could respect, and who is held in regard by the industry. Enthusiasm is underrated, but there is nothing like it for generating the genuine excitement and energy that has editors moving a manuscript to the top of the pile. But what if my book didn't sell straight away? I'd want my agent to have persistence. Next, and this may sound odd, I'd look for curiosity. Not only does it mean my agent would be open to the ideas behind my work and the directions it may take, but it would make them a better negotiator. A good negotiator asks questions even when they think they know the answer. Finally, to conclude in a rather circular way, I'd want to know I was working with someone who respects authors. This may seem a strange thing to say, but sometimes people in this industry forget that without authors there would be no industry.

Howard Morhaim: There are many successful agents out there whose style differs substantially. But at minimum, all agents should be able to identify talent and strong work, explain it and promote it well to editors. An agent needs to understand that creative people need a level of care and feeding that others do not, and that his or her own ego needs, as much as possible, to be put on the side. Above all of this, a good agent has to have the strength of character to understand what real negotiation is.

▶▶ Booksellers by James Crossley

With booksellers, nothing is more important than getting information from the source. I asked James Crossley, an experienced bookseller at Island Books on the West Coast who worked for Amazon.com "when it was just an independent book-store, albeit Earth's biggest," to share any relevant information. He came up with the following points for writer interactions with bookstore staff.

- If you're reading at a bookstore or participating in any other similar event, remember to be gracious. Audiences are forgiving of many faults, but they don't usually enjoy arrogance. One writer's opening appearance in front of a substantial, welcoming crowd consisted solely of staring at the lectern and saying, "I'll read for about fifteen minutes, and then I guess we're supposed to move on to a Q&A session, but hopefully we can dispense with that, because I don't really see the point." Now, these kinds of appearances can become tiresome and repetitive, but there's certainly a better way to express discomfort with the process than by announcing, in essence, that you don't want people to buy your book.

- Your graciousness should extend particularly to the store staff. Ideally, a reading will result in some immediate sales, but for a writer without an established reputation, the more significant impact will come later on as booksellers spread the word to their customers. If your book is of interest to the staff, it will be one that's remembered and recommended, and making a good personal impression can only help in this regard. I worked with a woman who was a big fan of a journalist who'd co-authored a couple of edgy and informative books about marginalized industries including punk music and the adult films, and she heavily promoted his work whenever she had the chance. She was delighted to help arrange an event for him, but in person he proved bizarrely hostile and demeaning, and by the end of the evening she'd been reduced to tears. Thereafter, his sales fell off more than slightly, not surprisingly.

- When trying to convince a retailer to carry your book, similar rules apply. Before you pitch whatever it is you'd like to sell, check the store out in person if you can and be honest with yourself about whether you can imagine a place for your book on its shelves. A shop that emphasizes business titles and vacation thrillers may not be suitable for your young adult novel. Try to engage with the staff about the place and what they like to read and sell, not in an artificial way, but to size up how well your book fits in. If you find someone who seems amenable to what you have to offer, expect to give away a copy to sway the decision maker. A bookseller will pay far more attention to an actual book than she will to a postcard or flyer. If you can't make an actual visit, at least research online as best you can to better target your approach.

- When you're communicating with a retailer, be conscious of how he'll sell your book even if he hasn't read it. What's its intended audience? Don't say everybody, provide a specific hook. "It's great for fans of smart, action-oriented historical fiction, like Patrick O'Brian's books," or "It has a very contemporary setting, but the characters are discreet and the story unfolds gently, so it has more appeal to the Jane Austen crowd than it does to *Sex & the City* viewers" or "It's for literary readers who find Pynchon too simplistic." If there's a local connection, highlight it. You may feel as if you're reducing your work to a caricature, but once you've shown that your book can sell to somebody, you've established a beachhead of sorts and word of mouth will begin to push it in other directions.

- If at all possible [if you don't have the support of a traditional publisher], make sure your book is available through the major distributors such as Ingram and Baker & Taylor. The terms won't be quite as favorable to you as they would be if you supplied copies yourself, but easier availability makes it much more likely that your book will be stocked. Many independent stores will work directly with you, however, especially if you're willing to consign your book. Self-publishing no longer carries the stigma it used to, but customers are still concerned with aesthetics, so pay attention to the design of your book if only to make sure it doesn't stand out in a negative way. This is an area where an expert can really be of service.

▶▶ Editors by Jill Roberts

Jill Roberts is the wonderful managing editor and head publicist at Tachyon Publications, the publisher of Booklife. *I've worked with her now on several projects and her attention to detail, along with a dogged, detail-oriented approach to edits and deadlines — including the deadline for* Booklife *— made her an ideal candidate to represent editors in this section of the appendices.*

■ What are the most important things for the writer to keep in mind or do during the publishing process — after edits are complete on the manuscript?

The main things is — unsurprisingly — to ramp up your end of the publicity efforts. After edits come advance review copies. Find out who is handling the publicity for your book (you should know already!). Let them know of anyone you think might review or blurb the book — something as simple as emailing a PDF out can result in a really great cover quote. Be as creative as possible in your promotional efforts (that's why you're reading this book, right?).

■ What are some common mistakes writers make in their interactions with the editor or publicist on their book?

Not giving the publicist enough information. A publicist is a rainmaker; the slightest bit of seemingly trivial information can lead to a downpour of publicity opportunities (OK, I'll stop with the sopping wet metaphors now). Stay in touch with, be extremely responsive to, and bounce your ideas off of your publicist. Not constantly — take their lead about how often to check in. Or just ask (politely).

James Morrow did really extraordinary promotion for his novel, *Shambling Towards Hiroshima*. (It's about a B-movie actor who is hired by the U.S. Navy to star as a Godzilla-like monster in order to end World War II. I'm not doing it justice.) Thanks to an inventive collaboration with our excellent publicist Matt Staggs, Jim did innovative events that included monster movie screenings — inexpensive yet priceless publicity.

Mistakes not to make with an editor? Never preface a conversation with, "Look, you chump." I'm just saying.

■ Do you have any advice about how a writer can optimize their impact on their book's success without stepping on any toes re the publisher/editor/publicist?

Ask what you can do. Be friendly, courteous, and appreciative. Be patient, flexible, and have reasonable expectations (I find most writers do). Be open-minded. Be amusing — publishing professionals like the funny, within reason. Breaks up the day.

■ Any anecdotes, anonymous, that you'd like to share re editor-writer interactions?

My best ones will incriminate me. I've had an author threaten to get on a plane and show up at the office (he didn't). I've had an author rewrite a large chunk of his book after it had been copyedited and typeset. I've had an editing team send me cat pictures that are too cute to be appropriate for a business climate.

■ What advice do you have for a writer who isn't outgoing and isn't Internet savvy? Is this definitely a deficiency in this day and age, or can you compensate?

Honestly, it is a difficulty to have an author who is reticent to participate in promoting their book. Seven years ago when I was new to this, I thought that sending out review copies and having a national distributor is enough. But it just isn't. You need to push.

Someone who's introverted in person might do better to focus on online efforts and vice versa (if you're better in person and not savvy online). Ask the publicist or people you know how to do the things you don't know how to do. You're a writer, you're really smart — I know you can figure things out! And especially, be willing to do things that are a bit uncomfortable. I've had very shy authors who were pleasantly surprised at how enjoyable doing an event can be.

■ What do you most love about your job?

I love working with authors and editors. They are some of the most amazing, creative people I have ever known. And they give fantastic email. Just off-the-cuff astonishingly clever and funny stuff. Someday I'm going to publish a Best Publishing Emails anthology. (Needs a snappier title…)

In the science fiction community there's this good-naturedly snarky archetype, the fangirl/boy. It's kind of the SF equivalent of a groupie (though much more nerdy and a lot less sleazy); it's someone who's not on the professional side of the industry. Those of us on the inside are supposed to be cooler. But almost everyone working in SF publishing is an unabashed disciple of the genre. We worship too. So yeah, I'm a fangirl and proud of it. I dork out over working with people I admire.

■ What's the hardest thing about your job?

Making the best book possible while being collaborative and pragmatic. I work hard to balance the author's vision with the marketability of the book. It's important to me even when I'm being pulled in a lot of directions — which is all of the time — to listen to and respect the people I work with. Even when I can't quite give them what they want, I'll have a very good reason why.

Can I change my answer? Deadlines. Deadlines suck.

►► Marketing Versus Publicity by Colleen Lindsay

Colleen Lindsay has worked as a publicist for, among others, Random House. Lindsay currently works as an agent for FinePrint. She also runs a lively and informative blog called The Swivet, which often addresses publishing-related issues. In both of her contributions to this appendix, Lindsay is writing in the context of what happens at major publishing houses. Some of her thoughts on book tours and contacting reviewers may contradict advice given in the Public Booklife section. Both her advice and the advice in Public Booklife is correct, depending on the context.

The first thing to understand about the publicity and marketing departments is the difference between them.

- The **PUBLICITY DEPARTMENT** primarily focuses on free (or nearly-free) promotion for the book and author: reviews, interviews, TV & radio appearances, feature stories in print periodicals and online, public appearances and — when warranted — bookstore or media tours.
- The **MARKETING DEPARTMENT** focuses on paid promotion of the book and author. There are variations of marketing.
  - **SALES MARKETING** focuses on putting together the sales conferences (where the marketing department "sells" — i.e., pitches your book to the sales force and tries to get them excited about it), in-store placement (also known as co-op, i.e., those big stacks of books you see on endcaps and tables in bookstores), sales materials, and special discount promotions geared toward large chains, jobbers, clubs, (Sam's, Costco, etc.) and indie bookstores.
  - **TRADE MARKETING** departments (the one most people think of when they think of marketing) also include online marketing, and focuses on consumer promotions, contests, book clubs, supplementary materials (reader's guides, bookmarks, t-shirts, etc), online promotions, website creation, email blasts, newsletters, etc.
- The **ADVERTISING DEPARTMENT** is an arm of the trade marketing department that focuses on paid newspaper, television, radio, magazine, and online advertising.

- There are also ACADEMIC (a.k.a. SCHOOL) MARKETING departments and LIBRARY MARKETING departments (self-explanatory), but for the general purposes of this post, we'll be focusing on the retail market.

To make it easy, just remember this formula:
- focus on the author + media +/- book tours = publicity department
- focus on the book + consumers + online + sales force = marketing department

The second thing to understand about publicity and marketing is that not every book gets equal treatment. Basically, the more money the publisher pays for your book, the more money they will put into promoting it. The majority of first-time authors — particularly debut fiction writers — will fall into the category of mid-list. (And contrary to popular belief, mid-list isn't a dirty word.)

With some rare exceptions, most new books *will* get galleys created (also called an ARC or advanced readers copy if the marketing department has gone to the trouble of having a fancy cover slapped on it) and mailed to the trades. These are the publications that are considered the most essential to the book trade; in the United States, these include *Publishers Weekly, Kirkus Reviews,* the *New York Times, Library Journal, School Library Journal*, and *Booklist.* A later mailing will go out to additional magazines, newspapers, and online reviewers. Your book will most likely get a finished copy mailing with a press release or press kit that goes out to additional reviewers, local and/or national media, and — if the publisher has a website and/or email newsletter — placement on that as well. Depending upon the book and author, the publicity department may try to set up phone, online, and print interviews as well.

What most new authors won't get is a bookstore/media tour. The vast majority of new books being published will have a publicity budget of less than $500. Unless the publisher feels the need to send an author out on a media/bookstore tour or spend money on a TV satellite or radio drive-time tour, then there is no real reason for a book to *have* a publicity budget. The truth is that, for the most part, bookstore/media tours are costly and ineffective, both for the publisher and the bookseller. They are especially ineffective for fiction.

Marketing is less set in stone and is more geared toward an individual book. The marketing department may arrange for you to do book club telephone tours. They may create a special *tchotchke* for the publicity department to send out with galleys, something that they hope will be talked about and create buzz. They arrange for the book to be featured at any appropriate conferences and book/media conventions. And although online marketing falls into this area, you shouldn't expect your publisher to build you a website or pay for you to have one built. The marketing department's sole purpose is to come up with creative ways to promote your book to consumers and booksellers. But they tend to spend a lot of time on a very few lead titles, so the chances are that you may never even speak to anyone in the marketing department.

The third thing to understand about the publicity and marketing departments is that they are not your adversaries. What they *are* — like most publishing departments these days — is underfunded and understaffed. Your publicist may be working on as many as forty titles in one three-month publishing span, possibly more if he or she handles a great many trade or mass market originals. Likewise, the experience of the publicist assigned to your book may depend a great deal upon the size of the advance you've received and whether or not your book is considered a lead or sub-lead title. An inexperienced publicist can still be a passionate advocate for your book, however. But even the most experienced, competent, and/or passionate publicist has only a limited amount of time to spend working on your book; the best thing you can do is make it as easy as possible for the two of you to work together so that your publicist can make the best use of his/her time on your project.

Sometimes an author can be overly helpful. An overly helpful author can sometimes be more frustrating to a publicist than an author who refuses to do any promotion at all. At least in the latter case, the publicist isn't being interrupted all day by a barrage of phone calls and emails.

First you need to understand what the window of time is for your book project; that's the time where your publicist is actively (or sometimes, not so actively) promoting your book. Here's a rough timeline of how publicity works (and do keep in mind that every publishing house is slightly different so this by no means should be taken as gospel):

- **INITIAL CONVERSATION WITH PUBLICIST:** The timing of this can vary. If the publisher is planning to send you on tour for your book, this conversation may happen as far out as a year before publication. After all, they'll need to ascertain your availability and give you ample time to arrange for time off from a day job, if needs be. They'll also need time to get your event booked into various bookstore calendars, which usually needs to happen about six months before pub date. If, however, you aren't being sent on a book tour, this conversation usually happens about four to six months prior to pub date.
- **AUTHOR QUESTIONNAIRE:** Sometime during the above time frame, you'll receive an author questionnaire (most publishers send one, but not all). This questionnaire may come from the marketing department, your editor, or your publicist, depending upon the publisher. The purpose of the questionnaire is to get as much useful information about you, your book, and any possible media contacts you may have as possible. It helps determine where to send the galleys, where to pitch you for local (and possibly national) media, and what kinds of things the marketing department might successfully try to promote your book. Don't ignore this questionnaire!
- **AUTHOR PHOTO:** Again, sometime during the above time frame, you will be asked for a high-resolution (print quality, which is 600 dpi or higher) head shot for an author photo. Some authors are under the mistaken

impression that a publisher will send a photographer out to your house for a photo shoot. If you're Stephen King, James Patterson or J. K. Rowling, this might happen. Otherwise, this is your responsibility. (Read your book contract; it says so right there.)

- **4-6 MONTHS PRIOR TO PUB DATE:** galleys sent to book trades.
- **3-5 MONTHS PRIOR TO PUB DATE:** remainder of galleys sent to long-lead media, magazines, newspapers and any other appropriate media.
- **6 WEEKS PRIOR TO PUB DATE:** Finished books are in the warehouse, finished book mailing w/ press release and/or press kit goes out to short-lead media, online reviewers, local and national media (TV and radio), and anyone else that may have been left off that initial mailing.
- **6 WEEKS PRIOR TO PUB DATE THROUGH 6 WEEKS AFTER PUB DATE:** Active window of publicity. This is the time during which your publicist will be focusing on your book, doing follow up calls to reviewers and media, booking interviews for you, keeping the sales force informed about breaking publicity news for your title, and generally trying to keep your book in front of the media and sales force. Communication with your publicist will vary from conversations every day (sometimes several times a day if you are on tour) to weekly updates. Your interaction with your publicist really depends on the amount of media coverage your publicist is able to get for the book; they'll need to touch base with you to fit interviews into your schedule and let you know of any new confirmed reviews.
- **6 WEEKS AFTER PUB DATE:** Your publicist is now actively moving onto other book projects. Unless your book is in the Top Ten of the *New York Times* best-seller list, or unless you are on an extended tour (for example, when I toured Matthew Stover for the book tie-in for *Star Wars* Episode III, he was on tour for thirty-two days straight, which meant that the active window of publicity was considerably longer than normal), you will be expected to start handling your own publicity. Communication will start drying up. It's perfectly okay to contact your publicist during this time if you have questions or need advice on something, but you shouldn't be hounding him/her for new interviews and/or reviews. This is the time period during which many authors become "that annoying author." Don't become that author!
- **3 MONTHS AFTER PUB DATE:** Your book publicity is effectively in your own hands from now on. Start thinking about the following things for your

next book: what worked for you, what didn't, what would you change if possible, were there any publicity opportunities that you think were missed, was there anything that surprised you (in a good way!), etc... When you have your initial conversation with your publicist (who may or may not be the same publicist, by the way — every house differs) for your next book, have your postmortem in front of you for easy reference. When I worked with Terry Brooks at Del Rey, this was always the first conversation we had when planning for the next book, and it was extraordinarily helpful for me in planning his upcoming publicity campaign.

So what can you do to work most effectively with your publicist? How can you make it easier for your publicist to do his/her job promoting your book?

- **GET YOUR AUTHOR QUESTIONNAIRE BACK AS SOON AS POSSIBLE, FILLED OUT AS COMPLETELY AS POSSIBLE.** This is the time for you to let your publicist know if you'd like copies of your book sent to specific personal contacts for either quotes or reviews. (And this shouldn't need saying, but I'm saying it anyway: do not list Oprah. You will lose all respect and your questionnaire will be passed around and laughed at for all eternity. Spare yourself this, please.)

- **LET YOUR PUBLICIST KNOW AS FAR IN ADVANCE AS POSSIBLE YOUR TRAVEL AND PERSONAL SCHEDULE.** If you will be unavailable for interviews on a certain day because it's your child's birthday or something, let your publicist know. If you are planning any travel at all, let your publicist know. Even if your publisher won't send you on a tour, your publicist may be able to set up a bookstore event or some local interviews in the city you'll be in. S/he'll also be able to arrange for you to do stock signings at local bookstores. If you are planning to attend a writing conference or convention, let your publicist know in advance. S/he not only can try to get you some panel programming or set up an event, s/he can also let the sales force know that you'll be in that city so that they can be sure there are books in the bookstores. Here's an example: fantasy author Greg Keyes is also a tournament-class fencer; he frequently travels to fencing competitions all around the country. When I worked with him as his publicist, I always tried to set up at least one bookstore event or local interview in the cities where the competitions were held. And if you having speaking engagements coming up, let your publicist know!

- **GET A CELL PHONE:** Yes, I know that some of you have an aversion to cell phones. Get over it. When your publicist needs to get hold of you to see about scheduling an interview, s/he doesn't want to keep a reviewer, feature writer, or producer waiting until you get home to check your messages. That's a great way to lose an interview altogether. If you're on a book tour, you absolutely must have a cell phone. Plans change, flights get delayed, interviews get postponed. You need to be accessible at all times. Get a cell phone.

- **HAVE ACCESS TO EMAIL:** I've worked with authors who insist on doing everything by telephone. It's time consuming and leaves no paper trail in case you need to access information later or need details of an interview in writing.

- **HIRE A PROFESSIONAL TO SHOOT YOUR AUTHOR PHOTO:** As sad as this may be, author image sells a book every bit as much as the content of that book. Having a great head shot for your book jacket can only work in your favor. It may be tempting to have your wife or brother-in-law or that Pakistani guy who runs the bodega down the street take a photo of you to save money, but you get what you pay for, and a professional head shot is well worth the money you'll spend. Make sure that when you do this, however, that you own the negatives or digital files. Get this in writing. Otherwise, your publisher will need to keep purchasing the rights to use the photo from the photographer, and that leads to a very annoyed art department.

- **DON'T BE A PRIMA DONNA:** Nobody likes a prima donna. Think about what you're asking for before you ask. Is it really necessary or did someone tell you that this is what you're supposed to ask for as an author? Difficult, high-maintenance authors develop a reputation with publicists, booksellers, producers, media escorts, and other authors. How do you know if you're behaving like a prima donna? Take this easy quiz: You're on book tour, have just arrived at the airport in Los Angeles at 8:00 PM and your car service hasn't arrived to pick up to take you to your hotel. You A.) pick up the cell phone and call your publicist at home in New York (where it is 11:00 PM), complain vociferously and wait for s/he to call the car service company to find out what happened, B.) hail a cab to take you to your hotel, save your receipt for reimbursement later, check in and after doing so, call your publicist's work number to leave a message letting him or her know about the mix-up with the car service. If you chose option A, congratulations! You're a prima donna! If you chose option B, you're a normal, rational adult, capable of surviving your first book tour without having your hand held. Does the publicist need to know that the car service screwed up? Absolutely! Does the publicist need to know this at 11:00 PM at night? Probably not.

- **UNDERSTAND THE HIERARCHY OF PUBLISHING AND TO WHOM SPECIFIC QUESTIONS SHOULD BE DIRECTED:** The only questions that you should be asking your publicist are those having to do with publicity, i.e., questions having to do with interviews, reviews, book tours, press materials, getting books to event venues, requests to send a book to a specific reviewer, etc. If you want to know how your book is selling, you ask your editor. If you want to talk about ways to best utilize your massive website email list, you talk to the marketing department. If you are getting calls from friends who are not seeing your book in bookstores after pub date, you call your editor who will inform the sales department. If you are doing a local event and notice that the bookstore in question has no display copies of your book, you call your publicist. You see the difference? And if you don't like a review of your book that you just saw on AMAZON.COM, well, you don't call anyone. There's nothing your publisher can do about that. Just suck it up and move on.

- **IF YOU HIRE AN OUTSIDE PUBLICIST, BE SURE THAT S/HE AND YOUR IN-HOUSE PUBLICIST ARE COMMUNICATING:** There's nothing worse than finding out that a freelance publicist is duplicating your hard work. Make sure that your freelance publicist is in constant communication with your in-house publicist. Have them coordinate who will be working on what part of your campaign. For example, your freelance publicist may be focusing on getting you online and podcast interviews while your in-house publicist focuses on radio and print media.

- **DO NOT EVER — I REPEAT — DO NOT EVER CONTACT A REVIEWER ON YOUR OWN:** You may be tempted to reach out to a particular reviewer to whom your publicist has sent a copy of your book, in order to "helpfully" follow up with that reviewer about your book. Don't. Do. This. Ever. It is incredibly unprofessional and can result in your books never being reviewed by that particular reviewer again. Additionally, you may be tempted to ask for a list of all the places your publicist has sent your book. This is perfectly acceptable, but understand that if your publicist sends you this list, s/he will do so without attaching any contact information. This is for two reasons: 1) to protect the privacy of the reviewer/producer and prevent what I mentioned in the first sentence, and 2) this information is proprietary and confidential; giving out contact information could result in your publicist being fired. (Likewise, as an unpublished author, you should never reach out to follow up with an editor to whom your agent has submitted your manuscript; this is one of the biggest mistakes a potential writer could ever make.)

- **KEEP YOUR AGENT IN THE LOOP:** Your agent is your advocate; keep him/her in the loop about anything going on with your book, including publicity and marketing plans. Too often an agent won't know about a potential problem until it's too late for the problem to be fixed. If your publisher wants you to come in and meet with the publicity and marketing folks, ideally your agent should accompany you. If you are having problems communicating with your editor or publicist, you need to let your agent know. Handling these kinds of situations is part of our job. Before you go to your publicist's supervisor, go to your agent. Your agent can try to remedy the situation first, and if not, then s/he can go to your publicist's supervisor on your behalf. We work for you; let us do our jobs.

- **DON'T BE AFRAID TO SHARE YOUR PUBLICITY AND MARKETING IDEAS; JUST DO IT THE RIGHT WAY:** If you have ideas for marketing and promoting and publicizing your book, share them with your publisher. Ideally, you should do this early on, in a written document that you send to your editor, who should then send it on to the marketing and publicity department. You can always ask your publicist if s/he received it. Schedule a telephone appointment to go over your ideas with publicity and marketing. (Hopefully, your editor and agent will be included on this phone call.) If some of your ideas are shot down, accept it gracefully and move on. Your publisher may not have the time or budget to implement all of your ideas. Likewise, some of your ideas may not be the kind of promotions that your publisher feels will drive sales. And selling your book is the whole point. And some of your ideas may just be plain stupid. (Hey, it happens to the best of us!) Also, don't be afraid to ask for certain things: postcards and bookmarks are fairly inexpensive and easy to produce; more often than not the marketing department will say yes.

- **DON'T BE AFRAID TO COMMUNICATE WITH YOUR PUBLICIST; JUST DO IT THE RIGHT WAY:** Don't call your publicist several times a day with new questions. Don't send your publicist more than one email a day. Instead, gather up as many of your questions as possible into one email, and then wait for an answer before sending off another. If your publicist hasn't responded within 24 hours, it is perfectly acceptable to leave a voicemail message follow-up. As a publicist, I received upwards of three hundred emails a day. Sending ten or twenty angsty/helpful/"hey, I've got an idea!" emails a day to your publicist will not help your book campaign, and can frequently hurt it, as your publicist is spending valuable time — time that s/he should using to pitch your book to media — placating a needy author. [See above re: prima donna.]
- **DON'T FORGET TO SAY THANK YOU:** It's not necessary to buy your publicist or editor or marketing person a gift. But it's absolutely proper to send a thank-you note or email after your campaign is over. And you'd be surprised at how often authors don't do this. Say thank you. It'll go a very long way toward earning you respect as a professional.

Appendix B
Content-Related

▶▶ Marketing/PR Campaign Summary (Example)

As DISCUSSED IN several sections of *Booklife*, you can have a say in the marketing and publicity for your book. The best way to present your ideas is through a simple, concise document that isn't longer than a few pages. This standard applies even if you are developing the document for your own use because your project has a non-standard path to publication. Here is the document presented to Tor Books in support of my novel *Shriek: An Afterword*. The original document I submitted was ten pages long and much more verbose. My editor, Liz Gorinsky, helped me trim it down, and explained that the document would be presented to both their marketing and PR departments. Not everything mentioned in the marketing summary could be implemented successfully, but that wasn't for lack of trying. This document also helped introduce me to the marketing department.

Every document of this nature is going to include a few unrealistic things, and every plan, from the perspective of a year or two later, may seem ridiculous in some detail. In this particular plan, those "ridiculous" things weren't as obvious as they might seem. For example, the virtual video/film book parties took place and were often successful. However, the attempt to leverage the novel both to mainstream as well as genre was at most a mild success, at worse a mild failure.

After the campaign for a book, always go back to the plan you presented to the marketing/PR department and determine what went right, but also figure out what went wrong, and why.

MARKETING SUMMARY
SHRIEK: AN AFTERWORD
Jeff VanderMeer
August 2006 Hardcover

TALKING POINTS

Shriek

- *Shriek* is the first ***original*** release from a major North American publisher by a unique, multi-award winning talent who can be compared to strong sellers such as China Miéville, Cory Doctorow, and Kelly Link (shared characteristics include considerable web presence, loyal fan base, etc).
- A *Shriek* Internet movie with an original soundtrack by legendary rock band The Church and a humorous *Rough Guide to Ambergris* Internet movie introducing readers to the fantasy setting will be released in August along with the novel.

Jeff VanderMeer

- Made the year's best lists of the *San Francisco Chronicle, Publishers Weekly, Publishers' News (UK), Amazon.com, SF Site, Locus Magazine,* and *LA Weekly,* as well as making the BookSense 20 and BookSense 76.
- Two-time World Fantasy Award Winner. Finalist for the Philip K. Dick Award, Theodore Sturgeon Award, British Fantasy Award, International Horror Guild Award, Bram Stoker Award, and the Hugo Award.
- NEA Florida Individual Artist Fellowship and Florida Artist Enhancement Grant winner.
- Named one of the top fantasy writers in the world by Locus Online in 2001.
- Grew up in the Fiji Islands because his parents were in the Peace Corps. Traveled around the world at an early age, which influenced his fiction heavily.
- Had extensive involvement with the "indie press" as an editor, publisher, and writer before his books were released by New York publishers.

- Attended the same Clarion East workshop as Cory Doctorow in 1992.
- Runs an entertaining and sometimes controversial blog at http://www.jeffvandermeer.com.

TOOLS FOR SELLING *SHRIEK*

City of Saints & Madmen (Bantam Spectra Edition)

The *City of Saints* PR efforts and PR page (http://www.jeffvandermeer.com/city/) will raise reader and bookseller awareness of the Ambergris setting. Parts of it can be re-used for a *Shriek* PR page in August 2006.

Limited Edition *Shriek* "Box"

VanderMeer is in the process of creating limited edition *Shriek* wooden boxes for devoted fans that will house Ambergris beer, a copy of *Shriek*, and other Ambergris-related novelties. Three of these will be created early to send to chain buyers along with copies of the ARC.

Action Item:
- Tor will pay $50 per box for the creation of three boxes.

Open Issue Needing Tor's Input:
- If the boxes cost slightly more than $50 each, will Tor pay Jeff for the full cost?

Rough Guide to Ambergris Movie

Humorous introduction to VanderMeer's fantasy setting, housed on his website. *Can Tor think of other marketing or PR uses for this film?*

Shriek Internet Movie

An Internet movie based on plot elements from *Shriek*. The movie will feature original music by legendary rock band The Church. It will be finished by June 2006. The idea is to create a "viral video" that people will link to. This movie will be self-contained so that viewers don't need to know anything about the book to enjoy it.

Leverage:

- Micha Hershman, the previous genre book buyer for Borders, has indicated that a link to the movie can be added to Borders e-newsletters. (Although Hershman is leaving for a position in the Borders Kids department, he indicates that Borders is still interested in partnering on this project.)
- The music tie-in will create possibilities for _Shriek_ promotion in music magazines and on music websites.
- Slashdot and Boing Boing may be interested in featuring the movie in some way.

Open Issues Requiring Tor's Input:

- Would Amazon.com be willing to host the movie? (VanderMeer's contacts have been unresponsive)
- Could Barnes & Noble be involved through national buyer Jim Killen?
- To what extent is Tor willing to send packages (with the book/ARC and a copy of the movie burnt to CD) and emails about the book to music and pop culture magazines to play up the movie and The Church's involvement in it?
- In what other ways can this movie be leveraged?

Shriek Internet Trailer

The trailer will be a one-minute version of the _Shriek_ movie that advertises the novel. It will be housed on the _Shriek_ website but will be a small enough file that it can be emailed to individuals targeted for sales or PR purposes.

Leverage:

- Housed on the _Shriek_ website.
- "Portable" and more PR-specific multimedia approach than the movie.

Open Issues Needing Tor's Input:

- Would Tor be willing to cover the costs ($300) of producing this trailer?
- What other uses can Tor find for this trailer?

Shriek Web Site (www.shriekthenovel.com)

Publicity about the *Shriek* movie will lead to additional traffic to the site.

Shriek Resource Page

VanderMeer has created a resource page ("fun stuff" and press kit) for the Bantam release of *City of Saints* (http://www.jeffvandermeer.com/city/). Elements of this page can be recycled and/or changed for a page devoted to the *Shriek* release.

White Box / Red Box Promotion

Bantam has included *City of Saints* in the BookSense "white box" promotion, which sent 900 independent bookstores a flyer that focused on *City of Saints* but also had information on *Shriek* and showed its cover. In August, Tor will reciprocate by doing a "red box" promotion featuring *Shriek* but also mentioning *City of Saints*.

Banner Advertisements

VanderMeer has reserved banner ad space on Locus Online for August and September 2006 ($400 per month). *Tor has indicated a willingness to pay for these banner ads. Is there final approval for this expenditure?*

Reader/Reviewer Contact Database

A very important yet often intangible element of VanderMeer's book promotion focuses on networking. VanderMeer has an impressive array of contacts in genre and the literary mainstream. This database contains 350 to 400 reviewer/media contacts, 40 to 50 bookstores, 500 emailable VanderFans, 700+ snail mail/email VanderFans, and other miscellaneous contacts.

"Virtual" Book Tour

Although this tour is still in the planning stages, VanderMeer hopes to leverage the *Shriek* movie into a series of same-day 20 or more book release parties in major metropolitan areas on the day *Shriek* is released. Each will feature the film, a video from Jeff, liaisons with local writers, and follow-up blogging by the VanderFans on the ground who helped organize each event. *What subsidiary support can Tor provide in the form of help booking readings; production of business cards, bookmarks, postcards, etc.?*

PAST MARKETING/PR EFFORTS

Several books written by VanderMeer appeared in the independent press before being picked up by major publishers in the United States and United Kingdom. VanderMeer did his own PR and much of the marketing for these indie releases. From this experience, VanderMeer has found that the following statements are generally true.

The Internet Provides VanderMeer with the Most Leverage

Marketing efforts that use the Internet tend to be very successful because *VanderMeer has a heavy Internet presence already, with a blog that gets between 4,000 and 10,000 unique visitors a day.* VanderMeer is also able to assist with such efforts much more easily. Most of VanderMeer's sales in the indie press came from Internet bookstores such as Amazon rather than brick-and-mortar stores, where the books had limited distribution.

Marketing Aimed at Genre and Mainstream Is Most Successful

VanderMeer is most successful when he reaches **both** a genre audience and a more general audience. Editing books such as *The Thackery T. Lambshead Pocket Guide to Eccentric & Discredited Diseases*, getting high-profile gigs at literary festivals, and being reviewed by mainstream journals such as *The Review of Contemporary Fiction* have all increased his visibility outside of genre. As possible, Tor should attempt multilateral marketing of VanderMeer's name and work. Although it is easier to market VanderMeer's work as fantasy to a genre audience, any inroads made into the literary mainstream ensure greater interest and sales over time.

Personality Positives Should be Accentuated

VanderMeer's high Internet visibility, confidence, and drive are three of his greatest non-writing assets and should be leveraged in all marketing and PR efforts. The more bookstore buyer/seller contact VanderMeer has through email, telephone calls, and personal visits, the better his books do.

QUESTIONS
(1) What are Tor's marketing and PR approaches to *Shriek*, and what are the specific events or actions associated with this approach?
(2) How much Internet advertising will occur?
(3) How much non-genre PR will take place?
(4) What actions can VanderMeer take to support Tor's efforts?

▶▶ Podcasts

At least as many people listen to or watch news as read it. One advantage is that you can multitask in a way you can't while reading the same information. Offering an excerpt from your book as a podcast — assuming you have publisher permission — may allow you to reach some people who wouldn't take the time to *read* the same excerpt as a download. What is a podcast? It's basically a spoken-word blog featuring a series of audio recordings (a feed) made available on the Internet. People subscribed to your feed receive new installments automatically.

Podcasts can be as simple as a recording of you reading from the book, or as complex as a full-cast audio drama complete with soundtrack and special effects. But to get started, all that's required is a microphone and recording software, which you can download from the Internet for free (try AUDACITY. SOURCEFORGE.NET). You can make podcasts available on your site. You also can submit your feed to Apple to be included in the podcast directory of the iTunes store.

Publisher Victoria Blake believes that podcasts "are starting to have real traction. I have huge faith in them as a way of building and gaining an audience."

Some writers have started out as podcasters and built a huge audience. Check out the websites of successes like Scott Sigler and J. C. Hutchins to get a sense for the podcasting subculture. Sigler's aggressive approach created a rabid fan base, with his podcasts leading to book deals for his fiction from major publishers. He's now a best-selling author.

Because you don't need much equipment to get started, podcasting can seem deceptively simple. However, as this advice from New Zealand writer and podcast narrator Grant Stone shows, it has hidden complexities:

> The most important thing right from the very beginning is getting high quality audio out of your hardware. You'll want to take a good look at where you're recording. Echoes bouncing from your walls or desk need to be avoided. Does your computer have a noisy fan? You'll find out soon.

When recording, here's what I do: start a track, then just read. If I make a mistake, make a loud noise that will be visible on the waveform — I just smack a pencil on the desk — and record it again. If you do this you end up with all of your takes in a single track, and it's just a matter of cutting the stuff you don't want. Because of that pencil on the desk, you'll be able to see your mistakes easily. Editing can take a while. Sometimes I'll spend three times as long editing as I spent recording, and I'm just doing a straightforward narration — special effects or music will add a lot of time.

As *TIME* magazine noted in a recent profile of Sigler and Hutchins, the investment of effort in self-defining as a "podcaster" and devoting your time to podcasting means that despite the huge success of a few this area probably shouldn't be your main focus. Better to use podcasting selectively, and try to leverage your work through successful podcasters who have already done the hard work of building up an audience. As Grant puts it, "Podcasting is a major timesink."

Another option would be to create an audio promo where you talk a little about your book, use a good soundtrack (make sure you have the rights to the music, many indie musicians online will be happy to work with you if you contact them), and tell them where they can find out more. Then approach podcasters you admire and ask if they will play your promo.

Lastly, there are many shows that focus on books, writing, and writers, and are happy to interview you for their show. Do a search online or in iTunes to find the names of these shows, listen to a couple, and contact the host.

There are several ways you can leverage podcasting in your Booklife, and not all of it requires you to be a DIY audio engineer. For example, PODOMATIC. COM provides an easy way to record a podcast online and find an audience for it.

▶▶ PR Plan (First Draft Example)

Below find the initial draft of the high-level PR plan for *Finch*, my latest novel. Although I believe in transparency, I have deleted a few sections and redacted information to protect confidentiality. Still, I think this public glimpse into my own strategizing is fairly unique. I've also included my initial back-and-forth with my editor, Victoria Blake at Underland, based on her reaction to the elements of the plan. As you might expect, there's no way to include the detailed plan that comes out of the finalized high-level plan — in part because too much of the information would be confidential and in part because the deadline for *Booklife* comes before my deadline for finalizing the detailed plan for *Finch*. Although I could include the high-level plan for *Booklife*, the problem is that it's less exemplary of the type of document due to *Booklife*'s unique qualities.

FINCH PR PLAN
Document Created by: Jeff VanderMeer

Pre-Publication

Advance Blurbs

We decided to focus on three or four groups: fantasy writers, graphic novelists, mystery writers, and literary mainstream writers (in that order).

** = top ten

- **Ben Templesmith
- **Mike Mignola — I have his email, but if you have it independent of me, even better — we have a good professional relationship and I don't want to abuse it.
- **Warren Ellis — I don't have his email, but he'd be perfect for this; I don't know him personally.

- **Michael Chabon — Chabon's probably too nice to like this book, but...
- **George R. R. Martin — don't know if his email address is confidential; he said he'd give it a look in bound form, so remind him of that, and we'll just have to create a special ARC for him, because he doesn't mean stapled or bound at Kinkos.
- Tom Piccirilli — he's gotten more and more popular in noir/mystery/thriller fiction and it would give us some street cred in that arena.
- Ken Bruen — One of the best noir thriller writers out there, and Tom P. has his email address. I don't know him personally.
- **James O. Born — a very popular thriller writer who now also writes SF.
- Elizabeth Bear — very popular SF/fantasy author right now.
- Peter Straub — *NYT* bestseller who blurbed my short story collection.
- Chuck Palahniuk — have his address somewhere if you don't; I don't know him.
- **Neal Stephenson — I don't know if this email is confidential or not.
- **Joe Abercrombie — hot new gritty epic fantasy author who I think would like this book a lot.
- Richard Morgan — he's a good candidate for this; don't know if this is a privileged email address.
- **Stephen R. Donaldson — would be a good match, given how brutal some of his stuff is.
- Brandon Sanderson — hot because he's the replacement for Robert Jordan — no idea if he'd like *Finch*; this is a privileged email addy; only know him from interviewing him for Amazon.
- **Joe R. Lansdale — just the nicest guy in the world, and would probably like it.
- Daniel Abraham — another nice guy, and a friend, whose fantasy novels seem to be doing well.
- Iain M. Banks — can't find his email address. I have it somewhere.

Early Adopters

The following bloggers, core fans, and others with gatekeeper status across the Internet have enthusiastically said yes to receiving a PDF of the finished novel, preferably by May. They have been told that any pre-publication coverage should be short and reveal no spoilers, and that they will be nudged in November for longer coverage. The point of early adoption is to make sure the book is on their radar, since sometimes books in November get short shrift, and because some of them do their best-of lists well before the last two months of the year. In addition, it makes sense for them to have Finch at the same time as some other noir fantasy titles — we might pick up some additional pre-pub publicity *embedded in the reviews of other novels.*

I am happy to send the PDF with appropriate verbiage to the following people who signed up:

- Abrams, Avi — Runs the hugely popular Dark Roasted Blend blog (will need the PDF to run on his iPhone!).
- Ayad, Neddal — Has interviewed me about the last two Ambergris books; will extend the interview to Finch and do a much longer full interview, to be placed somewhere.
- Bond, Gwenda — Runs the Shaken & Stirred blog.
- Champion, Ed — NYC-based blogger and podcaster who runs Ed Rants.
- Cheney, Matthew — Runs the Mumpsimus blog, which has solid literary street cred.
- Dudman, Clare — UK novelist and core fan.
- Duncan, Hal — UK author with cult following.
- Fernandez, Fabio — Runs the Post Weird blog.
- Gordon, Joe — Core fan who runs the awesome Forbidden Planet blog.
- Hindmarch, Will — White Wolf gamer who runs the Word Studio blog.
- Hogan, Ron — Mediabistro blogger.
- Jessup, Paul — Fan and general big mouth.
- Klima, John — Core fan and ex editor at Tor.
- Moles, David — Switzerland-based blogger and fan.
- Nolen, Larry — Runs the OF Blog of Fallen.
- Nordberg, Heidi — Core fan and runs Virushead blog (has academic contacts).

- Orchard, Eric — Illustrator who runs a Steampunk blog.
- Tan, Charles — Runs the Bibliophile Stalker blog.
- Thomas, Jeffrey — Core fan and writer friend.
- Tomio, Jay — Runs BookSpotCentral.
- Walter, Damien — Blogger and writer for the *Guardian* UK online.
- Wickett, Dan — Head of the Emerging Writers Network and associated blog.

Advance Reading Copies

Preferably, we would have access to between 150 and 200 ARCs so we can properly cover all applicable high-profile media outlets (traditional and non-trad) in fantasy/SF, mystery, mainstream literary, and pop culture contexts. Some might also be useful as freebies to influential booksellers at large independent brick-and-mortars, in addition to people like the books editor at Amazon.

The ARCs would also include the Murder by Death *Finch* CD (provided at-cost by the band), and a half-page press release explaining the genesis of that project, in addition to the main press release for the novel. If the *Finch* movie project is far enough along, that should be mentioned in the press release.

Although Underland Press's policy is to use a thumbnail of the cover on the ARC, we might be better off running the front cover at full-size, given the enthusiastic reaction to the art and design on the Internet. At thumbnail size, most of the details will be lost.

If budgetary constraints don't allow for 150 to 200 ARCs, then we'll need access to more finished copies for some venues.

On/After Publication

Finished Copies

Depending in part on the number of ARCs available, we will need to have between 50 and 100 copies of the finished book to send out as follow-up to reviewers. Typically, about half of these will be personalized by me and sent out by me. If this is an issue, I'll need some kind of discount to procure some copies myself. I can absorb postage costs regardless.

Finch *Soundtrack by Murder by Death*

Murder by Death plans to finish a 20-minute instrumental soundtrack by early June. It's meant to be included with the limited edition. In addition, Murder by Death will sell the CD off of their website and at their gigs. I will also have it available at my bookstore appearances, wherever possible.

The cost of the CD is being absorbed by Murder by Death. For the limited, a fair price should be negotiated that gives them some profit.

Murder by Death has a website here: www.murderbydeath.com.

Finch: *The Web-Based Movie*

Geoff Manaugh, founder of http://bldgblog.blogspot.com/, may be doing a short Internet film based on scenes from *Finch*. I will provide the script. He will provide the still photography from his huge archive of amazing urban scenes. I can provide the voiceover as necessary. Some of the music by Murder by Death will be used in the movie, so this project probably won't be completed until August or September. Initial plans include to possibly leverage it through GeekDad, but even if it's just leveraged through SF/fantasy blogs and through Bldg Blog, it should get good coverage. Manaugh has a book on cities out from Chronicle Books over the summer, and he wants to use this project to leverage that book as well. This project won't cost Underland Press anything.

Book Release Party

The World Fantasy Convention in San Jose, California, is the natural place for a book release party. Volunteering to host a party in the con suite for a couple of hours would mean the venue would be taken care of; all that would be required is promotional materials from Underland and enough decent food and drink so that no one is disappointed.

At the moment, vague plans would include teaming up with *Weird Tales* so that Ann is represented, along with a couple of friends who may have books being released then. This would cut costs and create additional interest, with the spotlight still firmly on *Finch*. However, this would mean that copies of the book must be available by that weekend (the last weekend in October).

World Fantasy would also kick off the book tour proper for *Finch*.

Endurance Tour

The proposed endurance tour for Finch would need to begin before World Fantasy, with three-to-four layover stops on the way to San Jose. (This would mean the book needs to be in bookstores.) Theoretically this leg of the endurance tour might receive some kind of support from: *Men's Health*, Delta Airlines, Amazon, and major blogs.

After World Fantasy, I would then spend roughly a month traveling back across the country by car, probably with one or two other writers. We would do a series of bookstore events and reading series at universities, depending on the opportunities. The trip would be run roughly diagonally, from San Jose up to the Northeast. Costs would be minimized by staying with friends and fans. We would team up with local writers for added interest. This would also serve as cross-promotion for *Booklife*.

For both legs of this endurance tour, the main issue is setting up the events earlier enough in advance, making sure the timing issues make sense (for car travel especially), making contact with local authors, and ensuring a place to stay in each location. Potential costs include the plane ticket, gas for the car, and food. I would also blog about the experience while traveling, and might be able to do so on various book blogs as well.

Additional Leverage

Other potential ideas for leverage include but are not limited to:

- Pursuing interviews on prominent sites.
- Encouraging legacy reviewers who like the Ambergris series to do extended pieces on all three books.
- Banner ads, postcards, and other virtual and hardcopy advertising.
- Viral guerilla PR based around various sayings by the Lady in Blue and the rebels, from the book.
- Podcast of the novel in segments by me.
- Appearances at book festivals, etc. (lots of invites beginning to pop up)

Other Ideas (currently on back burner)

The Booklife *Immersive Experience*

[For timing reasons, this idea has been redacted here, but will be fully explained and archived via the booklifenow.com site.]

Finch: *The Video Game*

A web-based three-dimensional video game allowing players to experience the world of Ambergris and the mystery plot central to the novel.

- Sponsored by Underland, third-party financing, advertising on the game site, and by possibly offering an add-on to the *Booklife* subscription price that allows "enhanced" subscribers to play the game.
- Supported by online mentions and reviews across many different subcultures (still to be explored).
- Created by Atomic Pistol (estimated time needed to complete a Beta version for release with the novel: three months).
- "Audience" for this is, well, just about everyone — video game players, fans of my work, etc.
- Budget: To be determined, but can be offset by including Atomic Pistol in the PR plan so they get maximum exposure.

[And here are Victoria's responses, with my comments on her comments all in caps.]

Pre-publication

—Advance blurbs: Doing them now.

CHECK!

—Early Adopters: Yes. The PDF in May won't be of the finished book, but pretty darn close.

CLOSE ENOUGH FOR EARLY ADOPTERS, MOST DEF

—Advanced reader copies: Yes, of course. Those are in addition to the 100 or so I'll be giving to the sales reps.

GREAT!!

On/After Publication

—Finished book to reviewers: I'm not sure what the difference between this and the galleys / arcs are. But I'm willing. Regarding the number of copies, I'm not sure how to handle that. The contract says that you can buy as many as you want at distributor's best discount. I go back and forth about this. I might be fine with you paying the actual per-unit plus the drop-shipment charge, making it a wash for me.

I CAN'T REMEMBER THE CONTEXT IN MY DOC, BUT IT'S MOSTLY ABOUT NUDGING PEOPLE WHO GOT THE ARC BUT DIDN'T DO ANYTHING WITH IT, AND THEN SOME MOP-UP. A LOT OF TIMES, PUBLISHERS GIVE ME AN EXTRA 20-30 BECAUSE THEY KNOW THE EFFECT I CAN HAVE.

—Finch Soundtrack: I need to talk to MBD about the cost of the soundtrack.

YEP.

—Web-based movie: Great.

YEP.

—Book release party: Good thinking. I'm down for hosting in conjunction with *Weird Tales*. I'm planning on having a table in the dealer's room.

GREAT. I CAN DO INITIAL RESEARCH ON THIS.

—Endurance Tour: What do you need from me?

ANY INTEL YOU HAVE ON BOOKSTORES OR OTHER VENUES THAT MIGHT BE AMENABLE TO THIS, AND ANY GENERAL OR SPECIFIC THOUGHTS ON THE IDEA AND EXECUTION, INCLUDING WRITERS TO TEAM UP WITH.

—Additional Leverage:

*Interviews: Yep.

CHECK.

* Legacy reviewers: Good thinking.

CHECK.

*Virtual and hardcopy advertising: I've printed postcards for the sales reps and for BEA. I'm not a fan of advertising. I'm not sure it actually works. I'd much rather spend money on co-op stuff.

THAT'S YOUR CALL, OF COURSE.

* Viral Guerilla: Sure, but how?

THAT'S SOMETHING FOR MATT STAGGS AND ME TO BRAINSTORM.

*Podcast of the novel: I'm super stoked about this. I have a podcast side of my website ready to go right now. We could start with the chapter releases before the hardcopy book release, to stoke interest.

WORKS FOR ME.

* Book festivals: Excellent. What do you need from me? I'm assuming a number of copies of the book for sale. If you want, I'd be willing to do this on consignment with you, so you don't have the shell out the cash and guess at the sales ahead of time.

MOST OF THEM WILL HAVE ASSIGNED BOOKSTORE SELLERS WHO WILL STOCK THE BOOK SO THIS ISN'T AN ISSUE.

Other Ideas

—*Booklife*: It is a fantastic idea. Truly. But it seems to me that there could be a larger-than-life size for this project, and there could be a human size. The human size: A very honest group blog about the process. We'd organize it by milestones, starting, as you say, 3 months before pub date. I'd be willing to commit a blog or two entry every week, from the publisher's perspective. But this seems a bunch more manageable. And by opening up the process to everybody, I think we'll be living the central lessons from *Booklife* (and the central philosophy of Underland online). For those who want to pay, they could go to the conference.

YES — I AGREE. MORE ON THIS SOON.

—Video game: I'm 51% against this, 49% for. How much would it cost? Should I write Atomic Pistol and ask, or should you? I don't know any third party off the top of my head who would want to finance, and I'm not sure

looking for special project funding is a good use of time / resources. But I'm
open to the idea, if we can make it work.

I JUST LEFT IT ON THERE SINCE WE'D DISCUSSED IT
AND BECAUSE LARGE PUBLISHERS HAVE HAD SUCCESS WITH
THIS. WE PROBABLY SHOULDN'T DO IT.

My thoughts:
—I'm exploring some co-op opportunities with [my distributor]. Some options:
tables at stores, face out shelving, newsletter mentions, reviews, etc. Amazon
bundling, etc. Amazon newsletter, etc. Co-op, co-op, co-op. Part of what we
can do depends on what the sales reps can get us. But co-op isn't cheap…

AGAIN, THAT'S UP TO YOU. GIVEN THAT I HAVE NO IDEA
WHAT CHAIN PENETRATION WILL BE LIKE, YOU ALSO NEED
TO LET ME KNOW IF PR EFFORTS SHOULD FOCUS ON DRIVING
PEOPLE TO CHAINS, INDIES, OR AMAZON FOR THE BOOK.
—Portland conference: I've been talking to venues. I have two that are
fantastic, and very close to each other. One has a full kitchen — a pleasant,
open bar that hosts readings. We could do a morning session there, staying for
lunch, then migrating over the other place, an old ballroom, for the afternoon
breakout sessions, adjourning for dinner, and then doing some smaller sort of
social event at then night. Anyway, totally do-able. And I'd love to do it.

OKAY — WHAT TIME? EARLY IN 2010?

I need to put a full marketing budget together for this. With the galleys, then
the finished copies, the Murder by Death soundtrack, the mailing costs, the
drop shipments, and the co-op stuff, we might be really pushing the limit of
what I can afford…

YES, IF YOU PUT TOGETHER THE FULL BUDGET AND
THEN TELL ME WHAT YOUR INCLINATION IS RE WHAT YOU
CAN AFFORD, THEN WE CAN DISCUSS HOW TO ACCOMPLISH
THE REST AND WHAT TO DROP

Victoria To Do:

1) Talk to Murder by Death.
2) Pin down co-op with [the distributor]. (I'm going to a sales conference on

the 15th. A lot will be talked about then.)

3) Continue getting blurbs.

4) Get room reserved for World Fantasy. Does Ann have a day she'd prefer? WE DO [AGENT] DINNER ONE NIGHT> WILL HAVE TO FIGURE OUT. MIGHT BE BETTER TO HOST THE CON SUITE.

▶▶ Press Releases (Example)

A press release should be concise. A press release should provide basic information about the book (who, what, where, when, why): author, title, publisher, ISBN number, general type of book, description, author information, advance blurbs (or appropriate comparisons to other writers), and the release date. A good press release should provide the reader with interesting facts about the book as "event" and why we should care about the author and the book. It should mention any promotion or publicity for the book, if unusual or different, especially: unusual and interesting facts about the author (or about author's expertise for writing this kind of book); a quote from the author and/or publisher about the book; anything timely about the book. It should also explain anything that might be difficult about the book in a way that makes it simple for the reader to understand.

Ideal press releases change for the audience. When I was running an independent press called The Ministry of Whimsy, we published *The Troika*, a book by Stepan Chapman. Chapman had published in literary magazines and in the fantasy markets. We created one press release for mainstream media outlets and one for the fantasy outlets. We also created a third press release for his local media in Arizona that stressed his roots to the community there.

Always give the important information up front, than include the less important details, just like in a standard inverted pyramid newspaper article. Slant the press release to the book or the author — i.e., if you need to introduce reviewers to the author, then slant it toward the author; if the author is established or the book is more important than the author's identity, slant it toward the book. Remember to mimic what you like in other press releases. It will also help to write a mission statement about what you want to the press release to accomplish before you begin writing it.

A good press release has an authority that a reviewer finds difficult to ignore. It positions the book in such a way as to emphasize its strengths while claiming it has no weaknesses. In many cases, a busy reviewer will just mimic or steal from the press release.

Here's the press release for *Booklife*. How well does it describe this book? How well do you think it would go over with a reviewer? Is there anything missing? If you think you could write a better press release, try to as practice for writing your own.

Tachyon Publications
1459 18th Street #139
San Francisco, CA 94107

tachyon@tachyonpublications.com
www.tachyonpublications.com
415.285.5615

Contact: Matt Staggs, Publicist
matt@tachyonpublications.com / 601.259.7779

for immediate release

Booklife: Strategies and Survival Tips for the 21st-Century Writer
Jeff VanderMeer

*The first book on writing that addresses the
challenges facing writers in the new millennium*

The world has changed, and with it the art and craft of writing. In addition to the difficulties of putting pen to paper, authors must now contend with a slew of "new media" outlets including blogs, social networks, mini-feeds, and podcasts. This has forever altered the relationship between writers and their readers, their publishers, and their work.

In an era when authors are expected to do more and more to promote their own work, *Booklife* steers readers through the bewildering options. What should authors avoid doing on the Internet? How does the new paradigm affect authors, readers, and the fundamentals of book publication? What's the difference between letting Internet tools use you and having a strategic plan? Most importantly, how do authors *protect their creativity* while still advancing their careers? How do you filter out white noise and find the peace of mind to do good work? Award-winning author, editor, and web-entrepreneur Jeff VanderMeer shares his 25 years of experience to reveal how writers can go about:

- Using new media: blogs, Facebook, Twitter, MySpace, YouTube, podcasts, and IM
- Effectively networking in the modern era (why it's not all about *you*)
- Understanding the lifecycle of a book and your role in the publication process
- Finding balance between your public and private lives and personas
- Creating a brand and identity tied to your strengths and your writing
- Working with your publisher: editors, publicists, marketing, and sales
- Taking the long view: establishing short- and long-term professional goals
- Getting through rejection and understanding the importance of persistence
- Enjoying and enhancing your creative process

Get a Booklife right now.

"Jeff VanderMeer has written a fascinating book on managing a writing career.... Recommended for anyone who writes, wants to write, or has written and now wonders what to do next."
—Nancy Kress, author of the bestselling *Write Great Fiction*

Trade paperback / $14.95 /326 pp. / 6 x 9 / November 2009 / Nonfiction / 978-1-892391-90-2

Planned Media: Print Advertising / Co-op / National Author Tour

Dedicated blog at Booklifenow.com & affiliation

with Publishers Weekly Booklife.com

Booklife West Coast/East Coast Endurance tour: 6 weeks, 20 cities, including readings and

workshops in Seattle, Portland, Los Angeles, San Francisco,

New York City, Boston, Philadelphia, and Washington D.C.

Highlights: The Hugo House in Seattle, MIT in Boston, and the Library of Congress in D.C.

Distributed to the trade by Independent Publishers Group

As more and more individuals become content providers through self-created platforms like blogs, it's important to re-state a few basic protocols for reviewing books. Also, book reviewing can be a modest but useful secondary stream of revenue in support of your Booklife.

The same things that bother me in reviews of my work that I think are unfair or poorly written, beyond simple errors of fact, are also things I try to avoid in reviewing other people's books. Although a one-paragraph summary of a book on your blog by no means constitutes a "review," anything longer becomes a potential influencer to your audience. You owe it to the writers being reviewed, and to your readers, to take your reviews seriously.

Here are things that I try to avoid doing as a reviewer, either on my blog or in my work for the *New York Times Book Review*, Huffington Post, the *Washington Post Book World*, and many others. Some of them are easy for me to avoid as a reviewer. Some are less so. But with every review, I think seriously about these issues.

BRINGING AN AGENDA TO A REVIEW THAT MAKES IT IMPOSSIBLE FOR THE REVIEWER TO APPRECIATE WHAT THE WRITER INTENDED WITH HIS OR HER BOOK. In most of these cases, the reviewer proceeds to hang the book on a gallows not one timber or thread of which came from the book itself (or, conversely, piles on undeserved praise). Thus, the review is a kind of closed system displaying certain aspects of the reviewer's mind — a psychological portrait of the reviewer, not an analysis of the actual book: a kind of alternate reality; ironically enough, a fiction. Since this is perhaps the number one or number two most annoying thing to encounter in a review of one of my own books, it is something I work hard not to do when reviewing.

MAKING A (VEILED) PERSONAL ATTACK ON THE AUTHOR. The easiest way for a reviewer to launch a personal attack is to imply base motives to the writer — to insinuate through word choice. Sometimes, of course, there are outright personal attacks, but these are usually so roundly denounced that the stealth attack has become the norm. As a reviewer, the easiest way to avoid personal attacks, if you have some issue with the writer that you cannot overcome, is to not review the book. The most ethical approach, however, is to recognize your bias, your particular weakness, and do your best to see the book as independent from the writer. This is the approach I try to take, although, admittedly, this sometimes leads to me being too easy on a book, perversely enough. As a writer, I find the personal attack bewildering, mostly because I could think a particular fiction writer is a jerk and it wouldn't affect my review of their book one iota. So, I wonder, "What did I do to piss this person off? Why'd they do this?" A personal attack makes a writer less sure of their place in the world and of their relationship with other people in the field. It's an awful thing to weather, although if you're in the business long enough you learn to live with it.

PLACING YOURSELF AT THE CENTER OF THE REVIEW. Overuse of first person and cloying personal anecdotes in lieu of penetrating analysis typify the kind of reviewer who believes, for whatever reason, that imposing their persona is more important than actually reviewing the book. In the case of an overblown ego, the reviewer tends to see reviewing as a way to garner leverage and power (however limited in scope). As a reviewer, I try, for the most part, to be nowhere in sight, unless as in my review of Erickson's *Zeroville* for the *Washington Post Book World*, a personal anecdote lends itself to discussing the book or easing the reader into the review. As a writer, though, I just find this approach hilarious — like watching a campy bad movie — and I've parodied it several times in my fiction. It *can* be entertaining, especially if it happens to someone else.

ENGAGING IN TERRITORIAL DEBATES. Every area of writing has Gatekeepers of the True Way, people who insist on engaging in territorial debates over whether something fits a particular genre or subgenre. This tends to involve generalizations about other territories — for example, a genre reviewer making generalizations about the literary mainstream, or vice versa. But beyond the fact that generalizations are usually false, the real problem with this kind of reviewing is that it clutters up the review with material that is ancillary to the book. As a result, such reviews tend to be less comprehensible, and readers often come away from the review having either no idea what the reviewer actually thought of the book or a sense that the reviewer liked or disliked the book for reasons that have nothing to do with the actual book itself. Every time I find myself drifting in this direction, I also tend to find the review harder to write, and, ultimately, writing the review becomes simple as soon as I strip away anything of this nature. As a writer, this kind of review is exasperating because I'm left with the feeling of a wasted opportunity — that the reader of the review will get no sense of the book at all.

EMPLOYING INAPPROPRIATE/SELF-IMPORTANT DICTION AND APPROACHES. Of all badly executed reviews, the worst in my opinion are those that cloak a core emptiness with "academic" terminology and references. The reason for this is that a poorly realized review in this guise has the appearance of authority — it trades the real authority of engaging a book honestly for the false authority of elevated vocabulary. It can be very difficult to unravel the language to get to the point where it's possible to see that the review actually has very little to say. It's for this reason that, except in analytical essays, I don't employ elevated or academic vocabulary. I believe there is an art to writing a good review, but, unlike in fiction, the range of prose styles is more limited by the need to be purely functional. As a fiction writer, I can't say this approach does more than give me darkly humorous amusement, although it makes me take the reviewer less seriously in future.

MAKING SNARKY, TANGENTIAL ASIDES. Sarcasm is not a welcome thing in any review, except in those rare cases where the book is itself sarcastic, thus opening the door (and even then it's not recommended). However, the worst kind of sarcasm or snark is the aside in a review that doesn't pertain to the book except in a tangential way. In these cases, the review writer cannot refrain from barking out some personal prejudice or pet peeve. Such a concern may be legitimate, but a snarky aside is not a legitimate way of expressing it. Whenever, as a reviewer, I feel the need to engage in this kind of behavior, I instead try to deal with my concern head-on by writing about it as the actual subject of a review or article. As a fiction writer, I hate this kind of zinger because it gets under my skin and colors the world around me. It's in a sense another form of personal attack.

ENCOUNTERING THE PROFOUND EVERY TIME OUT. Some reviewers feel the temptation to make a profound general statement about every book they review. These reviewers will never be content with engaging intimately with the book at hand. Each book is instead an opportunity to display an understanding of the Big Picture. Sometimes, this means the reviewer begins to have a thesis written before even reading a particular book. Sometimes, this means the reviewer believes he or she is more important than the book. The result is, oddly enough, a vast simplicity — a reduction of the book before the all-mighty altar of the Idea. Most good books, however, are complex, contradictory, contrary things. The best are not reducible to profound general statements. Admittedly, I can be as taken with my own pomposity as the next person, and so I'm on the lookout for this kind of thing as a reviewer. Which isn't to say that sometimes a grand, far-reaching approach isn't warranted, but a reviewer who does so every time out begins to seem oddly...desperate. As a writer, my reaction to this kind of review, whether positive or negative, is simply to parody it in my fiction (when the opportunity presents itself).

TRYING TO INTUIT PERSONAL DETAILS ABOUT THE WRITER FROM THE FICTION. Some of the very worst reviews, in my opinion, attempt to guess things like the writer's political motivation from evidence in the book itself. Obviously, when reviewing certain kinds of nonfiction this is unavoidable, even desirable. But when analyzing fiction, reviewers who make statements about the writer based on the actions of character or the machinations of plot or what they think they know about the writer are making a terrible mistake. The mistake they are making is a fundamental misunderstanding of the word "fiction." They also make a fundamental mistake about the relationship of a writer to, for example, even the text of an interview. I know from personal experience that during an interview a writer may say anything that comes into his or her head, may make things up with a kind of innocent honesty of wanting to be interesting — or simply do not want to engage some aspect of the book publicly, and thus misrepresent or change their real intent. Which is why reviewers should ignore most public statements by the author about their book, just as they should not apply their own attempts at playing amateur psychic. There is the book and there is you, the reviewer, and any *positive* context or experience you bring to the experience. (For example, you review a novel set in 1800s India and you have a background in the India of that era.) That is all, and that should be enough. I don't believe I ever make this mistake in my reviewing because, as a writer, knowing my own motivation for things and the effects I'm going for, it drives me nuts when I see it in other people's reviews — in either a positive or a negative context.

In addition to avoiding these kinds of mistakes, there are a few other things I try to keep in mind as a reviewer.

First, I always try to tell the truth as I see it, regardless of how others may perceive me or the review as a result. Admittedly, there are good reasons sometimes for revealing the truth gradually, or allowing the reader of the review to do some work in interpretation, but you must tell the truth.

Second, telling the truth doesn't require me to be mean. A good negative review should be written with respect and affection — and even praise where it can be applied. The fact is, writing any book is a gargantuan accomplishment, a huge application of time and resources on the writer's part. That some turn out to be lesser than others should not be a cause for a tone of triumph, elation, or smugness on the part of the reviewer. (My major flaw as a reviewer would be an unwarranted overenthusiasm at times; my mixed reviews tend to be more nuanced.)

Third, writing a positive or glowing review is as strenuous a task as a mixed or negative review. Nothing is worse than a positive review where the reviewer, for any number of reasons, manages to misunderstand the book. Most writers hate misguided positive reviews more than negative reviews.

All of this is simple. All of it is straightforward, and most of it has to do with being fair, honest, and forthright. In my opinion, reviewing a book ought to be a simple thing. You read the book. You think about what you've read. If you have time, you re-read the book. You think about it more, take notes. Then you report back to the reader your thoughts about the book. In doing so, you make sure to tell readers enough about the book to give them the context to understand your opinion…but not so much summary that readers feel they've read the book after reading the review. In your review, you analyze and synthesize what you've read, taking as your cue, your foundation, (1) what you think the book was trying to do, (2) whether it was done well or poorly, and (3) whether what the book tried to do was worth doing. In a skillful review, nothing in the middle should come as too much of a surprise after reading the opening. The writing should be clear, clean, almost invisible, and follow logical progressions. These things must be accomplished before a reviewer can think about going for more complex effects.

Traditional wisdom tells us that fiction writers shouldn't do reviews for fear of it hurting their careers. However, this approach ignores a rich history of past discourse and often raucous argument about books between various authors — in print. It also ignores the diversity created by the cross-pollination and interconnectivity of the Internet. More importantly, the health of any field requires open, transparent, honest, affectionate disagreement and discussion in order to strive to become better, more ethical, and more human.

Appendix C
Additional Notes on New Media
by Matt Staggs

Matt Staggs is a literary publicist and the proprietor of Deep Eight LLC, a boutique publicity agency utilizing the best publicity practices from the worlds of traditional media and evolving social technologies. He has worked in the fields of public relations and journalism for almost a decade. His clients include Tachyon Publications and Underland Press, and he has worked with a diverse group of authors, including Thomas M. Disch, Brian Evenson, James Morrow, Ekaterina Sedia, and Nancy Kress.

▶▶ Nodes and Influencers

As a book publicist, I've learned that embracing social media is an essential component in developing buzz about my clients' projects. At one time — as recently as five or six years ago — getting a title reviewed by critics associated with newspapers and other dead tree publications was the only way that you could establish an audience for a publication. Now, in an age where, thanks to blogs, podcasts, and microblogging platforms, everyone is a critic, these sorts of reviews are useful, but not mandatory. The traditional gatekeepers have been joined by the fans, readers, and a whole legion of creatives and Influencers, and this new environment presents both promise and peril for the publicist.

Properly identifying key audiences is the first step I take when developing a campaign. In addition to listing the obvious audiences (core genre, fans of the author's prior work), I always make a list of what I call "nodes" for each title. I define these nodes as large, general concepts that together form the story told by the author. For instance, a fantasy novel about an adventurer who discovers a hidden city beneath the earth could include such nodes as "underground," "mythology (hollow earth)," "fantasy," and "journeys." For each of these nodes, I then work out a list of potential audiences, and how I might approach them.

By identifying and dissecting the general thematic concepts behind any work you can increase your potential audience many times over. In this day and age, just going for the "easy" reviews alone is criminal. The Internet allows an individual practitioner to make contact with thousands of people and build networks of potential advocates for each and every title.

Identifying these advocates, these Influencers, is very important. I look for the movers and shakers who seem to pop up again and again in newsgroups, bulletin boards, blog comments, and more. I look for people who are sincerely interested in my title, people with an emotional and intellectual investment in the node I've developed, as well as the means to tell the world about it. You need to include podcasters, bloggers, and other broadcasters in your media plan. Your Influencer should have access to at least one of these social mediums, as well as the willingness to utilize them on behalf of your title.

Many pieces have been written about how to properly approach bloggers, podcasters, and other Influencers, and to tell you the truth, I don't think that there's any "right" way to do it. I think that at the end of the day it's about sincerity. You, as the publicist, need to care about what you're offering — in most times this is media content in the form of author contact and potential review copies — and to approach people as you'd like to be approached. Carefully study what your potential Influencer's "beats" are, and *don't* approach him or her unless you are sure your pitch is appropriate.

If you've done this, you need to give your Influencer everything he or she needs to spread the word about your title: enable them to evangelize. If they need author contact, make sure they get it. Do they need an extra copy of the book to give to a friend or maybe for a contest? Make sure they get that too. I try to serve in a support capacity at all times because at this point the Influencer is my "client" too. You should make sure that nothing stands in his or her way to tell the world about your title.

Honesty, sincerity, and patience are the hallmarks of this sort of campaign, and here's the peril that I referred to in the first paragraph. Taking people for granted — and this includes both blowing off potential interviewers just because their audience is smaller as well as simply assuming that a big Influencer will do what you want — is a sure way to kill your title before it hits store shelves. Remember: for the most part, bloggers and podcasters are online because they get a personal sense of satisfaction from what they're doing that extends beyond simple material compensation. *They deserve your respect, and giving them anything less than this can result in repelling the very audience you want to cultivate.*

▶▶ Reputation Management: Telling Your Story Before Someone Else Does

One of the most important things an author should learn about this new era of social media is that the means of production and dissemination is no longer in the hands of an anointed few. Bloggers, podcasters, forum participants, and others are talking, and collectively their voices can be louder than any single newspaper columnist or critic could ever hope to be.

An author can and should now actively engage his or her potential readers by finding where they read their news, which blogs they favor, and what kinds of message boards they frequent. Utilizing this strategy can be an advantage for authors otherwise limited by small publicity budgets and time constraints. However, writers seeking to enter the evolving world of social media should be aware that these engagements are conversations, not monologues and unless you are willing to fully extend yourself — and this involves some amount of vulnerability — you'd be better off not getting involved at all.

Social media thrives on authenticity and honesty, and nothing will sour outreach efforts quicker than the appearance that you are insincere. Problems will happen, scandals will occur, and it's important that when something potentially destructive rears its ugly head — be it about you or your book — that you be the first to talk about it. By telling your story first, you have the opportunity to shape the conversation before someone else can. Your instinct may be to cover up any controversy and hope that no one notices, but this instinct is very nearly always wrong.

People are going to talk about you — they probably already are — and it's up to you as to whether you want to sit quietly or take an active role in the conversation. It's understandable that you might be a little wary to admit to faults and actively engage your critics in open, honest communication online, but this is the only way that you can gain and maintain credibility among your audience. People aren't going to want to listen to you any more if they perceive you're not willing to be honest with them.

I have a very simple formula that I very nearly always recommend to someone involved in a potential crisis. Here it is:

1. Admit that you're wrong. I know that it's hard, but it's going to come out anyway, and you're not going to do yourself any favors in the long run by denying the truth.
2. Explain why and how you're wrong. Sometimes people can be a little more sympathetic when you take the time to tell them exactly what led you to make the poor decision that you did. Everyone has had the experience of making a mistake. They can relate.
3. Make any necessary apologies. Yes, Mom was right. A sincere apology is the best tool that you have in your crisis communication toolbox.
4. Explain how and why this error will never happen again. Each mistake is an opportunity for a lesson learned, and by showing that you're only human and honestly trying to improve, people may be more likely to trust you again.

▶▶ Sipping from the Fire Hose: Online Search Tools

I use a lot of online search tools in my work as a publicist, some of which are extremely valuable. The first thing that you should know is that no one tool is going to be able to do everything you need it to do. You'll need to use several. Secondly, even the best tools depend on their user, so you'll need to know how to use them well. This advice especially applies to the essentials in information gathering: RSS readers, Google Alerts, and regularly targeted web searches.*

---

* Everyone leaves a digital trail these days, and Google is probably the best search tool I've

The web is an organic, growing thing. It's constantly changing and interdependent. One tiny post on an obscure blog in the darkest corner of cyberspace can result in an explosion of remarks, retorts, and referrals from a million different points — a potential conflagration of information. How do you keep track of it all? RSS readers.

RSS — "Really Simple Syndication" — is a system through which web users can subscribe to multiple websites and read their latest updates consolidated in one place. It's an amazingly cool and useful tool for anyone who has a number of different sites they enjoy reading. So how do you take advantage of RSS? It's simple. The first thing that you'll want to do is look for a RSS reader or aggregator. This is the tool through which you'll read all of your subscriptions, and there are tons out there. Some of them work as desktop applications and others are web-based; you'll have to decide which is right for you. Just do a web search. I use Google's web-based Google Reader. It's incredibly simple, and since it's web-based it doesn't take up any room on my already crowded hard drive.

Once you've signed up for a reader, you'll need to start subscribing to the websites you'll want to monitor. Visit your targeted website and look for the orange-and-white RSS symbol. It's usually either next to the URL address or located somewhere on the website itself. Depending on your reader, you should be able to just click the symbol and subscribe automatically. Once you've subscribed, you should be able to read any further updates directly in your reader.

You may wonder where you'll find the blogs and websites that cover the sort of material that you're interested in. There are a number of different ways to do this. The first way is to do a few basic web searches on your topic. Since

---

found for uncovering them. I use it all the time to research potential reviewers for the books I promote. Don't have an email address? Use a wildcard search. If you know the domain for the site that publishes your target's work, you can likely find your subject's email address. Do a search for email associated with that domain with an asterisk in the place where the person's name would be, like this: "*@DOMAIN.COM." This will uncover all email addresses associated with that domain, and if you can decipher a pattern, like "FIRSTNAME.LASTNAME@DOMAIN.COM", you'll be able to deduce your target's email address from that. Be sure to run a general search for the target's name, as well. Google can uncover MySpace and Facebook pages, Twitter accounts, blogs, and more that the target may be utilizing. You can read these to gather intelligence about the target's likes and dislikes. This can help you craft a good pitch letter for your book.

we're talking about books, I suggest that you Google terms like "litblogs," "book reviews," and your particular genre, like "horror" or "steampunk." You should find quite a few sites, all of greater or lesser relevance. In addition to general searches, you can use specialized blog search tools. There are many out there, like Icerocket and Twingly. One of the best known is Technorati, which monitors and aggregates information related to blogs.

You can search and find dozens of blogs on a variety of topics quickly and easily. Technorati provides data that can tell you how popular these blogs are as well through a measurement called "authority." Authority counts how many other blogs have reacted to posts on your targeted blog, reactions being blog posts that link to the targeted blog. The idea is that a frequently referenced blog is more authoritative than one which few people recognize or react to. My own site ranks a modest "145" at the time of this writing. That's not too bad, but let's look at some others for comparison. Bookslut, one of the best known book review sites on the web, weighs in at 1,062 reactions. Fantasy Book Critic, another niche blog focusing on speculative fiction like my own, rates in at a comparable "197." Using Technorati to find popular blogs that focus on your sort of material is a good way, but perhaps not the best, to start to build your subscription base. A supplementary method — but one that takes a lot more time — is to find a few popular blogs on your topic matter and then subscribe to the sites that they link to. After a while you should be able to build up a comprehensive database of blogs.

Depending on your reader or aggregator, you should be able to sort and organize your RSS subscriptions by topic ("books," "popular culture," "science fiction") or any other criteria you can think of. RSS subscription can save you a lot of time, but only use them to your best advantage. Subscribe to those sites that normally feature the topics that you're interested in, and monitor your feeds at least once a day. Be judicious about canceling subscriptions that aren't useful or germane, or you'll become overwhelmed. Another great advantage of RSS Readers is that with most of them you can actually search for specific keywords within your subscriptions, so once you've got a good database built up you can look for mentions of your book or name and quickly go to those relevant posts and respond to them as needed.

Even with a masterful list of RSS subscriptions you should never assume that you have a complete overview of what's happening on the web. That's where our next tool comes in: Google Alerts.

Google Alerts allows anyone with a free Google account to plug in up to 1,000 search terms and receive daily or even as-it-happens email alerts of when and where a keyword is mentioned. Begin at WWW.GOOGLE.COM/ALERTS. You can even customize whether you just want mentions, Google News, blogs, or something else in your alerts. It's that simple. However, like RSS subscriptions, Google Alerts can become overwhelming unless you handle them correctly. The first thing you'll want to do is to choose the right search terms. If you use something too general like "books" you'll be overwhelmed. The second thing you'll want to do is to establish a special folder in your email client only for Google Alert updates. If you do this, then you can search through all of them once a day and respond accordingly. Like your RSS subscriptions, you'll want to avoid the temptation to check these things constantly. They can really burn a lot of time. When you do check your alerts, be sure to check where each is coming from: you may discover new blogs or websites to consider for RSS subscription.

These two rather specialized forms of information gathering are important, you shouldn't forget about web searches. You can use your usual web search engine to do some amazing stuff if you only take the time to check the advanced search features. Limit your search results by date, excluding occurrences of specific words and focus on certain kinds of content. If you've just been using your search engine for basic searches then you're probably missing a lot of information. Again, I use Google, but no matter what kind of search engine you're using there are always ways to narrow your focus.

Another great search tool is called Addictomatic. Addictomatic searches across live web resources (blogs, Twitter, YouTube, and more) and generates one page with all of the results in a neatly ordered format for your perusal. It's a great tool to get a top-down look at the recent material on the web, but like the rest, it shouldn't be used exclusively.

Appendix D
Nurturing Creativity

▶▶ Chasing Experience by Nathan Ballingrud

Nathan Ballingrud is a remarkable short fiction writer who has won the Shirley Jackson Award and had his work reprinted in year's best anthologies. I first met him at the Clarion Writers Workshop in 1992. Pertinent to his discussion of "Chasing Experience," I remember that the first day he locked himself in his dorm room and typed furiously for a couple of hours. Suitably intimidated, we all thought Nathan was incredibly committed to his art. But, as he told me many years later, in fact he wasn't typing anything: he was just nervous about meeting the other writers attending the workshop. Although "Chasing Experience" refers to genre writers, I believe it has universal application to all writers.

WHEN I WAS twenty-one years old, I didn't know a goddamned thing. I was poorly read, socially awkward, and a virgin. I was perpetually embarrassed, and had lived as tentatively as I could manage. By any measure, I was woefully ill-equipped to become a writer; yet somehow, in 1992, I contrived to be accepted to the Clarion Writers Workshop in East Lansing, Michigan. Expecting to emerge, resplendent, from my chrysalis, I instead spent six weeks in reeling disorientation as my peers spun out reams of stories, while I struggled to come up with a single idea that wasn't nakedly ridiculous or even — on one occasion — stolen outright. I'd arrived on the Susan C. Petrie Scholarship, and I'm informed that, after the first week, there was speculation that I was just there as a charity case.

By the time it was all over, I knew I was in over my head. But I thought I could just write my way through it. After all, that was the advice we'd been given. Write every day. Saturate the market with submissions. Eventually you will break through the editorial wall and achieve total enlightenment — or, you know, get a story published in *The Magazine of Fantasy & Science Fiction* or something.

So I heeded the Word, and lo, a few months later I sold a story to *F&SF*. It was a little fingernail paring of a story, and although I thought the prose was pretty good, I felt the story itself was a sham: a meaningless little vignette which pretended to be about more than it was. And I felt that my story's publication was indicative of a problem pervasive throughout the genre, one that perhaps I was in an ideal position to recognize. To wit: the lack of a broad life-experience.

To be more specific, I believed that the genre suffered from being mired in a rigidly narrow perspective. I believed — perhaps unfairly, perhaps not — that most of its writers were well-educated, generally comfortable middle class folk, with the bulk of their own experiences coming from a fairly specific stratum of the socioeconomic spectrum. I recognized my own shortcomings in everything I was reading. Furthermore, the characters in the stories did not seem to reflect the kind of people I knew in my own life. The people I knew were buffeted by feelings of rage, pain, and loneliness, which made a lot of science fiction and fantasy ring false to me.

I reacted with hostility. To my own diminished ambitions as much as to the limited scope of the stories I was reading. Clarion taught me craft, but that was only half of what I needed. I didn't want to spend my energies writing filler for the digests. I resolved to write more honestly about the emotional experiences I was familiar with. And I decided that I needed a corrective to the insular life I'd led.

So I moved to New Orleans within the year, without employment or a place to live, with the intention of working menial jobs and exposing myself to what I imagined was a more immediate, more "real" sort of life.

I did manage to collect quite a few interesting experiences over the next several years. I was a cook on barges and oil rigs in the Gulf for a while; I used to go up to the helicopter pad in the middle of the night and stare into the long night all around me, oil rigs which were too far away to see in daylight suddenly ringing the horizon like Christmas lights. Once we were caught in a tropical storm, and I went out on deck, gripped the railing for everything I was worth, and watched as the ship heaved through the enormous waves (one of the stupidest and yet most awe-inspiring things I've ever done). I did drugs for a while — cocaine, acid, ecstasy — and once spent a terrified few hours when a friend paced the room with a gun, convinced a dealer he claimed to have ripped off was coming for him. (He wasn't.) I was roommates with a prostitute for a while, and occasionally had to pretend to be a tough guy for people who harassed her outside of work. And finally I just settled down as a bartender and stopped seeking out derangement, letting it come to me instead.

These were calmer and more rewarding years, and while life was still full of criminals and prostitutes and cops, they were just regulars now. Often they were friends. Then came marriage and a child, and later a divorce, and a whole different set of experiences. I finally got to the point at which I was comfortable writing again. And the writing did benefit from all of this, though not in the way I would have guessed.

It turned out that physical experiences were less valuable to me than emotional and cultural ones. A lot of the details of physical experience can be faked in prose. Getting into a fistfight, for example, or whitewater rafting. There will be certain details unavailable to you unless you actually do experience them, but generally these are not damning.

What will stunt your writing is a lack of emotional and cultural experience. And I think it is incumbent upon us to actively seek out a broader range of these kinds of experiences. By that I mean ranging well outside your comfort zone and immersing yourself in a lifestyle that scares you at first, because of its difference and its strangeness, and getting to know people you've been conditioned to think of as throwaway people, or as corrupt people, or sometimes only as "those" people. This broadens perspective, which is one of the most important tools at a writer's disposal. We have to learn to look outside of our own lives; sometimes, in order to do that, we have to change our lives.

It is in this sense that manufacturing experience will produce flawed work. I won't say don't do it — I don't feel morally or ethically capable of telling anyone what they can or cannot write about — but I feel a lack of personal experience, and the perspective and empathy it provides, will be obvious to most readers, and will ultimately subvert the readers' trust.

We're seeing this play out online, in what's been dubbed RaceFail '09 [on the Internet]. I believe the science fiction and fantasy genre has been so insular for so long, the question of an honest and accurate depiction of any culture other than white middle class culture was just never given a lot of consideration. Not on a systemic level, and not by more than a handful of writers. I doubt this was conscious; I think it's a direct result of a narrowness of perspective — a lack of real experience with any culture other than the dominant one. I suspect the feelings of bitterness and frustration that seem to have caught so many by surprise are not new; it's just that the Internet has given readers a means of communication on a scale that didn't exist before. A lot of writers are being called out on a problem they didn't know they had, and are too proud or embarrassed to acknowledge. It turns out liberal politics are not a cover for limited perspective.

On a personal level, all those experiences I so self-righteously sought out did find their way into my stories. I can point to a few specific examples, but generally it's more organic than that. I've drawn a little on my time as an offshore worker or as the owner of a painting business to inform some of the characters. But in most cases reality is just the backdrop. It informs the imagination. I've yet to transcribe an actual event from my life into a story, but I've drawn heavily from emotional experiences. I exaggerate certain qualities in myself — anger, pettiness, anxiety — so that I can prosecute them in a fictional context, and maybe achieve some kind of catharsis. Or at least remind myself of the bad places they can take me, if I let them. I've discovered that I write a lot about issues of masculine identity, about men who fail to live up to what their own expectations of what a man should be. I never thought I held those notions myself — I've always congratulated myself as being a more enlightened person than that — but when I read over my own stories it becomes obvious to me that I'm trying to come to terms with those expectations myself, however absurd or outdated they might be.

I tend to be pretty confessional in my stories, even if it's only on the metaphorical level. I love reading stories in which I feel the author has a personal stake. There doesn't seem to be much point to it if you're not trying to reveal something fundamental of yourself. That's what I was missing all those years ago when I was pouring through the digests. It's likely that I was actually reading some good stories in there and just didn't have the apparatus to recognize them. In some ways going out and chasing down varieties of experience was just a way to shock myself into adulthood. I became a better writer, a better reader, and a better human being.

I wouldn't advise anyone to go to the lengths I did; I'd argue that my case seemed particularly dire, and required strong action. I was also young, and responsible for no one but myself. I'm a single father now and today such a radical jump would be impossible. What I would advise is a harsh self-appraisal. Find a way to address your limitations. Be suspicious if your solution seems too easy.

The world is choking on mediocre writers. Make yourself better. Even if — especially if — it hurts.

▶▶ Luck's Child by Marly Youmans

Marly Youmans has published young adult, genre, and literary fiction in a variety of publications and in book form for publishers including Farrar, Straus, & Giroux, Penguin, and many others.

Although the daydreams of a young writer seldom involve bad luck but are castles in the air, pleasantly sprinkled with stardust, she soon becomes acquainted with many inhabitants of the Land of Luck, some of them lovely and some twisted and harsh. It is impossible to live a writer's life without some meeting up with bad luck. It is possible to create one's own good luck.

Bad luck arrives in the shape of those things that happen to books that writers have not caused and cannot control. Bad luck is random, sometimes catastrophic, a source of frustration, and hard on unfortunate souls who have a too-permeable skin that refuses to transform into protective chitin. In my experience, such ill luck can come from any or many directions — as, poor book design, a publisher who collapses and slashes imprints and cuts staff, an editor's private woes that spill over into work, and events of historic scope.

In 2001, bad luck swirled up around a book of mine called *The Wolf Pit*. First, the editor departed the house unexpectedly, leaving the unfortunate book an "orphan" up for adoption. Second, the book was postponed until mid-September. It made an appearance in the world not long after 9-11, a day of destruction that made worrying about a new novel feel silly and wrong. Bookwise, the result of such an event was to launch a craze for nonfiction books about terrorism and the Arab world and to put a tight squeeze on the review space available to novels. Third, the book appeared on the publisher's fall list in the wake of Jonathan Franzen's *The Corrections*. Franzen and his encounters with Oprah — or his Bartleby-like refusals to encounter — seemed to consume much of the remaining oxygen at Farrar, Straus, and Giroux.

While two out of those three happenings are a bit unusual, the fact of un-controllable bad luck is common among writers. If I look around at friends, I see one writer with an especially memorable case: his novel was six weeks away from being made into a movie with Jack Lemmon and James Garner when Lemmon abruptly dropped out, scuppering the project. What a difference such visibility might have made to his career! Another friend who recently chose to move from one publishing house to another has been told that the new publisher can pay neither the second half of his advance nor his tour expenses. Meanwhile, his editor has fallen under the cost-cutting axe. A third friend is coming to realize that an editor simply does not like the subject matter of her novel, even though he had discussed and approved a detailed proposal. Alas, the partial advance has already been spent on living expenses.

None of these events or changes could be halted by a writer; not one could be foreseen. In each case, bad luck's causes and nature were unexpected, its messages as arbitrary as the gnomic predictions that come to us in fortune cookies. Bad luck was simply to be endured, for the most part, though damage control might salvage something. In the case of my 9-11 book, I managed to improve my own feelings about the situation by writing some editors a letter to ask whether they would consider reviewing a book that had been overlooked during that tumultuous fall. This strategy helped in terms of gathering many reviews, although they arrived very late — really too late to help in a landscape where books are quickly returned by booksellers. The book did, however, go on to nab one piece of good luck, winning the Michael Shaara Award for 2001.

An opposite to overpowering bad luck exists — an overwhelming good luck that is suddenly shed on an author when a publisher chooses to invest mightily in a particular book and then to push hard. Because the number of books produced is so high, a push often strikes even the recipient as arbitrary and surprising. Few books are lead books. In addition, celebrities of various sorts have their own large luck, compelling the devotion of many publishers.

But what writers mean when they talk about good luck is far simpler.

For most writers, particularly mid-list writers, good luck in publishing springs from the work itself. Persist, and eventually requests arrive from editors at magazines and presses. Awards come, as well as what is better: the gift of respect from those writers and editors a writer admires. By not losing hold of the joy that gives birth to creation and by keeping faith with the vocation, a writer can flourish despite the pesky tweaks and harder blows of ongoing randomness and bad luck. A writer makes friends and advocates for the work by doing the work and sharing her words. And that is as it should be because literature declares by its very existence that other people matter.

▶▶ Workshops by Cat Rambo

Cat Rambo has attended the Johns Hopkins Writing Seminars, Clarion West, and Taos Toolbox, and taught writing at Johns Hopkins, Indiana University, and Bellevue Community College. She serves as the editor for Fantasy Magazine.

Writing workshops are great in that you can learn tremendous amounts from them. You can network effectively and, if you are willing to pay attention, move your career along faster than you might be able to move it otherwise. You can hear people who have grappled with specific writing issues talk about them and learn from their experience. You can be challenged and inspired and forced to write good, solid stuff.

Writing workshops are terrible in that they have the potential to exacerbate psychic problems, render your ego to a shred of its former self and even impose a profound writer's block. Bad people can ruin a workshop easily. This is a sad thing, but sometimes it happens. Make the most of it by connecting with the people you like and who have useful energy, feedback, and inspiration to give you.

Go with reasonable expectations. Do not think a workshop will spiritually enlighten you or provide a parental figure or mentor that will guide the rest of your existence. You will be given neither a secret decoder ring nor a tamed muse in a box. This is not to say that, if you are the personality type who does this sort of thing, you will not find spiritual enlightenment, but generally most of us will come away with a few more tricks in their writing toolbox, some good contacts, and some new stories. Which are all good things to come away with.

Writing workshops are not a bad way to spend money if you have it to spend. At worst, you will have some time away from home in which to write. A writing workshop's cost may be tax-deductible. Consult your accountant.

In workshops, as with writing groups, you want to be with people who are better than you, whose examples will push you and instruct you. This is true of both fellow students as well as instructors. Google around and find out what other people have thought of the workshop and instructors and factor that research in when deciding whether or not to apply or go.

Cultivate both a hide and ego of iron. Take criticism humbly and consider it for what it's worth. If you don't agree, that's fine.

In workshops, be kind, but honest. Don't tell someone else how you would write their story. Tell them what works and what you would like to see more of.

If many people are pointing at the same thing in a manuscript as broken, they are likely all correct that the piece in question is broken. It is unlikely that any of them are proposing the right fix, however.

If you want to get more out of a workshop:

- Take the time to read some stuff by the instructors beforehand. You don't need to go overboard with it.
- Try and fail. There is no better time to try and fail than in a workshop. Failing shows that you're trying something new, that you are working at your craft. You learn more from trying and failing than trying and succeeding, particularly if you try again.
- Go prepared to focus. Get rid of things that worry at you as much as you can and give all of your attention to the work you are doing.

A workshop should push you well out of your comfort zone. It should make you change at least one thing about the way you write. It should make you write at least one thing you would have never written otherwise.

Keep making use of writing workshops after you've gone. Keep in touch with at least a couple of people in it. Six months to a year later, go through the notebooks or files from the workshop and see what new work or practices they inspire.

▶▶ Sacrifice: Without Hope, Without Despair by Matthew Cheney

Matthew Cheney's writing has appeared in a wide variety of publications, including One Story, Weird Tales, Locus, English Journal, Rain Taxi, Las Vegas Weekly, *and the anthologies* Interfictions *and* Logorrhea. *He is a columnist for* Strange Horizons *and currently lives in New Hampshire, where he teaches at Plymouth State University. Knowing his balanced approach to the idea of sacrifice for one's writing, I invited him to expand upon our email conversations about the subject...*

> Isak Dinesen said that she wrote a little every day, without hope and without despair. I like that.
> —Raymond Carver, *Paris Review* interview

1.

When I was in grade school, a professional writer came to talk about his life and work. Later, one of my teachers, a man who occasionally thought about writing short stories and essays of his own, said to me, "You know, I just don't think I'd really like being a writer — all those hours alone, staring at a page, stuck in your own head. No, not the life for me."

To me, even at that age, it sounded like heaven.

2.

It is a fact: If writing becomes part of your life, it will consume, at least occasionally and perhaps frequently, significant amounts of attention, energy, and time. Sometimes you will become distracted, absentminded. You will forget birthdays and anniversaries and appointments and deadlines. Phone calls will go unreturned, email will accumulate, bills will go unpaid. If the project you are working on is particularly consuming, you may even forget to eat or to change your clothes or to take a shower. You neighbors may gossip.

If writing is something more than an idle hobby, more than an amusement you indulge in only when most convenient, then it becomes a significant gravitational force in your life. In *About Writing*, Samuel Delany offers advice to an aspiring writer: "One difference between your situation and mine may simply be [...] that when I was nineteen years old, I decided in no uncertain terms that all my first energies would henceforth go directly into my writing. Only when whatever piece I was working on was as fine as I could possibly make it, would I put any leftover energy whatsoever (and only that) into living what others think a decent and reasonable life. Family, friends, lovers, education, and even my health have all taken second place to my writing."

3.

The fact is not a justification for bad behavior. The decision to commit your life to any serious activity will lead to consequences, and the difficulties of a writing life should not be glorified or used to buffer an image of the Romantic suffering artist. All people choose what to do with the limited time, resources, attention, and energy given to them in life. Many people are limited in other ways — by circumstances of birth or geography, duty or desire. Note that Delany says "I decided in no uncertain terms." It is a choice, and a strong one. *This is what I will do, this is who I will be.*

Delany admits that his is not the only way to write, but he says he suspects that, had he chosen to prioritize differently, he would have published only half as many novels as he has, and no nonfiction. "My only point," he writes, "is that every artist — not to mention you or me — must begin by saying: Is there any more I *could* have done? Is there any more I must do now, in terms of the work itself?"

Those questions are valuable, but taken to extremes they will backfire. There is always more you can do, more you can sacrifice. It has become a cliché to say that no work of art is ever finished, only abandoned, but just because it is a cliché does not mean it is wrong. There is a point of diminished returns, and it is important to keep in mind another question: "Would the work and I benefit more by moving on?"

The sacrifices, too, may become more harmful to the work than beneficial. You could, yes, spend twenty hours a day, seven days a week, fifty-two weeks a year writing. This would not be good for you or for your writing. (Have you seen Jack Nicholson in *The Shining*?)

We need experience — to get out in the world, to be among people not like us. We need to daydream and goof off. Joyce Carol Oates, one of the most prolific American writers of recent decades, has said she spends an awful lot of time looking out the window.

4.

Sometimes the sacrifice is too large, too much. One has to live, one has to support oneself. Tillie Olsen chronicled the ways writers have been kept from writing throughout her book *Silences*, one of the essential texts for any aspiring artist:

> The habits of a lifetime when everything else had to come before writing are not easily broken, even when circumstances now often make it possible for writing to be first; habits of years — response to others, distractibility, responsibility for daily matters — stay with you, mark you, become you. The cost of "discontinuity" (that pattern still imposed on women) is such a weight of things unsaid, an accumulation of material so great, that everything starts up something else in me; what should take weeks, takes me sometimes months to write; what should take months, takes years.

I've seen various writers cite advice from Flaubert: "Be regular and ordinary in your life like a bourgeois so that you may be violent and original in your work." Yet what is it that allows a person to have a "regular and ordinary" life? Do we all have access to enough privileges that even if we don't have the luck to be among the bourgeois, we can at least pretend?

To admit sacrifices, shouldn't we first admit privileges?

5.

Many places in the world have no libraries or bookstores, no publishing infrastructure to create and distribute books and magazines, and hence no literary culture. Few writers are bred in such conditions. The ones who write against that silence — that silencing — are more likely to be swallowed by it than to have even their loudest scream get heard. The idea of such writers sacrificing for their art is absurd; they are the sacrificed.

Or consider what Nadine Gordimer said in a *Paris Review* interview published in 1983, during the vicious reign of South Africa's apartheid regime:

> I come to America, I go to England, I go to France...nobody's at risk. They're afraid of getting cancer, losing a lover, losing their jobs, being insecure. It's either something that you have no control over, like death — the atom bomb — or it's something with which you'd be able to cope anyway, and that is not the end of the world; you'll get another job or

you'll go on state relief or something of this nature. It's only in my own country that I find people who voluntarily choose to put everything at risk — in their personal life. I mean to most of us, the whole business of falling in love is so totally absorbing, nothing else matters. It's happened to me. There have been times in my life when I have put the person I was in love with far ahead of my work. I would lose interest, I wouldn't even care if the book was coming out. I'd forget when it was being published and I wouldn't worry about the reception it got because I was in such a state of anguish over some man. And yet the people I know who are committed to a political cause never allow themselves to be deflected by this sort of personal consideration or ambition.

Look at the sacrifices there, on all sides. Writing sacrificed to love, everything sacrificed to politics. Imagine the other sides of what is said. The love that could have been sacrificed to writing. The political cause that could have lost an activist to a novel. What of the people for whom everything is at risk, but who did not volunteer to put it there? What of the people who didn't get to write novels because, for the accident of skin color, they were relocated, banned, left to die, tortured, beaten, hanged?

What of the people who have sacrificed for you — so you can be what you are, do what you do? You can't even know all their names.

All does not have to be lost. I think of a visit I made to Nicaragua, and a woman who spent nearly eighteen hours every day selling bits of fruit on buses, a job for which she was grateful, because the only other occupations she knew of were provided by sweatshops and prostitution. And yet, she could recite entire poems by Rubén Dario from memory. So could taxi drivers, mothers, factory workers, children. Someone told me about Ernesto Cardenal, Nicaragua's first Culture Minister, founder of the Solentiname Island community of artists who are ordinary people, and thus extraordinary. Someone told me about the literacy campaigns in the early days of the Sandinista government — campaigns that brought words to a citizenry which had previously been dominated by illiteracy. Imperfect, scattered, its funds forever bled dry by years of war sponsored by the United States, nonetheless the campaigns taught people of all ages to be poets, to sing their sacrifices, to share their souls. It's a beautiful ideal, even if the reality may have been messier than the memory years later made it seem. Shards of beauty from the reality remain.

6.

The same 1983 issue of *The Paris Review* that contained the interview with Nadine Gordimer contained an interview with the American writer Raymond Carver in which he spoke candidly about his battle with alcoholism. "I suppose I began to drink heavily," he admitted, "after I realized that the things I'd wanted most in my life for myself and my writing, and my wife and children, were simply not going to happen."

Ambition's edges are sharp. Ambition fuels us to seek publication for our work, an audience, somebody with whom to communicate, eyes to receive our visions and minds to receive our written thoughts. It inspires us to make things and then to shout at the world: "Look at me!" And then it slices us open with ever-shifting goalposts for failure: one reader is not enough, there must be a thousand; this magazine is a nice enough place for a story to appear, but it would be better to have been in that one; getting paid for a piece of writing is exciting, but it's still not enough to live on; making a living from writing is extraordinary, but it would be better to be rich; being rich is magnificent, but respect would be more fulfilling...

Ambition tells us that fame will heal our wounds. Once the masses love us, we will overcome the shame of having been born. But there are never enough masses, and they have as much power to smother as to love. The wounds from which we write are gaping, an abyss at the heart of the self.

Maybe once we wanted to frighten our parents and scandalize our friends by joining a cult and following a guru; now ambition makes us ache to be the guru ourselves. What better way to feel good than to conjure wisdom for wide-eyed minions? But what if the minions don't arrive? What if they refuse to open their eyes? Can there be a guru without followers? Can there be a cult writer without a cult?

And yet what of the opposite? A writer without ambition — without dreams and hopes and yearnings and crazy power fantasies — is probably not a writer. At best, such a writer is invisible, and will always be so, having destroyed whatever manuscripts were created long before another person got to lay eyes upon the words. Having killed the words, that writer does not exist.

Tillie Olsen quotes Miriam Allen deFord:

Some of what I know to be my best writing will never be published... many of my most cherished projects will never come to fruition; many of my aspirations forever unfulfilled. I am always surprised when a stranger recognizes my name...but for more than half a century I had had my work published...at 77 I am busier with my writing than ever before and expect to continue until I die.... When I was young I was going to be a great poet...now I am happy that at long last I did get one volume [of poetry] published...I was also going to be a famous short story writer and novelist. How many years of disappointment and rebellion and grief to realise that I was never going to be anything of the kind; [there are only] my dozen books, my moderate recognition in two or three specialized fields.

It is what you aspire to rather than what you attain that brings into being even what you do attain. Never set your sights too low.

There is no disgrace in joining us Almosters. At least a little of what we had to say has been said and a few have heard and even listened.

7.

When I was in high school, I met the novelist and screenwriter Calder Willingham, whose first novel, *End as a Man*, published when he was in his early twenties, had become a best-seller. He had hung around with such writers as Norman Mailer and Gore Vidal and William Styron in the 1950s. He had never achieved their critical success, nor had his other novels done as well as *End as a Man*, though I met him when one of his last books, *Rambling Rose*, was being filmed from his screenplay. He had not published a novel in fifteen years by then, though he had continued to work as a screenwriter, often on projects that didn't get made, or that other people rewrote significantly. Still, the projects paid better than novels. Such is the way of Hollywood.

Calder Willingham held a lot of bitterness toward the literary community by the time I met him. He attacked my youthful idealism and egotism with sharp glee. I had told him, in a letter, that "I have to write." He replied with words that still whisper at me now and then: "You say you *have* to write. Why? Who is holding a gun to your head?"

His point was, I think, a good one. We make choices. We follow the paths that seem most appealing at the time. I have never *had* to write. I have often *wanted* to write, because writing seemed like a way to relieve built up pressure, or to amuse myself, or to share an idea. I have written because I was better at writing than at other things, and so writing was more appealing. I would love to be a musician, but I have no sense for rhythm and little sense for tone. I wouldn't mind being a physicist, but I have no head for mathematics. I would like to change the world, but I'm quickly exhausted by all the people in it.

In *The Writing Life*, Annie Dillard says, "It should surprise no one that the life of the writer — such as it is — is colorless to the point of sensory deprivation. Many writers do little else but sit in small rooms recalling the real world."

Sitting in small rooms, recalling the real world...this is when I have been happiest. And so I write. I am wary of ambition, and often think that writing is not a calling or a choice so much as an affliction. But small rooms are comforting, and the real world more appealing in recollection than in fact.

8.

I adore Samuel Johnson mostly for his sentences, which are long and complex things of pure formal beauty, but now and then I adore him, too, for his sentiments. The eighty-eighth of the weekly essays he published as *The Idler*, for instance, "What Have You Done?", seems to me a work of perfection. "He that in the latter part of his life too strictly enquires what he has done," Johnson writes, "can very seldom receive from his own heart such an account as will give him satisfaction. We do not indeed so often disappoint others as ourselves."

When we realize the choices we have made in life, how do we weigh them? What do we value? Have we sacrificed, or have we simply chosen ourself over other selves? Would it have been better otherwise? Were there choices we were blind to?

Or have we achieved more than we admit? Only the tamest aspirations are always met. Why sneer at the Club of Almosters when its members can all claim to have made some small mark against a fleeting life? Allow reality its shards of beauty; claim some for yourself.

And remember the end of Johnson's eighty-eighth *Idler*:

He that has improved the virtue or advanced the happiness of one fellow-creature, he that has ascertained a single moral proposition, or added one useful experiment to natural knowledge, may be contented with his own performance, and, with respect to mortals like himself, may demand, like Augustus, to be dismissed at his departure with applause.

Appendix E
How to Write a Novel in Two Months

THE MODERN ERA, with its increased interconnectivity between pop culture, genre, and the literary mainstream, has forever scrambled the distinction between low and high art. As a result, it's become more acceptable for a writer to take on the kinds of gigs that in the past might have weakened a "serious" reputation. In my case, my entry point to combining pop culture with my own vision came when I had the opportunity to write a novel in the *Predator* universe for Dark Horse Books. Taking on such a project confounded a few of my readers. Some thought that my background in "literary fantasy" meant I couldn't pull it off. Others thought I just shouldn't attempt it because of the debased reputation of tie-in novels. The fact is, though, that I accepted the assignment without a second thought for two reasons: (1) I'm a huge fan of the *Predator* movies and it's one of the few movie franchises for which I'd already developed a couple of ideas and (2) my friend Brian Evenson, the creative writing director at Brown University, was writing an *Aliens* novel.

What I didn't anticipate is that due to a variety of circumstances, including sickness and an unexpected trip to France, I would wind up with a deadline for the novel that seemed to preclude being able to produce anything of quality. The result is that I basically wrote *Predator: South China Sea* in two months. I had more than six months to work on it, but only spent about eight weeks at the computer and writing longhand.

This may seem like a short time period. That's because it is a short time period. Some ideas, some novels, require a long gestation period and an equally long time in which to revise, revisit, re-envision. For example, it took a decade to put together the stories that comprise *City of Saints & Madmen* and eight years to work on *Shriek: An Afterword* on-and-off. In my twenties, I was known to spend six months on a single short story or novella. Factored into this time span, however, were all of the editing, publishing, nonfiction, and hours spent at a full-time job. You would also have to factor in that as a writer in your twenties and, to some extent your thirties, you are still getting comfortable with your writing. You don't know how to do a lot of things and so some of your time is spent puzzling out how the pieces fit together, how this or that technique works, why this doesn't, etc.

Now that I don't have a full-time job and am over forty, two things have happened: (1) I can put more of the full force of my attention into a novel or short story more intensely over a short period of time and (2) I'm much more relaxed and as a result my rough drafts tend to be more complete than in the past; I still do a ton of rewriting, revision, and line editing, but I find that more of the initial vision in my head is in the draft right away.

These factors helped in writing a novel so quickly (for me). However, there were other little tricks and factors that allowed me to work this fast without sacrificing quality. (From the enthusiastic reaction to the novel, it would appear I've written something sea-worthy, but, of course, you can judge the results for yourself.)

So, here's what I've learned. With the caveat that...I don't know how *Star Wars* and *Star Trek* writers do it, because they have huge bibles of information to absorb while all I had was three sheets of info on the Predator, prior *Predator* novel tie-ins to read, and the two *Predator* movies. For this reason, what I learned really has less to do with writing a tie-in novel than just with having to quickly writing *any* novel while trying to make sure the quality control is still there.

■ Support

Before you can even entertain the idea of writing a novel in two months, you need to have adequate support. Support constitutes a form of strategic planning. Here are just a few elements that go into such planning.

ALLOCATE ENOUGH TIME DURING THE TWO MONTHS TO MAKE YOUR GOAL POSSIBLE. If you cannot find six to eight hours in a day to write, you may need to set yourself a different goal. If you can only find four hours a day to write, set a goal of four months and stick to that goal as strictly as if you were writing the novel in two months.

MAKE SURE YOUR PARTNER IS WILLING TO GIVE YOU THEIR FULL SUPPORT. My wife Ann made the experience of writing this novel an easy one. I rarely left the house and she did a lot of things I usually do for the household. I can't thank her enough for that, and I still owe her some kind of reciprocal sacrifice.

ACQUIRE CONTACTS THAT YOU CAN USE FOR SPECIALIST INFORMATION SO YOU DON'T HAVE TO DO RESEARCH. This ranges from small stuff to huge stuff. For example, Dave Larsen (DAVIDLARSEN.COM) was my guns and heavy artillery guy, and he came through in a big way. I think his expertise probably saved me twenty to forty hours of work. In addition, because he's fired guns before and also has made knives, he gave me invaluable personal experience that enhanced the reality of the novel. However, I also had sources for information on a small scale. The Australian writer K .J. Bishop was able to give me information on the rough parts of Bangkok. Russian immigrant Ekaterina Sedia was able to find just the right Russian word for "freedom," which led in turn to a character coming to life that had not been as fully-fleshed out before that intervention.

MAKE SOUND LIFESTYLE CHOICES. I have to admit I exercised less and drank more during the two months than is normal for me. However, I still managed to do two-hour weightlifting sessions at least three times a week and limited the drinking to a couple of drinks a day. Eating healthy also helped keep my energy level up. This is important, because you're doing a lot more typing and longhand writing per day than you normally would, and you have to make it count for more, as well. You can easily find your body beginning to break down — wrist sore, shoulders and back aching.

MAKE SOUND PROCESS DECISIONS. Most of the time, I wrote new scenes in the mornings, revised existing scenes in the afternoons, and spent my evenings on line-edits and rewrites of individual paragraphs here and there. By structuring my time this way, I made better progress than if I'd just focused on doing new scenes all day until the novel was done. By the time I'd finished writing the new scenes, most everything up to that point had already been through a second or even third revision.

HAVE A GOOD GROUP OF FIRST READERS WILLING TO READ THE NOVEL IN PIECES OR IN COMPLETED DRAFT FORM. These readers should be a mix of people who usually read the kind of novel you're writing and people who *don't*. They should *not* all be fellow writers. A good percentage of them should be pure readers, because you are not really looking for the kinds of things a writer may be more invested in than a reader.

▊ Writing-Related

Here's the scenario for my novel:

> *On a remote South China Sea island, a hunt is going on...but not the hunt the participants expected.* Ex-Khmer Rouge Colonel and lodge owner Rath Preap knows something odd is happening — security fences have been cut and big game animals run amok, surveillance cameras reduced to white snow, members of his small private army disappearing...Is it a demon or one of his own men?
>
> *The hunters...*
> John Gustat, billionaire entrepreneur, haunted by a secret and the owner of a mysterious black box. Nikolai and Marikova, supposedly part of the new class of wealthy Russian oil aristocracy, but a little too proficient with a knife and a sniper's rifle. A Romanian ex-professional wrestler turned mobster who knows Gustat is hiding something. A South African arms dealer. A Washington D.C. liquor baron. And a Thai pirate captain out to avenge the murder of her sister...
>
> Full-on battles in old temple ruins. Deadly African crocodiles. A secret

Thai military base. A strange alien virus. Double crosses and last stands. Love and death in the tropics.

Something is beginning to hunt the hunters. Something that has endured a thousand battles on a hundred worlds. Something entirely too familiar to the mysterious John Gustat...

That description masks an underlying strangeness in the novel, but at least gives you the general context. My task in setting down to the actual writing was to play on the tropes of traditional thriller/adventure fiction while adding my own unique point of view. I was not attempting to create something completely new, but to renovate an existing genre. On a general level, this also helped in speeding up the writing process as I was able to rely on the shorthand of the genre's conventions — and then play off of them at will.

The completed novel was 85,000 words. In the two-month period I wrote several drafts of every scene. Here are the specific writing decisions I made that allowed me to finish the novel in such a short time without sacrificing quality.

CREATE A STRUCTURE THAT WILL ALLOW YOU FLEXIBILITY BUT ALSO MAKE SURE YOU DON'T LOSE FOCUS. Your initial synopsis should be detailed enough that you can divide it into chapters when you start the actual writing, and, if possible, make sure that you have a one- or two-line description of the *action* for a particular chapter or scene. Know going into the writing for a week exactly what each scene is supposed to do and why. If you know that, you will find it is still possible to be highly creative and surprise yourself in the individual scenes. If you don't know that, you will spend most of your creative energy just trying to figure out what general action should be occurring in a particular scene. You may find the purpose and action of a scene changing as a result of other decisions you make, but it's easier to manage such changes within an established structure.

MAKE SURE YOU KNOW WHAT KIND OF NOVEL YOU'RE WRITING. I know this sounds basic, but be able to create a mission statement along the lines of "I'm writing a relatively fast-paced action-adventure story with a subplot involving espionage and a tragic love relationship." You may vary from that description, but being able to on the macro level tell yourself what it is you're trying to do is very useful. You'll note my example did not read "I'm writing a multi-generational saga about a powerful crime family." There are some kinds of novels you cannot write in two months.

MAKE SURE YOU ARE USING A RELATIVELY TRANSPARENT STYLE. I don't believe it's possible to write a good novel in this limited amount of time if you're using a more baroque, layered style (and by that, I mean styles like those used by writers like Vladimir Nabokov or Isabelle Allende). This doesn't mean that you can't have complexity of character and complexity of style, but it has to be a more invisible complexity. Good examples of invisible complexity include Lawrence Block and Ken Bruen. The layering process, otherwise, will take too much time. In this case, writing a *Predator* novel, this would've been my approach anyway. Note that less layering usually means less subtext, but you can make up for that in the pacing, and by leveraging the hidden motivations and conflicts of the characters in different ways.

BASE AT LEAST SOME OF YOUR MAIN CHARACTERS ON PEOPLE YOU KNOW AND REALLY LIKE, BUT NOT PEOPLE YOU HAVE SPENT A LOT OF TIME WITH. I know this advice may sound paradoxical, but it turned out to be a very effective way for me to generate depth of character. It was almost like having some of the work done for me, but not all of it. The character "Horia Ursu" — named after my Romanian editor — provides a good example of this effect. Horia is a dear, dear friend who I correspond with via email and who my wife and I have met twice. We have spent perhaps a total of seven days together. I feel very close to him, I admire him greatly, but I don't know him in the way I know Eric Schaller, for example, who illustrated *City of Saints & Madmen*. I've known Eric for more than a decade and we've spent a lot more time together. I could never use "Eric Schaller" as a name to animate a character quickly because I know too many details about his life. With Horia, there is a *space* there, a lack of knowledge, that allowed me to create a very entertaining character in the novel by riffing off of what I *did* know and then filling in and making up details. I used this technique with at least three characters in the novel and it worked extremely well. Usually, thinking about character would take a lot more than two months — it, along with structure, would be the biggest impediments to finishing a novel in such a short time. But, with the help of these real people who are my friends, by literally invoking them through using their names, I was able to find an effective shortcut.

DON'T BE AFRAID TO USE SEVERAL VIEWPOINT CHARACTERS. The quickest way to create drama in a scene is to make sure that the character with the most at stake is the viewpoint character. Early on, I had a very rigid view of this — I was going to have two or three viewpoint characters, and I would rotate them in a strict sequence. It soon became clear this would not work if I wanted to finish the novel within the allotted time. So I switched to the idea of shorter chapters, with several viewpoints threaded through the novel. Each time, the viewpoint was of the character with the greatest stake in the scene in some way. This is especially true in the last half of the novel, which rises to a crescendo of action. To avoid making the novel seem too fragmented, I anchored the novel with a simple formula: the longest chapters were all from the viewpoints of major characters. The effect is simple: it takes less time to write a scene because you already are in the head of someone who wants or needs something from what's going on. Then it's just a matter of making sure you have enough subplot and enough overarching plot (in terms of character scheming) that this approach doesn't begin to seem repetitive.

CREATE TENSION BY CUTTING SCENES IN HALF. Every scene has a point of greatest dramatic potential, and every scene then falls away from that moment. In most novels, the writer decides where to cut away from a scene depending on what kind of effect he or she wants to create, within the greater context of the entire novel. Where you cut a scene also largely determines the pacing of the novel. But there is another way to actually create tension: cut the scene at a moment of confrontation, or right before a confrontation, and either leave the rest of the scene unwritten or provide it to the reader after another scene with other characters. Although this may seem artificial, it is less artificial than writing your way to a cliffhanger at the end of a chapter (as is the case with a popular but extremely manipulative novel like Dan Brown's *The Da Vinci Code*). The advantage of using the approach is that it automatically creates tension because the reader wants to know what happens next, and can heighten the tension in almost any scenario. In writing the rough draft of my *Predator* novel, some scenes naturally ended at a moment of tension. If they didn't, or seemed sluggish, I would cut them in one or two places and thread them through other narratives. In some cases after cutting apart scenes in this way I realized I didn't even need the second half of the scene. Overall, this technique established a protocol for structural edits that meant I didn't have to analyze each unique situation, which saved me time. When I cut a scene in half, it also allowed me to come back into the second part of the scene in the viewpoint of another character, which solved other potential problems.

REUSE ELEMENTS OF THE SAME SETTING. Managing your settings in any novel can be difficult — figuring out how to provide the right level of detail, for example. How much information do you give for a setting you only use once? In the case of my *Predator* novel, I decided to use an island setting because it meant I could describe the island once and then any time I wrote that the characters were, for example, near the ruined temple complex, readers would be anchored without me having to provide additional description. Although this meant that the beginning of my novel is slower because of fleshing out the setting, it also means I had fewer constraints later on than if I'd set my novel in several different locations.

MAKE SURE ANY EXOTIC SETTINGS ALLOW YOU TO FIND PARALLELS IN YOUR OWN IMMEDIATE SURROUNDINGS OR "IF YOU'RE GOING TO CHEAT, MAKE SURE MOST READERS WON'T NOTICE." I didn't do much research on South China Sea islands for the novel. I just made sure the island had a semitropical climate like Florida and then I riffed off of the Florida landscape, with a few altered details. Since I hike a lot in the wilderness of North Florida, this allowed me to add some nice description that had a specific, accurate quality to it. As a result, the novel had more authenticity than if I had tried to completely fake a setting. (I do admit that a reader from the South China Sea might find the setting unbelievable.)

DON'T ANIMATE WHAT DOESN'T NEED TO BE ANIMATED. This might apply to any novel, but it's especially true when you're under the gun deadlinewise. There's a lodge in my novel and separate rooms for all of the guests, along with one common room. There are only two scenes in the separate rooms and lots in the common room. So I spent my time detailing the common room and really didn't describe the other parts of the lodge at all. There was really no point. In a more leisurely kind of novel with a more leisurely time frame, this might've been something I'd have liked to explore, but it wasn't necessary here.

PLAY AGAINST TYPE TO CORRECT A MISTAKE. Dave Larsen pointed out that his Cambodian friend says Cambodians who speak English drop their plurals. I'd already written my Cambodian main character's dialogue. I was also afraid of making the character sound too much like a caricature, no matter how true Dave's observation was. So, my character was raised by Western missionaries until he was ten and is proud of the fact he doesn't drop his plurals when speaking English. Thus, I turned a possible lack of authenticity into a more unique detail, saved time rewriting the lines, and provided additional insight into a main character's background.

LEAVE ROUGH WHAT SHOULD BE ROUGH ANYWAY. My novel features a few full-on battle scenes at night, inside an old temple complex. After mapping out the general dimensions of the temple, and the general flow of the fighting, I left the actual writing in those scenes a little raw, a little confused, because that's what war is like; the film equivalent of a handheld camera. You don't want some elements to be too polished because the prose should mimic the action. However, the other rationale for adopting this approach is that I didn't have to spend as much time rewriting those sections.

STEAL FROM OTHER, MORE IMMEDIATE MEDIA. Mimicking the examples provided by other creators can help save time, but if you have to quickly steal a technique or idea from another writer you run the risk of not changing it enough when you use it in your book. Although not strictly plagiarism, it does mean you don't transform the technique or idea enough for it to be effective for you. However, if you steal from other media, the act of placing the technique or idea in another context usually transforms it sufficiently. For a scene involving a fight between the Predator and an opponent, I stole a great idea from an Orson Welles movie. In the movie, Welles starts out showing a battle from overhead, far away, and then gets closer and closer in until the final scenes are so close all you see are arms and swords and blood. Then he cuts away abruptly to the scene from afar, and this time you see the battlefield filled with the bodies of dead men. In applying the mechanics of this scene to a novel, and changing the context further to a scene involving single combat,

I made the technique completely new, and also added value and depth to the scene without having to spend a lot of time on it.

■ Conclusions

Although I had to write a novel in two months, I don't actually recommend doing so if you have the choice. I was successful in my effort, but I could easily not have been — the demands of the novel could have been more complex, unexpected difficulties could have arisen, or my stamina could simply have given out. In fact, NaNoWriMo (National Novel Writing Month)'s famous novel-in-a-month competition seems crazy to me, in how it condenses the inspiration/thinking-about-it aspect so severely. I, at least, had several months to contemplate my novel before I began to write it.

That said, I don't regret producing a novel in such an abbreviated span of time. It made me humble. It made me think about audience in a different way, and it taught me techniques I now use in my original, more leisurely fiction.

Another, final, element that animates any such effort is passion. I had a passion for my characters and the situation while I was writing the novel. I welcomed the opportunity to engage with the text each and every day I was working on it. If you plan to write a novel in two months, try to bring that passion with you as well.

Appendix F
Evil Monkey's Guide to Creative Writing

As a kind of coda, I offer up the "guide to creative writing" ostensibly written by my alter ego Evil Monkey and originally posted on my blog. Although Evil Monkey likes to be funny, I wouldn't discard his advice as mere mischief...

More than half of all writing advice you receive will be incorrect, incomplete, or howlingly wrong. You will encounter advice driven by neuroses, bitterness, failure, ego, and arrogance. In books and in writing workshops, you will have instructors who mistake their own path to success as the only path to success.

Yet others will try to impose upon you their own writing style, their own list of valid subject matter and approaches. Anecdotal evidence will loom large. Some advice, some instructors, will be actively obstructionist, driven by the belief that "toughening beginners up" — discouragement — is good practice for the real world of writing.

Some of your instructors will be drunk. Some will be sleeping with some of the students. Some will be going through painful divorces and believe the world is a rotting peach pit of unhappiness and despair. Some will be Pollyannas who love every word you write and will appeal to your sense of vanity, your ego, your own love of every word you write. Hacks will give you good advice.

"Literary" writers will give you crappy advice. Some will exhort you to lie down in the gutter. Others will beseech you to remain in the tower. (Some of your instructors will be wise and happy and playful and wonderful, but it is boring to write about that which does not contain the seed of conflict.)

Within writing books you will find pathetic attempts by almost every writer to give you good advice equally on every aspect of writing, even those aspects the writer has little or no experience with, or is not good at. Some writing books will display a desperate reaching for a different structure — dividing up parts of a story or novel into esoteric or exotic categories, simply to be different.

Beware the instructional books that include information like "your hero must be handsome or attractive in some way so that readers identify with him or her." Beware the writer who justifies their own hedonistic, experience-is-everything approach by codifying it in their instructional manual as Law. Beware people who always talk in terms of "trends" and "publicists."

Never seek validation from others. Some people will always think you should not be a writer. Some people will always think you should be a writer. All of these people are fools. There is only one way to determine whether or not you are a writer: you must find the secret tunnel leading to the hidden door. Once there, you must place your hand upon the doorknob. If you are really a writer, the door will open. You will be ushered into a magical palace. Inside of this palace, a beautiful woman (or man, depending on your wont) will take your hand and whisper in your ear, "I'm glad you made it here. I need someone to mop the marble floors. I'll pay you good money. This will keep you from starving while you write." Of course, everyone is chosen. The door opens for everyone.

Never sleep with a ghost writer; that person will replace your words with their own and leave your skin covered in strange tattoos. Do not go to a writer's workshop and wind up in a cult. Do not seek advice from Ouija boards or from scientists in lab coats.

Never trust writers who not only dress in black but also wear black pajamas and underwear to bed. No one has ever written truly immortal poetry about how good their dog looks in knitted garments. Waistcoats and pocket watches are signs of lunacy and therefore lack of authority when it comes to writing advice. Those who must display their bodices incessantly have a hidden agenda. Alcohol is not your friend. Cigars are neutral.

Computers are overrated. Haste is overrated. Sloth is just as bad as haste. Ten words are better than ten thousand, if those ten are right and the ten thousand are wrong. Personal experience is useless if you cannot leverage it with imagination. If you have no imagination you are dead to me. If you don't realize writing is hard work, I keel you with my eye bullets. If a man in a black cape approaches you in the back of a bar and promises to make you a bestseller, beware! For He is either Agent or Devil.

For all of these reasons and more, writing is perilous work. It is more deadly than special ops. It is more boring than selling insurance. It is more exhilarating than jumping out of an airplane without a parachute. You may die from writing, but more probably you will be disappointed. That is okay, too. Disappointment, as we all know, builds character.

As for this guide and this writer: everything you read was true. Everything you read was a lie. I am the wisest monkey who has ever lived. I am a fool. Both may be true for you, sometimes on the same page.

Acknowledgments

Thanks to everyone who contributed to *Booklife* in the form of quotes and examples. Thanks to the great staff at Tachyon, including Jacob Weisman, and to developmental editor Juliet Ulman, who also gave me my first big break in the U.S. when she worked for Bantam Books. Special thanks to my wife Ann for helping me with everything from structure to edits on the paragraph level to printing out the damn thing when our printer broke. Additional special thanks to Tachyon managing editor Jill Roberts for her comments, edits, and care with this book. Thanks also to first readers Tessa Kum and Matt Staggs, Matt for his analysis regarding new media and Tessa for being a constructive curmudgeon who challenged several of the concepts in the early draft, to the book's benefit. Conversations with Matt also provided the genesis for several sections of this book. Thanks to Mur Lafferty for consulting on the section on podcasting. Additional thanks to the students at Clarion South 2009, who gracefully allowed me to experiment on them to perfect some of *Booklife*'s text. Further thanks to such beta readers as Desirina Boskovich, J. T. Glover, and Angela Slatter, whose questions, suggestions, and copy edits made the book better. Finally, *Booklife* owes a huge debt to every writer, editor, and other individual who was willing to give me advice or other help ever since 1985, when I began to seriously consider devoting my life to writing. Thanks to all of you — your example keeps me focused not just on what's important, but on paying it forward.

About the Author

JEFF VANDERMEER has been involved in the publishing industry from almost all perspectives for more than twenty years as fiction writer, book reviewer, editor, publisher, publicist, teacher, and creative consultant. In that span, he has had novels published in fifteen languages, won multiple awards, and made the best-of-year lists of *Publishers Weekly*, the *San Francisco Chronicle*, the *LA Weekly*, and many others. His award-winning short fiction has been featured on WIRED.COM's GeekDad and TOR.COM, as well as in many anthologies and magazines, including *Conjunctions*, *Black Clock*, and in *American Fantastic Tales* (Library of America), edited by Peter Straub. His nonfiction has appeared in the *New York Times Book Review*, the *Washington Post*, the *Barnes & Noble Review*, the *Huffington Post*, and hundreds of others. He is a regular contributor to Amazon's book blog. In addition, he has edited or co-edited more than a dozen influential fiction anthologies for, among others, Bantam Books and Pan Macmillan. On the pop culture front, VanderMeer's work has been turned into short films for PlayStation Europe and videos featuring music by The Church. With his wife Ann, he has lectured, conducted master classes, and given workshops all over the world, including at the Brisbane Arts Center in Australia, the University of California at San Diego, and Wofford College, in South Carolina. He is a frequent guest of conferences around the world, including such events as Utopiales in France, the Bumbershoot Festival in Seattle, the Brisbane Writers Festival in Australia, Finncon in Helsinki, and the Walker Arts Center in Minneapolis. For more information, visit JEFFVANDERMEER.COM and BOOKLIFENOW.COM.